Knocking on the Back Door:

Canadian Perspectives on the Political Economy of Freer Trade with the United States

Knocking on the Back Door:

Canadian Perspectives on the Political Economy of Freer Trade with the United States

Edited by
Allan M. Maslove and Stanley L. Winer
School of Public Administration
Carleton University

The Institute for Research on Public Policy/
L'Institut de recherches politiques

Canadian Cataloguing in Publication Data

Main entry under title:
Knocking on the back door : canadian perspectives
on the political economy of freer trade with the
United States

Foreword in English and French.
ISBN 0-88645-058-6

1. Free trade and protection — Free trade. 2.
Canada — Foreign economic relations — United States.
3. United States — Foreign economic relations —
Canada. 4. Negotiation. 5. Social sciences.
I. Maslove, Allan M., 1946- II. Winer, Stanley
L., 1947- III. Institute for Research on Public
Policy

HF1766.K66 1987 382.7'1'0971 C87-090355-1

The camera-ready copy for this publication was created
on a Xerox 6085 Desktop Publishing System.

The Institute for Research on Public Policy/
L'Institut de recherches politiques
P.O. Box 3670 South
Halifax, Nova Scotia B3J 3K6

Contents

Foreword

Negotiations for a comprehensive Canada-United States trade agreement have been underway since the spring of 1986 and are expected to be concluded in the autumn of 1987, at which time the proposed text is to be submitted for ratification in the legislatures of both countries. These negotiations are aimed at sweeping away remaining barriers to cross-border trade in goods and services, and at putting in place new rules for this trade that would better accommodate the large, close and intricate trade and economic relationships between the two countries. A successful outcome to these negotiations would be of historic importance, building a free trade arrangement upon the impressive process of bilateral trade liberalization that has already been achieved over the past half century.

The consequences for the future development of Canadian social and political structures may also be dramatic, serving not only to integrate the North American economies more fully, but also to bind Canadian political and regulatory decisions more tightly into American mechanisms, reflecting American values. While one might hope that mutual acceptance of agreed rules and dispute resolution mechanisms would offer greater insulation from American political pressures, and hence greater scope for independent economic and social policy in Canada, experience to date with examples like softwood lumber or natural gas pricing suggests that the price of more assured access to U.S. markets for Canadian exports of manufactured goods may well be the extraterritorial application of American standards and criteria in the appraisal of Canadian economic, cultural, or social policy. The determination whether, on balance, this further economic integration might prove to be in the broad national interest is therefore complex indeed, and the choice facing Canadians in the fall may be a tough one.

A conference organized by the School of Public Administration, Carleton University, in Ottawa on September 25-26, 1986 was therefore very timely, and made a valuable contribution to understanding the issues involved in the negotiations. This volume contains the proceedings of that conference; and whatever the outcome of the negotiations, the papers presented at the conference and the introduction by the editors will be of permanent value in illuminating the importance and complexity of the Canada-United States relationship.

The Institute for Research on Public Policy is pleased to publish these proceedings of the Carleton conference as a further contribution to the understanding and public debate of policy issues of vital concern to Canadians.

Rod Dobell
President

October 1987

Avant-propos

Des négociations ayant trait à un accord commercial global entre le Canada et les États-Unis sont en cours depuis le printemps 1986, et l'on s'attend à ce qu'elles aboutissent en automne 1987, après quoi le texte proposé devra être soumis au corps législatif des deux pays en vue de sa ratification. Ces négociations visent à éliminer les derniers obstacles au commerce des biens et services et à mettre en place de nouveaux règlements régissant ce commerce dans le but d'améliorer les relations commerciales et économiques étroites, complexes et de grande envergure entre ces deux pays. Un succès résultant de ces négociations aurait une valeur historique, car il mènerait à un accord de libre échange rendu possible par la libéralisation impressionnante du commerce bilatéral déjà réalisée lors des cinquante dernières années.

Il se peut aussi que les conséquences pour le développement futur des structures canadiennes politiques et sociales soient considérables, servant non seulement à intégrer encore plus les économies nord-américaines, mais aussi à lier encore plus les décisions politiques et régulatrices prises au Canada aux mécanismes américains qui reflètent des valeurs américaines. Bien que l'on puisse espérer que l'acceptation mutuelle de règles et de mécanismes permettant le règlement de conflits nous mette plus à l'abri des pressions politiques américaines, permettant ainsi une meilleure perspective pour une politique économique et sociale indépendante au Canada, à l'heure actuelle, certaines expériences, telles que les questions concernant le bois d'oeuvre où la fixation du prix du gaz naturel suggèrent qu'un accès plus sûr de l'exportation canadienne de produits manufacturés aux marchés américains s'achètera peut-être au prix de l'application de normes et critères américains à l'évaluation des politiques économiques, culturelles ou sociales canadiennes. Il est donc bien difficile de déterminer si cette nouvelle intégration économique s'avèrera être dans l'intérêt national. En effet, le problème est complexe, et la décision que les Canadiens devront prendre en automne pourra être difficile.

La conférence organisée par l'École d'administration publique les 25 et 26 septembre 1986 à l'Université Carleton, à Ottawa, a donc été très à propos et a contribué de façon importante à comprendre les questions impliquées dans les négociations. Ce volume contient les actes de cette conférence. Quels que soient les résultats des négociations, les communications présentées à la conférence ainsi que l'introduction des éditeurs seront toujours valables, car elles soulignent l'importance et la complexité des relations entre le Canada et les États-Unis.

L'Institut de recherches politiques a l'honneur de publier les actes de la conférence de Carleton dans le but de permettre aux Canadiens une meilleure compréhension des problèmes politiques les plus importants et de stimuler un débat public.

Rod Dobell
Président

Octobre 1987

Acknowledgements

We would like to thank Xerox Canada and the Social Sciences and Humanities Research Council of Canada for funding the conference on which this volume is based. We are also indebted to Martha Clark for serving as conference secretary, and to the staff of the School of Public Administration for their help in preparing the manuscript.

Beyond the Gains from Trade:
A Brief Introduction

Allan M. Maslove and Stanley L. Winer

The papers in this volume offer a wide range of perspectives on the Canada-United States free trade debate, and on Canada-U.S. trade relations generally. They are for the most part revised versions of papers delivered at a conference organized and sponsored by the School of Administration at Carleton University in the fall of 1986. By and large the papers focus on issues of process and politics, including the problems of adjusting to trade liberalization, sovereignty, the negotiating process and the role of social science as well as others that we shall introduce below. These sorts of issues are less well studied and understood than are the welfare gains from free trade. But it is at least as important to study the broader economic and political issues and the problems of policy implementation as it is to measure the static welfare gains from free trade arrangements.

The first paper, by Bruce Wilkinson, introduces the free trade debate, surveys the narrow economic arguments for free trade with the United States (including measures of the welfare gains to be expected) and then moves on to question whether an emphasis on bilateral trade liberalization with the United States is preferable to greater efforts in a multilateral context. Peter Cornell, in his response to Wilkinson's paper, disagrees with the suggestion that bilateral and multilateral approaches are not complementary, and reasserts the case for bilateral free trade with the United States.

Choosing a direction in which to pursue trade liberalization is one thing. Actually implementing a trade agreement is another. Usually free trade wins out in academic forums but loses badly in the ballot box. The reason for this may largely be due to our failure to cope with the losses to individuals, groups and firms which follow any substantial change in economic policy. How we might reshape public policy processes to ease the hardships of adjusting to stiffer international competition is the topic of Michael Trebilcock's paper.

In his contribution to the study of adjustment, Donald Daly looks closely at the past behaviour of business people to see how they have adapted to the trade liberalization introduced by the General Agreement on Tariffs and Trade and by a host of bilateral arrangements since 1945. John Baldwin, in commenting on Daly's paper, discusses the same issue using different data sources as a basis for his conclusions. The tone of both of these papers is hopeful. Canadian entrepreneurs do not seem to have succumbed to trade liberalization. Indeed, the evidence points in the other direction.

The discussion next turns to the question of sovereignty. What is it? Will it be diminished by free trade with the United States? And does it matter? This is a subject even harder to deal with in a careful way than is the adjustment problem. Denis Stairs introduces the issue, and deals directly with the central question of whether sovereignty really matters. We shall not reveal his answer here. Glen Williams attempts to redefine the sovereignty issue within the context of a general theory of Canadian trade relations. This paper relies on a tradition of political economy that originated with Harold Innis. It views the recent trade negotiations as part of a wider process involving economic and political relationships between centre and periphery in a world economy.

The next section of the volume considers the negotiations *per se*. Gilbert Winham regards the Canada-U.S. trade negotiation as a troubled affair, partly because of the nature of existing negotiating structures and because of unfortunate timing. To a considerable extent, these problems originate in the United States. Winham suggests that we conduct ourselves in a manner that would allow us to salvage as much as possible. He argues for maintaining momentum as long as possible, for preparing for scaled down talks in the likely event that the current, ambitious round is unsuccessful, for using the talks to stimulate debate about our trade relations generally, and, finally, for stimulating discussion between federal and provincial governments over the internal common market. He suggests that the Trade Negotiation Office may have a useful life after the free trade talks as an agency devoted to reducing barriers to interprovincial trade.

The role of the provinces in the negotiations is the subject of the next paper. The Barrows-Boudreau paper argues that the provinces have legitimate claim to a major role in the negotiations. Because so much of the discussions involve non-tariff barriers, they also involve areas of provincial jurisdiction and long-standing provincial economic development policies. They go on to outline the framework proposed by Ontario for provincial participation in the negotiations and ratification of any agreement that emerges.

Finally, we return to the role of social science and social scientists in the free trade debate. It is important to consider the role the social sciences have in informing debate on one of the most important public policy issues in recent years. Mel Watkins gives us a European perspective on the role of economics and economists using the entry of Britain into the European Economic Community as a background. The entry of Britain into the EEC worked no magic for the British economy, he argues, and he sees a disturbing similarity between the rhetoric being used in the Canadian debate and the language of the debate surrounding British entry into the EEC. It is disturbing to him because he thinks the basic economic argument for free trade is flawed. Watkins questions whether access to a larger market is a necessary and sufficient condition for economic prosperity. He questions whether we are being given useful economic analysis by the economics profession, or rather simply pro-market ideology.

In the next paper Gilles Paquet argues that the social sciences as a whole have become more disconnected from the ordinary questions that led to its creation than ever before. He sees the free trade debate as one which will expose social scientists more than they would like, because social science, in his view, has drifted away from a form that would allow useful interventions in policy debate, towards a barren positivism which even the physical sciences have begun to move beyond. In his view, economists have little of use to add as economists and it is not surprising that they have resorted to rhetoric rather than substance in their contributions. He proceeds to analyze economic arguments using the logic of literary criticism, describing the use of metaphors, irony and other literary devices. In the end, he finds the stories unconvincing, and he suggests a direction we might take in reconstructing economics in particular and social science in general so as to provide effective policy analysis.

While the Watkins and the Paquet papers are pessimistic concerning the usefulness of economics in the free trade debate (and if economics is not useful here, then where?), the following contributions are much more optimistic.

Sharon Sutherland, a political scientist, implicitly defends the contemporary positivistic social scientist in her comment on Paquet's paper. Sutherland disputes Paquet's contention that we should return to ordinary forms of discourse and forsake "the trained lunacies of the econometrician" (Sutherland's phrase). She sees serious limits to the ability of the human mind to process complex decisions, as revealed by much recent research on cognitive psychology. As she puts it, ordinary knowledge is not an Olympic athlete stripped for speed. She argues that it is not unreasonable, given the great complexity involved, to make the best guess one can after relying on the most highly developed and analytical of the social sciences, and particularly after relying on quantitative techniques that help us to overcome our individual cognitive limitations. While she does not say so, we are tempted to see this argument as support for "a leap of faith" into free trade after carefully considering the quantitative estimates of the gains from trade.

Finally, Richard Lipsey, in a strong response to Watkins and Paquet, defends the contributions to the free trade debate of social scientists in general and economists in particular.

The immediate focus of this volume is on bilateral free trade arrangements with the United States. But as the above brief introduction demonstrates, a discussion of free trade involves us in issues which are much broader than the term "free trade" might at first seem to suggest. A debate over Canada-U.S. free trade also leads us into a discussion of multilateral trade policy, the nature of industrial policy, the meaning of cultural sovereignty, federal-provincial relations and the nature of the social sciences, among others. This wider debate may be, in the end, one of the most important contributions of the most recent Canada-U.S. free trade talks.

Multilateral Versus Bilateral
Trade Liberalization

Canada-United States Free Trade: Setting the Dimensions

Bruce W. Wilkinson

In this paper I provide an overview of the debate concerning freer trade with the United States including the meaning and scope of "free trade," and an assessment of the economic pros and cons of Canada entering an agreement with the United States. I will discuss these topics in that order. My role is to focus primarily on economic issues. Yet, as will be seen in what follows, political and legal issues of necessity often have to be introduced.

The initiation of the negotiations, the negotiations themselves, and the consequences of the negotiations involve political as well as economic factors. Economics by itself provides too narrow a perspective.

My conclusion is that the attitudes of many Canadians toward bilateral free trade with the U.S. can best be typified by two of Shakespeare's seven stages of man. At first many Canadians were as "the lover, sighing like a furnace with a woeful ballad made to his mistress' eyebrow." But, as the realities became clearer regarding the extremely nationalistic U.S. attitudes and what they might require Canadians to give up in return for a deal, more Canadians are beginning to look like they have reverted to Shakespeare's second stage of man—"... the whining school boy with his satchel and shining morning face creeping like snail unwillingly to school." It is my hope that as events unfold we do not finally end up in the initial stage of the infant in the nurse's arms.

The Meaning of Free Trade

According to the General Agreement of Tariffs and Trade (GATT), a free trade area is "a group of two or more customs territories in which duties and other restrictive regulations of commerce ... are eliminated on substantially all the trade between the constituent territories in products originating in such territories." (GATT 1969, 43). The exceptions allowed include some export and import quantitative restrictions and some restrictions for special purposes such as balance of payments needs. GATT rules also stated that the purpose of a free trade area is "not to raise barriers to the trade of other contracting parties with such territories." (GATT 1969, 41).

In Canada our understanding of what bilateral free trade (BFT) with the United States entails has been evolving over time.

Two decades ago, when Canadians considered free trade with the United States, the focus was primarily, if not exclusively, upon the effects of removing **tariff** barriers on trade in manufactured goods alone. Although the removal of non-tariff measures was provided for in GATT (with some exceptions as in Article XI-2), their magnitude was not deemed of great significance relative to tariffs. Agricultural products were specifically excluded from GATT—at U.S. insistence as a condition of joining GATT. (It was in the U.S. interest to have this exclusion at that time.) Services trade and the issues involved therein did not then appear to be of much importance. Thus, it is not surprising that the classic 1967 study by Paul and Ron Wonnacott was confined to the implications of removing tariffs on manufactured goods.

As the Wonnacott volume was being produced, and for several years thereafter, a number of studies sponsored by the forerunner of today's C.D. Howe Institute, the Private Planning Association of Canada, were published. They also focused primarily upon manufactured goods trade, although one of the research monographs (Trant, MacFarland and Fischer 1968) as well as the final volume (English, Wilkinson and Eastman 1972) did recommend that agriculture be included in any negotiations. But non-tariff measures were given almost no attention, and trade in services was very much ignored.

A few years later the Economic Council (1975) clearly recognized the growing importance of non-tariff measures and some background work by Roma Dauphin (1983) attempted to estimate their magnitude for Canada. Still, the role that they were to play, especially in gaining access to the U.S. market, was not yet fully understood. The council did recommend that agriculture be included in any bilateral or multilateral trade liberalization negotiations. Services trade was still not given much attention, however, and oil and gas were to be excluded, at least initially, in any trade agreement with the United States.

Shortly thereafter the Standing Senate Committee on Foreign Affairs (1976) echoed the council's concern about the restrictive effects of non-tariff measures and recommended BFT with the United States as a means of reducing such measures facing Canadian products. But once again services (apart from tourism to which several pages were devoted) were given scant attention. And, in a step backward from what the

Economic Council had recommended, agriculture was to be exempted from the negotiations.

By the time the Senate committee's third and final volume came out in 1982, the Tokyo Round of GATT negotiations had been concluded. It was then apparent that by 1987, when the Tokyo tariff reductions would be in effect, a very large proportion of Canada-U.S. commodity trade would be tariff free or facing tariffs of five per cent or less (see Table 1). The possibility of Canada and the United States taking a "declaratory approach" to a free trade area without necessitating a formal application for approval to GATT was considered. It would have meant that the two countries would have been able to move on to negotiating the remaining tariff reductions without seeking GATT approval or exemption. But, by this time, the spectre of U.S. non-tariff measures had become more evident. The committee, therefore, felt that, even if this approach were accepted by the United States and GATT, it would not eliminate these barriers which they now saw as the main source of obstruction to, and uncertainty in, the U.S. market (Senate Committee 1982, 34). Hence it recommended that a bilateral free trade area should be negotiated between Canada and the United States to eliminate them. However, it continued to assume that agriculture could be or should be excluded from negotiations, and it still gave no real attention to trade in services. Free trade in manufacturing, especially secondary manufacturing, was envisaged as the only objective that mattered to Canada and presumably the only one that the United States would be much interested in negotiating on.

The most recent study to have a major impact upon Canadian public opinion and policy-making has been the Report of the Royal Commission on the Economic Union and Development Prospects for Canada (the Macdonald report).[1] This 1985 report made BFT with the United States the kingpin of its recommendations and the key to Canadian industrial survival in today's world. It strongly emphasized that "security of access" of Canadian products to the U.S. market meant that Canada would need to negotiate restraints on American contingent protection such as "anti-dumping duties, countervailing duties and safeguard or 'escape-clause' actions" (v. 1, p. 312), government procurement preferences, and various product-quality, safety standards, and other restrictions on market access (v. 1, p. 313). The Macdonald commission, however, like the Senate committee before it, chose to exclude agriculture (v. 1, p. 308).[2] And, while recognizing that the massive service sector was one in which the United States wanted to see trade liberalization on a world scale, it quickly removed this sector from its general discussion after a mere three paragraphs (v. 1, pp. 291-292 and 308-309), saying that "future negotiations on services should be conducted on a sectoral basis" (v. 1, p. 309).

Cultural activities, most of which are within the service sector, were also quickly disposed of by the commission with the statement that

> Canada could insist on explicit treaty provisions that would authorize
> public funding of its cultural activities and permit affirmative
> discrimination for Canadian producers, in order to compensate for the
> handicap of our small domestic market. The examples of the European Free
> Trade Association (EFTA) and the European Community demonstrate that
> substantial subsidization of cultural activities is possible within an
> effective free-trade framework. (v. 1, p. 310).

Table 1
Trade-Weighted U.S. Average Tariff Rate on Imports from Canada, Post-Tokyo Round

	Per cent
Agriculture	1.6
Food	3.8
Textiles	7.2
Clothing	18.4
Leather Prod.	2.5
Footwear	9.0
Wood Prod.	0.2
Furniture & Fixt.	4.6
Paper Prod.	0.0
Printing & Publ.	0.3
Chemicals	0.6
Petrol. Prod.	0.0
Rubber Prod.	3.2
Non-metal Min. Prod.	0.3
Glass Prod.	5.7
Iron & Steel	2.7
Nonferr. Metals	0.5
Metal Prod.	4.0
Nonelec. Mach.	2.2
Elec. Mach.	4.5
Transport Equip.	0.0
Misc. Mfr's	0.9
AVERAGE	0.7

Source: Based on data supplied by the Office of the U.S. Trade Representative as reported in Drucilla Brown, "Testimony Regarding United States – Canada Free Trade" before the subcommittee on economics stabilization of the committee on banking, finance, and urban affairs. United States House of Representatives, August 5, 1986.

The commission also made its BFT recommendation more palatable to Canadians by indicating that Canada would undoubtedly be able to retain control over the pace of its natural resource development, as well as its taxes on resources and resource exports – all in accord with GATT provisions (v. 1, p. 310). By stressing that it was recommending a free trade area and not a customs union or a common market, the commission was also able to submit that Canada would be able "to reserve the right to exercise some controls over the movement of U.S. capital into this country . . ." (p. 306) and retain independence in its tax policy generally and "regulations for goods entering from third countries" (v. 1, p. 307). Finally, it stressed that any agreement would have to permit Canadian policies "intended to encourage local, regional or sectoral economic development" (p. 358) and leave intact our social security and health care network. It did, however, recognize that the Canadian provinces would have to surrender certain protectionist measures such as their government procurement policies.

After two decades, then, Canada – or at least some Canadians – arrived at a definition of what free trade with the United States would entail: removal of U.S. tariffs and, more important, removal of, or clear restraints upon, U.S. non-tariff measures restricting access for Canadian manufactures. Canada would, in turn, reciprocate in these same areas, but would reserve the right to control or regulate:

- U.S. capital inflows in Canada

- the pace of our resource development and exports

- our regional development policies (which often involve subsidies of one sort or another)

- our subsidized support for and protection of Canadian cultural activities

- our taxation policies

- our rules on trade with third countries

In addition, agriculture and services would be excluded from negotiations (services would supposedly be dealt with in separate sectoral negotiations), as would our entire network of social support policies, including unemployment insurance and health care. Finally, two common themes of all Canadian studies was that Canada should be given more years than the United States to adjust to free trade and that the Canadian dollar should be allowed to fluctuate *vis-à-vis* the U.S. dollar. This flexible rate would be a final safety valve to enable Canadian industry to be competitive with U.S. industry.

The federal government announcement in the autumn of 1985 that the United States was being approached to commence BFT negotiations, and subsequent announcements by the government, reflected this definition – although they recognized that agriculture and services would have to be included. Yet, what services would be comprehended was not well-defined. Agricultural marketing boards and the Auto Pact were to be exempt from negotiations, however. The need for tax or other policy harmonization was downplayed (e.g. Mulroney 1985; Clark 1985; Kelleher 1986a and 1986b). With this conception of what BFT meant, it is not surprising that initial Canadian enthusiasm for it was substantial.

There was only one problem. The United States did not have the same definition of what BFT should encompass. Their interest in a bilateral agreement has not been just to gain greater access to the Canadian market for U.S. firms than they already have, but to set an example for the world of what they wanted the non-U.S. tariff and non-tariff measures to look like after any multilateral talks (Wilkinson 1986). As the months have passed, the list of what the United States wants to see altered or removed in Canada (in addition to the removal of all tariffs) has been steadily expanding. It includes our agricultural protection and support programs, including federal and provincial marketing boards of all types, as well as all perceived subsidies, even those on transportation; the control of grain sales by the Canadian Wheat Board; the Auto Pact, as well as our duty remission programs to encourage overseas automobile producers to locate in Canada; possibly unemployment insurance measures to the extent that, in U.S. eyes, they constitute export subsidies; Canadian royalty or other government rent-extraction measures such as stumpage charges on timber harvesting; provincial protectionism such as that related to alcoholic beverages, government procurement, and trucking regulations; programs designed to protect or stimulate Canadian cultural industries; and all restrictions on U.S. participation in our service industries which include the entire communications sector, involving telecommunications, radio, TV, newspapers and publishing, advertising, transportation, and consulting.[3] The most recent item of apparent U.S. interest is whether, from a U.S. perspective, the production of hydro-electricity is subsidized. In addition, the United States also wants its corporations to be able to invest freely in Canada with no government surveillance or regulation. (This is a characteristic of a common market which many economists and politicians in Canada have assured us is not being negotiated).

Simultaneously, the United States has indicated that a general provision for a longer period of adjustment for Canada than the United States before all trade barriers are removed is not likely (Merkin, cited in *The Globe and Mail*, February 28, 1986). Again, the United States does not view bilateral removal of government procurement restrictions as an equal exchange. Canadian firms would obtain access to a market in the United States over 20 times larger than that which U.S. firms would gain in Canada (Ibid.).

The United States also perceives the intercorporate relationship between Bell Canada Enterprises Inc. and Northern Telecom as "unfair" because it gives Northern Telecom a privileged market at the same time that Northern Telecom has been able to sell its products widely in the United States. Yet the United States does not seem to comprehend that the massive U.S. direct investment in Canada gives their parent firms and accompanying long-established suppliers in the United States privileged access to the subsidiaries in Canada. The far higher proportion of purchases imported by foreign-owned, especially U.S.-owned, firms in Canada from their home country than is done by Canadian-owned firms, is a long-established statistical fact about Canadian foreign trade (Wilkinson 1968; Statistics Canada 1981). The United States wants to expand this privileged access to the Canadian market by having Canada remove all constraints on U.S. capital inflows to Canada and all regulations about the performance of foreign firms in Canada. To them this means the establishment of a level playing field, and letting the market work. Yet, when Bell and Northern Telecom do it in our own Canadian market, it is a discriminatory behaviour which ought to be eradicated.

These widespread differences in perceptions of what bilateral free trade should involve strongly suggest—as Mr. Reisman and Mr. Mulroney have now come somewhat belatedly to understand—that the negotiations will be extremely difficult. Because the United States is much larger and Canada is far more dependent upon its exports to the United States than is the United States upon Canada, our negotiating position is weaker. The likelihood, then, is that any agreement reached will match more closely the U.S. model than the Canadian one. Economic history tends to confirm that a nation is able to make more advantageous trade deals the more dependent the partner countries are upon it (Rooth 1984, 1986).

The major reason that I have spent this length of time on the meaning of free trade is that the economic arguments made in favour of BFT as well as the calculations of net benefits that are supposed to accrue to Canada from BFT, have generally been based more on the Canadian model, not the current U.S. one. For that reason and for a variety of other reasons too, they are deficient and have tended to create inflated economic expectations for many Canadians of what can be achieved at this time from BFT, given the current U.S. trade balance, political system, and long-standing, extreme nationalism.

Let us consider these matters.

The Benefits and Costs of BFT

The economic argument of BFT is very well known in Canada. It is that unhindered access to the vast U.S. market, including the purchases of U.S. governments, would permit Canadian manufacturers to achieve economies of scale that they cannot obtain within the much smaller Canadian market. Accordingly, they would be able to attain increases in productivity and would have an incentive to adopt new technology more quickly, undertake more research and development themselves, revamp their managerial techniques to enhance their efficiency in the more highly competitive environment that would evolve, and generally avoid the need to relocate in the United States or at least to establish subsidiaries there. More processing of primary natural resources before they are exported, and possibly lower foreign ownership are hypothesized as other benefits. Employment in Canada would increase. Consumers would gain from the lower prices made possible by the removal of Canadian barriers to imports and the augmented productivity of Canadian producers.

I and others have expressed our reservations about the importance of many of these arguments on other occasions (Barber 1985; Stern 1985; Daly and Rao 1985; Wilkinson 1980, 1982, 1985a, 1985b, 1986), so there is little need to go into great detail here. Very briefly, many estimates of net benefit attached to these claims are exaggerated and present an over-optimistic picture of what BFT will do for Canada. I will present only a few examples. One fairly recent set of estimates which has received much attention, the Harris-Cox model, projected real income to increase by about 9 per cent, and employment to rise by over 5 per cent. The evidence now suggests that for a variety of reasons the estimates of net real income gains are much too high and that 2 to 3 per cent gains are a much more likely figure – *provided that some sort of guaranteed access to the U.S. market can actually be negotiated* (e.g., Economic Council 1986). If the United States is unwilling to depart from its current countervail, anti-dumping and general safeguard laws, then the net advantage of BFT to Canada could well be less than this. (I will return to this particular issue shortly.)

The employment gains presented in these large scale models are also highly suspect. In the Harris-Cox model the improvements for manufacturing are supposed to come mostly in industries such as clothing (259 per cent), textiles (156 per cent), transportation equipment (59 per cent), knitting mills (48 per cent), paper and allied products (31 per cent), urban transport equipment (28 per cent), and printing (13 per cent). Yet, Canada would be very foolish to count on trade diversion from developing countries sources to expand its labour-intensive industries such as clothing and knitting mills, or industries with highly standardized technology such as textiles. Also, Canada and the United States already have essentially something like free trade in the automobile, aircraft and pulp and paper industries, with the exception of fine papers (Wilkinson 1986). Thus, one cannot put too much reliance on the estimates of aggregate employment gains this type of model provides.

Peter Cornell has argued that these large-scale models are not appropriate for determining the effects on aggregate employment, but are only useful for highlighting the changes in employment in individual industries. But one has to have doubts about this too. For example, a comparison of the Harris-Cox results with those of the University of Maryland's INFORUM model reveals that for only 4 of the 20 manufacturing industries involved are the signs of expected employment change even the same. All the rest show opposite signs and frequently involve large divergences in the numbers (Table 2). Similar discrepancies arise between these two models and the Informetrica model, TIM. (TIM, unlike the other two mentioned, also shows employment in manufacturing actually decreasing from what it would be in the absence of free trade—and it has some fascinating predictions, such as major gains in shipbuilding).[4] It is evident that we should not rely too heavily on the results from these macromodels in estimating the net benefits from BFT or in devising policies for negotiating free trade. The diverse results are largely the result of variations in assumptions processed through sophisticated programs. At most they tell us that we do *not* really know in any detail what the industrial consequences of BFT might be. Perhaps the most disturbing feature about the discrepancies in these models is that, in the documents which the Department of External Affairs made available to the public last May reporting on the models, such discrepancies were not drawn to the attention of the reader or the policy maker.

Other points that need to be noted are as follows. First, a number of our resource sectors, such as agriculture, fishing and forestry, have had very small productivity gains since 1970. Yet many of the products in these industries have had tariff-free access to world markets for many years. Such access has not been sufficient to ensure productivity growth. Of course the EEC agricultural policies and now the U.S. agricultural export subsidy program have made things more difficult for agriculture. But quite apart from these factors, many of the reasons for failure in domestic output and efficiency improvement are of domestic origin. We have simply not adopted policies within Canada that could have enhanced the performance of these sectors (Wilkinson 1985). Our focus on BFT should not distract us from the need to make a wide range of policy improvements in agricultural land conservation, new crop and varieties development, and grain grading and handling, forestry management and restoration, fisheries and fish processing rationalization, and new product development for metals and minerals.

Second—and this is very important—many of the areas where improvements in efficiency may occur if BFT comes about are actually improvements which we could undertake domestically without facing some of the difficulties that BFT might produce

Table 2
Employment Effects of Bilateral Free Trade

	Manufacturing Harris-Cox: (%)	University of Maryland INFORUM (Changes by 1995) (Thousands)
Food and Beverages	-2.3	+4
Tobacco Products	-10.2	0
Rubber Products	+4.9	-4
Leather Products	-7.8	-2
Textile Products	+156.1	-6
Knitting	+48.2	} -26
Clothing	+259.2	
Wood Products	-12.8	+36
Furniture and Fixtures	-38.1	-2
Paper and Allied Products	+31.3	+4
Printing and Publishing	+12.7	+2
Primary Metal	} -7.9	+14
Metal Fabrication		+4
Non-Agricultural Machinery	-34.6	} +46
Agriculture Machinery	-26.7	
Urban Transport Equipment	+28.2	} +36
Other Transport Equipment	+58.7	
Electrical Products	-22.7	+8
Non-metallic Minerals	-1.4	+3
Petroleum and Coal	-7.7	0
Chemicals	+.4	-1
Miscellaneous Mfg.	-33.2	-18

Sources: Col. (1) R. Harris and D. Cox (1985) "Further Calculations on Sectoral and Bilateral Free Trade" in *Canada United States Free Trade*, eds. John Whalley and Roderick Hill. Toronto: University of Toronto Press. Table 8-A2.

Col. (2) Department of External Affairs, Government of Canada (1985) *Interim Report on the Implications of a Canada/U.S. Enhanced Trade Agreement*. Table 2, p. 11.

for us. These policy changes are ones we should be making in Canada anyway, regardless of whether we negotiate free trade. They include:

- getting rid of our marketing boards such as those for dairy products, poultry and eggs

- reducing provincial production subsidy programs, such as for hogs, which prevent provinces fully exercising their comparative advantage on trade within Canada

- removing interprovincial restrictions on liquor sales

- eliminating "buy-provincial" policies for both goods and services

- liberalizing interprovincial trucking restrictions

All of these existing policies discourage the development of more efficient scales of production, reduce incentives for technological change and other efficiency-improving measures to be undertaken, and raise production costs and therefore prices to consumers. Some provinces may see the giving up of these balkanization policies as a cost rather than as a benefit of free trade which they are not prepared to face. But if we want to prosper as an independent nation we need to undertake them regardless. If we do so, prices for consumers would be reduced so that real wages would rise somewhat without any increase in the nominal or real wage cost to manufacturing or other sectors.

Third, with the Canadian dollar now less than US$.75, Canadian industry, by and large, is already quite competitive with most U.S. industry. One of the major studies released in May by External Affairs on unit costs in Canadian and American industries found that after taking account of the exchange rate, Canadian industries generally were "more cost-competitive than their U.S. counterparts in 1984" (Data Resources 1985). Thus, setting aside for the moment U.S. non-tariff measures, if this evidence is correct, it implies that with the existing, low U.S. tariffs that exist on most industries, a large number of Canadian industries already have the potential to specialize more, find market niches for themselves in the vast U.S. market, lower their costs with increased production and export more to the market. The fact that any firms, often of small size, have already done so suggests that this is a realistic possibility that should not be overlooked or discounted by any more firms and by policy makers. Moreover, since the Canadian dollar has followed the U.S. currency down by 40 per cent or more *vis-à-vis* other major currencies in the last year, Canada should also be able to achieve new markets in other developed nations as well as in third countries where those developed nations are now selling. Such policies, of course, require new vision and initiatives on the part of the Canadian entrepreneurial class. This is true whether we have BFT or not.

What the foregoing paragraph implies is that the current economic argument for BFT stands or falls almost entirely upon whether, at this time, with surging protectionist and nationalistic forces in Congress and throughout the United States, Canada can, through bilateral negotiations, secure any exemptions for itself from the awesome battery of U.S. contingent protection, and thereby avoid, or even reverse, the decision of the U.S. authorities to impose new duties on Canadian exports. The U.S. laws permit countervailing duties against foreign products produced with any government assistance to industry, anti-dumping duties, and provisions to counter or retaliate against **any** foreign practices which, from a U.S. perspective, are "unjustifiable, unreasonable, or discriminatory, and burden or restrict United States commerce" (Section 304 of the 1984 Trade Act). There are also "escape clauses" which permit the blockage of imports if "serious injury" to U.S. industry can be demonstrated, even if the foreign producer has not violated any other U.S. law. Other countries of course have countervail, anti-dumping, and escape clauses in accord with the relevant sections of GATT. But it is the increasingly aggressive way in which the U.S. laws are being applied and the fact that *any* action by a foreign government or producer becomes unfair if the U.S. authorities choose to define it as such that is the disturbing thing. The best example of this is with regard to the U.S. view that Canadian stumpage laws give Canadian lumber firms a cost advantage in the U.S. market and therefore justify a high U.S. tariff on imports of lumber from Canada. Stumpage is identical in principle to royalties that our provinces or federal government levy on oil and gas production and other such taxes on mineral extraction. What is at issue, then, is the sovereign right of Canadian governments to determine resource taxes and, by implication, the pace of our resource development and our exports thereof. Also at issue is whether Canada, which has a relative abundance of natural resources, will have the right to exercise its God-given comparative advantage in such resources in its trade with the United States. These are the same issues that the pending U.S. Gibbons bill raises.

Many suggestions have been made regarding how Canada might negotiate to exclude from U.S. countervail action certain Canadian policies such as regional development grants, providing they only counter the economic disadvantage of a firm locating in a particular region, or subsidies up to a certain maximum (Lipsey and Smith 1985, 152-153), or extra unemployment insurance for fishermen facing a short inshore fishing season, or other current assistance programs (Steger 1985, 26-28). It might also be possible to negotiate stricter standards when injury is being determined, or at least have "injury" defined more clearly so as to reduce the number of injury complaints that might be filed (Steger 1985, 29). All of these are useful ideas and worthy of exploration by our negotiators. But recent indications from the United States are that there will not be any waiver of existing U.S. countervail, anti-dumping or escape clause provisions.

The U.S.-Israel agreement did not make any dent in U.S. contingency law or its application. The U.S. view was that such laws exist "to keep the trade free and open." They were not open for negotiation (Gibbons 1984). Note also that in Annex Four of the U.S.-Israel agreement, it was Israel that agreed to discontinue several subsidy programs. Moreover, up to the end of 1990, Israel must discuss with the United States any measures it would like to institute to encourage the development of new industries. After 1990 Israel must get U.S. consent before instigating any new industrial development policies. Some economists (such as Cornell) argue that Canada is much more important economically to the United States than is Israel, so that we should not see the U.S.-Israel agreement as any guide to what the United States would want from Canada. I would suggest that if the United States wants control over even tiny Israel's industrial development policies, how much *more* will it want control over what Canada does – while giving up very little or no control over its own contingency measures.

In brief, it is not inconceivable that merely in return for reductions in the remaining, modest U.S. tariffs and with little or no change in U.S. contingency protection, Canada will have to surrender or alter substantially the wide range of its domestic programs and laws mentioned earlier in this paper. Also, the U.S. agricultural exports subsidization program is not likely to be negotiable in a purely BFT context, since the major U.S. concern in having it is to counter the EEC export subsidy program and eventually bring the EEC to the bargaining table, presumably in the next GATT round.

There is, of course, nothing inherently wrong with Canada altering its domestic laws and programs. If, as with marketing boards and provincial protectionist practices discussed earlier, they are contributing to domestic economic inefficiency, then we should alter them ourselves. But it is highly questionable whether we should make additional changes in our policies in return for the minimal improvements in our access to U.S. markets such as we might get from only a removal of the remaining, generally small U.S. tariffs.

This is particularly true if we retain the freedom of a reasonably flexible exchange rate. Should a decline of a few more percentage points in the rate be necessary to achieve competitiveness and a balance on current account appropriate to any long-run objectives we might have with regard to capital inflows, this should not be avoided. One would hope that the Bank of Canada would be open to this possibility, for any inflationary pressure resulting is likely to be modest, given our continuing unemployment problem.

Under BFT it is far from clear that Canada would be able to have a value for its currency that reflected our trading position. Utterances from several high-placed U.S. officials such as Treasury Secretary James Baker, Trade Representative Clayton Yeutter and Commerce Secretary Malcolm Baldridge[5] suggest that the United States may well expect there to be some commitment forthcoming from Canada in the BFT agreement to holding the Canadian currency within some particular range — presumably one that keeps the Canadian merchandise trade balance with the United States at some level acceptable to the United States. The adjustment safety valve that many ardent free traders see Canada as possessing may not be open to us.

There is a related point to be made with regard to exchange rates. It is well known in the international trade literature that the beneficial effects of a devaluation or depreciation of a nation's currency often take two years to be in full evidence. The U.S. dollar commenced it decline *vis-à-vis* the yen and several European currencies in the autumn of 1985, and then continued for a number of months thereafter. If the past is any indication, we should not expect to see a **major** turnaround in the massive U.S. trade deficit for perhaps another year or more. The protectionist, nationalistic pressures are likely to remain at peak levels during this period. Yet it is precisely in this time span that Canada is attempting to negotiate a BFT arrangement with the United States, namely, before the U.S. negotiating authority runs out at the end of 1987. It is the **worst** possible time to be doing so. A good argument can be made that Canada would be better off working through the multilateral negotiations of GATT which will be going on beyond 1987. By that time the U.S. trade balance is likely to be much improved and the highly protectionist mood may well be considerably assuaged.

Another weakness of the pro-free trade position is evident in the External Affairs documents released in May 1986. A tendency exists to minimize the problems of adjustment to BFT. The government generally has tried to downplay the extent of the adjustments that will be necessary. Although adjustment is discussed in more detail in other papers of this volume, one issue is not given much attention by other participants. It is the question of how the adjustment is to be financed.

This matter often seems to have been ignored, apparently because of the belief that our national income would grow sufficiently that financing would not be a problem. Yet, Canada would lose about $2.1 billion of customs duties each year, which would have to be made up by either higher personal income tax, or higher corporate taxes (through equalizing taxes across industries or eliminating various tax privileges). Also, the profits of many import-competing firms will decline, at least until they can rationalize in some way, even if other firms' profits may improve. If the Informetrica model has the sign right on what happens to total federal government revenues in the longer run, the federal deficit will increase – unless, as the builders of the model suggest, federal transfers to the provinces are reduced as provincial revenues rise somewhat.

It is not clear, however, that the macro-models allow fully for the demands that will be placed upon the federal government by business firms for assistance in their rationalization – not to mention all the demands by workers for assistance as they have to change jobs, relocate, and retrain. When one hears claims from an industry such as brewing, with its long history of high returns on capital, that it will need several billion dollars of government assistance in order to adjust to free trade, one wonders whether the expectations on government are not going to be far greater than any government could tolerate. Tax reform, as is currently being discussed, involving a reassessment of the entire range of grants and assistance to businesses, will be a necessary adjustment to any BFT agreement.

Another subject all too glibly slurred over by advocates of BFT is the extent of policy harmonization that will be necessary. Economists supporting BFT constantly remind us that we would be negotiating a free trade agreement, not a customs union or a common market like the EEC. Therefore harmonization and integration generally would not be nearly as great between Canada and the United States as they have had to be within the EEC (Brean 1985, 27). In contrast to this view, note what one student of the two situations has to say:

> ... there is a much greater degree of integration in North America in transportation and communications systems, technical standards and ownership and control of industries and intercorporate links than exists in Europe today, even a quarter of a century after the EEC came into being. (Lane 1985, 35)

Also, with regard to the individual states in the EEC, Lane (1985) had this to say:

> Not only did they all have programs designed to aid particular industries and regions, they also had powerful general instruments of policy at their disposal which could be used to influence the response of their firms to the problems and opportunities of integration. These ranged from relatively modest devices like special depreciation and other tax concessions to more interventionist mechanisms such as using the economic power of nationalized industries and infusing capital into certain private enterprises through control of the banking system or special investment funds. (p. 14)

Notice, then, that the types of legislative prerogatives that individual governments in the EEC were able to retain for themselves in their customs union or common market are many of the very prerogatives that the United States wants Canada to dispense with in a mere free trade agreement with them. If the United States insists on an across-the-board "national treatment" policy for all its firms in Canada and in Canadian trade with the United States — as Prime Minister Mulroney has said he wants — the extent of policy harmonization could be enormous.

Economic empirical work and theorizing on free trade in Canada all too often ignore the political and economic realities of U.S. aspirations today. On the harmonization issue we have such high-sounding statements as:

> The pursuit of (the) gains from free, international trade need not compromise national policies that alter the outcome of domestic market forces because of social decisions to produce a variety of public goods and to achieve a more equitable distribution of income. Fiscal sovereignty must take precedence over commercial arrangements for free trade ... National policies that ... are essential to the pursuit of Canadian objectives ... must be respected in any international trading arrangement that falls short of complete economic integration. (Brean 1985, 28-29).

I agree. But whether Professor Brean and I agree does not really matter. It is whether U.S. congressmen see it that way. All indications are to date that they do not. Again we have such statements as this regarding the BFT negotiations:

> The fourth source of negotiating pressures is a set of political and legal pressures that, for want of a better name, we call 'philosophical.' For example, the United States might decide that it just does not like the tenor of Canada's unemployment insurance system or Canada's health-financing system. It might feel Canada's regulatory policies are not sufficiently market oriented, and so on. In such cases, it could put pressure on Canada to abandon these systems just because it did not like them. **Once again, there is no reason for Canada to accede to these pressures**. (Lipsey and Smith 1986, 18). (boldface is mine.)

Yet a little earlier in the same paper the authors say:

> Given the current protectionist climate in Congress, it is no longer unreasoned hysteria that makes one wonder how soon the United States will decide that Canada's unemployment assistance, health and welfare policies, or domestic regulatory policies are unfair trade practices and apply legal sanctions against them. (p. 9).

The authors do not make a convincing case as to why we might be subject to U.S. action against our domestic policies at the moment, yet will somehow be able to negotiate these pressures away in a BFT agreement. In brief, much more careful work is necessary on the harmonization issue. It cannot be readily assumed aside by arguing that having a flexible exchange rate will reduce or eliminate the need for such harmonization. As already noted, we may even have difficulty retaining the flexibility of our currency *vis-à-vis* the U.S. dollar.

Another area where oversimplification or at least misunderstanding has occurred in Canadian economic discussions of BFT is with regard to the "fast-track" procedure. Under this U.S. procedure the president has been authorized to negotiate an agreement with Canada. Then the president must submit it to Congress which has a limited time in which to approve or disapprove it, with no amendments being permitted. There has been a tendency in Canada to think that this procedure will make for easier negotiation for it is only the executive branch of government which is directly involved. However, congressional members and their constituents are entitled to have and will be having a continuous input into the substance of the negotiations. The fast-track procedure only limits the time spent in Congress. It does not in any way limit the horse-trading, log-rolling, or other processes that go into the negotiation of an agreement.

Concluding Comments

These comments bring me back to the theme with which I opened this paper, namely, that much more than narrow economic analysis is involved in BFT. Economists have tended to shy away from or assume aside a number of the most difficult issues in making their economic assessment of the net gains from free trade. When these are introduced, the outcome is not nearly so evident, and neither is the exact magnitude of the net gains. There may well be a significant loss of Canadian sovereignty in the process.

Yet, I also see that as a consequence of the debate over the past two years, there has been a deepening of understanding of the issues by all participants in that debate, and a coming together on a number of key issues. For example, even some of the strongest advocates of BFT, such as former Premier Peter Lougheed, or Professor John Crispo, have come to recognize that if items like exchange rates, our social policies, health care policies, tax policies generally or other demands which undermine our political or cultural sovereignty are items which the United States wants to negotiate, then we should **not** continue the negotiations.

Canadians often have a tendency to want a "quick fix" for their economic problems. A number of years ago, the control of inflation (which no one denies was necessary) was offered as a means to stabilize our economy, restore the confidence of our business community, and prepare the way for a new surge of economic growth and greatly reduced unemployment. We controlled inflation, but that was not enough. Many other factors would have had to come together as well before our unemployment problems would have been resolved. Again, it was only two or three years ago when there was a tendency to believe that if we just got rid of the most important of the rules on foreign investment inflows under the Foreign Investment Review Agency (FIRA), this would restore the confidence of the foreign business community and bring about a new inflow of foreign firms anxious to capitalize on the opportunities in the Canadian market. FIRA was in due course eliminated, but the domestic advantages of eliminating it were hardly noticeable. Finally we have had the "leap of faith" into BFT and this is offered as the way to establish a more favourable environment for new investment in Canada, restore business confidence, and increase our prosperity or at least prevent us from losing whatever prosperity we now have.

If our negotiators are able to prevent the United States pressing through with all its extravagant demands and continually exercising its formidable contingency protection laws against Canada, there certainly should be gains for Canada. But negotiating by ourselves with the most powerful and certainly one of the most nationalistic countries in the world is not an easy proposition. That is why I would prefer to see us take the longer route via the multilateral framework and in the meantime simply fight U.S. protectionist measures one by one as they arise.

One author (Young 1986) has suggested that it might be best to try negotiating **only** a government procurement agreement with the United States whereby each nation's businesses would have free access to the government purchases of the other nation. But as mentioned earlier, given the U.S. propensity for wanting equal benefits from any agreement, Canada would have to give something besides access to government purchases in Canada to bring such a deal about. What that something else might be is anyone's guess. Would it be worth it?

Finally, I will let Ron and Paul Wonnacott have the final word at this time. This quote is taken from their 1967 study on BFT:

> Because a free trade arrangement is bound to create a number of specific problems (regardless of its overall desirability), it would best be undertaken when major disturbances, such as widespread unemployment or an international financial crisis, are absent. (307).

With that I concur.

Notes

1. Other studies have come forth over the years, such as J. Williams (1978), but they have not been given as much public attention as the various studies mentioned here have received.

2. Although it had admitted just three pages earlier that "free trade in wine might not be sustainable without free trade in grapes if U.S. growers enjoy substantial cost advantages over their Canadian rivals." (v. 1, p. 305).

3. Banking and other financial services would apparently be excluded from the BFT negotiations as the U.S. Treasury apparently believes that they can do a better job of negotiating changes in this sector outside BFT.

4. Peter Cornell takes issue with me for questioning that Canadian shipbuilding would gain from a bilateral agreement with the U.S. He argues that this result takes into account the removal of U.S. non-tariff measures on ship imports, and therefore should be quite reliable. If he really believes the Informetrica results, and that bilateral free trade as he envisages will come to pass, then my

recommendation would be that he invest heavily in the shares of Canadian shipbuilding firms and other such industries identified by the model of his choice.

5. Note that these men are not just some radical protectionist group as Cornell has attempted to suggest.

References

Barber, Clarence. 1985. "Manitoba's Interest In and Attitude Towards A Proposed Canada-United States Free Trade Area: A Study Prepared for Manitoba Industry, Trade and Technology." September.

Brean, Donald J.S. 1985. "Fiscal Policy Harmonization and Negotiation of a Free-Trade Area," Toronto: Institute for Policy Analysis. December.

Brown, Drucilla. 1986. "Regarding United States-Canada Free Trade," Testimony Regarding United States-Canada Free Trade before the Subcommittee on Economic Stabilization of the Committee on Banking, Finance, and Urban Affairs, United States House of Representatives, August 5.

Canada, Department of External Affairs. Clark, Joe. 1985. "A Speech to the Foreign Policy Association New York." November 18.

Canada, Department of External Affairs. 1985. "Effect of Enhanced Trade on Investment: Survey Evidence." Ottawa.

_____. 1985b. *Competitiveness and Security: Directions for Canada's International Relations*. Ottawa: Minister of Supply and Services.

_____. 1985c. "Interim Report on the Economic Implications of a Canada/U.S. Enhanced Trade Agreement." August 23.

Canada, Minister for International Trade. 1985. *How to Secure and Enhance Canadian Access to Export Markets*. Ottawa.

Canada, Senate. Standing Senate Committee on Foreign Affairs. 1982. *Canada-United States Relations, Vol. III. Canada's Trade Relations with the United States.* Ottawa: Queen's Printer.

_____, Canada-United States Relations, Vol. II. *Canada's Trade Relations with the United States*. Ottawa: Queen's Printer.

Daly, Michael J. and R. Someshwar Rao. 1985. *Scale Economies and the Gains from Free Trade*. Ottawa: Economic Council of Canada.

Data Resources. 1985. *Unit Cost Comparisons For Canadian and American Industries.* Prepared for the Department of External Affairs. September.

Dauphin, Roma. 1978. *The Impact of Free Trade in Canada*. Ottawa: Economic Council of Canada.

Economic Council of Canada. 1975. *Looking Outward: A New Trade Strategy for Canada*. Ottawa: Supply and Services.

_____. 1986. *Twenty-Third Annual Review: Changing Times*. Ottawa: Supply and Services.

English, H. Edward, Bruce W. Wilkinson, and H.C. Eastman. 1972. *Canada in a Wider Economic Community.* Toronto: University of Toronto Press, for the Private Planning Association of Canada.

General Agreement on Tariffs and Trade. 1969. *Basic Instruments and Selected Documents.* Geneva: GATT, v. 4.

Gibbons, Sam. 1984. "Statement to the Deputy U.S. Trade Representative and the Deputy Undersecretary of Agriculture for International Affairs and Commodity Programs." Proposed United States-Israel Free Trade Area: Hearing Before the Subcommittee on Trade of the House Committee on Ways and Means. 98th Congress, 2nd Session, 26.

Globe and Mail. 1986. February 28, p. A11.

Harris, R. and David Cox. 1985. "Summary of a Project of the General Equilibrium Evaluation of Canadian Trade Policy: Appendix, Further Calculations on Sectoral and Bilateral Free Trade." In *Canada-United States Free Trade*, ed. by John Whalley and Roderick Hill. Toronto: University of Toronto Press, 171-177.

Informetrica. 1985. *Economic Impacts of Enhanced Bilateral Trade: National and Provincial Results: Executive Summary.*

Kelleher, James. 1986a. "Speech at University of Western Ontario." January 22.

_____. 1986b. "Notes for an Address to the Canadian-California Chamber of Commerce for the California Council for International Trade." January 16.

Lane, A.W.A. 1985. *Economic Integration – Some Aspects of the European Experience.* October 21, p. 35, 14.

Lipsey, R. and M. Smith. 1986. *Policy Harmonization: The Effects of a Canada-United States Free Trade Area.* Toronto: C.D. Howe Institute.

_____. 1985. *Taking the Initiative: Canada's Trade Options in a Turbulent World.* Toronto: C.D. Howe Institute.

The Macdonald Report. 1985. *The Report of the Royal Commission on the Economic Union and Development Prospects for Canada.* Vols. I, II, and III.

Mulroney, Brian. 1985. "Statement in the House of Commons on Canada/USA Trade Negotiations." September 26. House of Commons Debates, September 26, 1985, p. 7055-7056.

Rooth, T.J.T. 1986. "Tariffs and Trade Bargaining: Anglo-Scandinavian Economic Relations in the 1930s." *Scandinavian Economic History Review*, XXXIV, No. 1, 54-71.

_____. 1984. "Limits of Leverage: The Anglo-Danish Trade Agreement of 1933." *The Economic History Review*, Vol. XXXVII, No. 2, May, 211-228.

Shakespeare, William. *As You Like It*. Toronto: Longmans, Green. Act II. Sc. 7.

Statistics Canada. 1981. *Canadian Imports by Domestic and Foreign Controlled Enterprises: 1978*. Ottawa: Minister of Supply and Services.

Steger, Debra. 1985. "The Impact of U.S. Trade Laws on Canadian Economic Policies." Toronto: McCarthy & McCarthy, December.

Stern, Robert. 1985. "Book Review of Richard G. Harris with David Cox, Trade, Industrial Policy, and Canadian Manufacturing." *Journal of International Economics*, v. 19, pp. 189-192.

Trant, Gerald I., David L. MacFarland, and Lewis A. Fischer. 1968. *Trade Liberalization and Canadian Agriculture*. Toronto: University of Toronto Press, for the Private Planning Association of Canada.

Wilkinson, B.W. 1986. "Canada-U.S. Free Trade: The Current Debate." A paper presented to the Overview Conference, "The North American Political Economy in the Global Context." Sponsored by the Canadian Institute of International Affairs. Toronto: February 27-28.

_____. 1985a. "Commercial Policy and Free Trade with the United States." In *Canada Among Nations, 1984: A Time of Transition*, ed. by Brian W. Tomlin and Maureen Molot. Toronto: James Lorimer and Company, 164-184.

_____. 1985b. "Canada/U.S. Free Trade and Canadian Economic Cultural and Political Sovereignty." *Canadian Trade at a Crossroads: Options for New International Agreements*. Toronto: Ontario Economic Council, 291-307.

_____. 1985c. "Canadian Foreign Policy: Comments on the Green Papers." *Behind the Headlines*, XLII (6)/XLIII (1) 62-65.

_____. 1982. "Canada/U.S. Free Trade and Some Options." *Canadian Public Policy*, VIII (Supplement), 428-439.

_____. 1980. *Canada in the Changing World Economy*. Toronto: C.D. Howe Research Institute, Appendix D.

_____. 1968. *Canada's International Trade: An Analysis of Recent Trends and Patterns*. Montreal: Private Planning Association.

Williams, J. 1978. *The Canadian-United States Tariff and Canadian Industry: A Multisectoral Analysis*. Toronto: University of Toronto Press.

Wonnacot, Ron and Paul Wonnacott. 1967. *Free Trade Between the United States and Canada: The Potential Economic Effects*. Cambridge, Mass.: Harvard University Press.

Young, Robert. 1986. "A Way Out for Mr. Mulroney." *Policy Options*, v. 7, #4, May 3-8.

In Support of Trade Liberalization:
A Comment on Bruce Wilkinson's Paper

Peter Cornell

It is indeed a pleasure to take part in this very topical discussion and to come up once again against as formidable a representative of many (though certainly not all) views that run so counter to mine on trade policy.

Perhaps as a continued unrepentant proponent of trade liberalization, and one who does not see the multilateral and bilateral approaches as being mutually exclusive, I should entitle my discussion of Professor Wilkinson's paper "We Never Promised You a Rose Garden." In fact, I am in agreement with many things he has to say in his paper — though sometimes with qualifications — but to a very considerable extent he sets up a straw man (my "rose garden") as a basis for comparison. He then proceeds to knock it down — even at times resorting to the use of "pink" if not "red" herring. I must say that I would not mind at all having Professor Wilkinson as my defence lawyer if I were up on an indictable offence (perhaps, as a proponent of trade liberalization, I am) but I do find his argument rather unbalanced.

Let me comment first on some of the areas where I agree with Professor Wilkinson, though often with certain qualifications.

I agree that:

- Economics by itself provides too narrow a perspective when talking about Bilateral Free Trade (BFT) in particular. (I do note, however, that when it comes to political views, those of any or all economists are of equal weight.)

- Our understanding of what is actually meant by BFT has been evolving over time. There is certainly much more emphasis now on Non-tariff Measures

27

(NTMs), especially perhaps contingency measures although, as Professor Wilkinson admits, these were not entirely absent from earlier discussion. Most certainly, U.S. contingency measures are a key element in the present discussions and these will make the negotiations very rough to say the least. But few, if any, proponents of BFT have ever held that we should go ahead at any cost. We have, as Professor Wilkinson has, looked at both costs and benefits, but we have disagreed and still do on the relative size of those. I will come back to this point. Nevertheless, I would caution against forgetting about tariffs entirely. True, the average levels are much lower now but there are still some outstanding examples of tariff barriers (e.g., fruit and vegetable preparations, U.S. tariff 10.70 per cent).

- Trade in services is now also a much more important element. This is, of course, true in the NTM framework also and there may be a lot to be said for a bilateral approach to some of the service trade issues.

- More homework has been needed on both benefits and costs. On the cost side, the Economic Council of Canada has done a good deal on adjustment but no one, to my way of thinking, has done much on harmonization issues. (Note here the expansion of the Economic Council program on the adaptation process including examination of dynamics.)

- Free trade is not a panacea. The problem is that I am not aware of many proponents of trade liberalization who think it **is** a panacea.

- Economic models are not by any means entirely satisfactory. But the modellers themselves are usually the first to point out that their results are only a rough guide and that they depend heavily on some key background assumptions and, of course, on the structure of the particular model. General equilibrium models (e.g., Harris) are not, of course, designed to tell us what will happen to total employment, only how it may be redistributed under the impact of trade liberalization. I note, too, however, that there continue to be attempts to improve the realism of the modelling work, e.g., by introducing more NTM effects, and that the models of impact as well as the mounting work on the adjustment process continue to accumulate evidence that points in the same direction at least.

In this respect I wonder why, for example, Professor Wilkinson takes a crack at the shipbuilding results contained in Informetrica's work. He argues first that we need to know more about the impact of NTMs. The Informetrica results were the direct reflection of including the potential removal of an important U.S. non-tariff measure in that particular set of simulations.

Perhaps I might touch, too, on the question of the calculated benefits of BFT. Professor Wilkinson rightly observes that he and others have expressed reservations about the size of those gains (while exaggerating the costs?). There has indeed been a good deal of criticism of the potential gains calculation and most of it surrounds the scope for economies of scale. (I would prefer "economies of market size" as a more all-inclusive term.) And it may be that some of the earlier suggestions, in particular, were somewhat exaggerated. Yet we still get evidence that there are potential gains for a variety of Canadian industries from access to larger markets. And even when we use rather conservative estimates of productivity improvements, some preliminary work at the Economic Council indicates substantial gains in Canadian real income and price performance.

But I have to ask another question as well. Why do the opponents of BFT – and some of them I suspect are not too keen about Multilateral Free Trade (MFT) either – continue to rely on anecdotal evidence or their critiques of other people's models? When are they going to contribute to the homework?

I agree that many of the areas "where improvements in efficiency may occur if BFT comes about are actually improvements which we could undertake domestically without facing some of the difficulties that BFT might produce for us." Certainly the Economic Council and others have said much the same, but we must at least ask why we have not cleaned up our own domestic act. Maybe, just maybe, external pressures *are* required.

So you can see that even where I agree with Professor Wilkinson, I think that in many cases he, too, glosses over some of the issues in order to make his case. Going further, however, I am disturbed by the way in which he arrives at his description of the definition of what is now meant by BFT. On the Canadian side he does this by a fairly careful review of the various analytical contributions to the debate. Whether they add up to what Simon Reisman has in mind at this point I am not sure.

But I am even less sure that his adding up of anecdotal evidence of statements by outright opponents of trade liberalization in the United States, of congressmen with their districts in mind, add up to the official U.S. position. I agree they indicate that the going will be tough, but I am not sure that this is very newsworthy.

I am concerned, too, with what he is using as a base for comparison of the results of BFT (or even MFT). To my mind, what many of the U.S. statements he uses indicate is that the base we should be using for comparison is much worse than the status quo, if we can even use that term for the present situation.

I am concerned as well, as I noted earlier, that there is a rather fishy smell surrounding some of his additional arguments. I find it difficult to accept that recent problems with respect to employment and productivity, whether in the European Economic Community or Canada, should even be related to the results of trade negotiations. The real question is:

> Would we have been worse off in the face of oil price shocks, severe cyclical movements and a long period of low aggregate demand if the previous trade negotiations had **not** taken place?

And I hardly think that the U.S.-Israel free trade agreement can be used to illustrate much about a potential Canada-U.S. agreement. Surely U.S. economic interest in Canada is much greater when one thinks of the size of our trade with the Americans relative to that of Israel. And as Data Resources International (DRI) has pointed out, some individual U.S. industries have a far higher stake in the Canadian market than is generally realized.

The Adjustment Problem

Can We Become Better Losers?
The Problem of Disinvesting
from Declining Sectors

*Michael J. Trebilcock ***

The (Macdonald) Royal Commission on the Economic Union and Development Prospects for Canada identified the overriding public policy issue on its agenda as follows in its interim report, *Challenges and Choices*: "How can we better manage and adjust to change? If there is a single major concern among Canadians, it relates to that question."[1]

Adjustment to changing economic challenges and circumstances is both necessary and vital in a dynamic economy but also often painful. A well-functioning market economy yielding high rates of economic growth over time requires risk-taking, innovation, and dynamic adjustment mechanisms that quickly reallocate resources to higher-valued uses, but also implies, by necessity, a degree of economic uncertainty and, above all, winners and losers. In Schumpeter's memorable phrase, market forces tend to entail "a perennial gale of creative destruction."[2] However, as a society becomes more prosperous by virtue of these economic processes, it may well come to feel that assuming large negative risks is something it can afford to dispense with and hence will vote to establish collective programs that minimize certain classes of risk—hence free public education, health insurance, public pensions, workmen's compensation, unemployment insurance, etc. These safety nets are seen as the mark of a prosperous, civilized, compassionate society and offer the promise of individual or family security that stands in contrast to the risks assumed by citizens in poorer, Third World countries facing a

* This paper is drawn from Michael Trebilcock. *The Political Economy of Economic Adjustment* (Ottawa: Research Study No. 8, 1986, for the (Macdonald) Royal Commission on the Economic Union and Development Prospects for Canada, 1986).

continuous battle for survival against pestilence, famine, malnutrition, floods, drought, economic and political disorder, etc. Thus, collective decision making is frequently directed to reducing risk and enhancing security, the market system to fostering risk taking and concomitant uncertainty.

Yet, despite these tensions between our economic and political systems, the fact remains that no genuine democracy has existed in recent times outside a capitalist economy, and few capitalist economies have existed outside democratic politics. This suggests that viable compromises between the inequalities required by an economic system predicated on the importance of incentives and the equalities of a political system predicated on egalitarian democratic entitlements are attainable. Public policies toward the costs of economic adjustment very much entail a focus on what form such compromises might take. However, these compromises will never be easy to fashion. Throughout most of 1984, Britain was embroiled in a coal miners' strike, marked by bitterness and violence, over proposals by the government-owned National Coal Board to close down 20 uneconomic pits and terminate 20,000 jobs. The steel riots in Paris in early 1979 over proposals to phase out steel production and jobs in regions with obsolete plants entailed a similar reaction to the prospects of economic change. Both events are in some ways reminiscent of the Luddite movement in early nineteenth century Britain, protesting technological unemployment induced by the industrial revolution. This similarity of public concerns over the span of almost two centuries is striking.

Alternative Perspectives on Government Intervention in the Adjustment Process

The Economic Perspective

From a neo-classical economic perspective, the case for intervention in economic adjustment processes is tightly circumscribed. Rapid adjustment to changing economic circumstances is viewed as central to high rates of economic growth, as resources are quickly reallocated out of lower-valued uses to higher-valued uses. Economic Darwinism — unconstrained market forces — is thought to be most conducive to this process, as a multitude of private sector actors make their best judgments as to the future in making investment and vocational decisions and are rewarded or penalized pending the soundness of the judgments.

Private capital markets, with large numbers of expert actors with large personal stakes in the soundness of their decisions, are seen as much more likely than government to make appropriate evaluations of the future value of given economic activities. Thus, government intervention in the economic adjustment process to alleviate the consequences of private risk taking by owners of financial or physical capital is viewed as having little merit.

In the case of human capital, or labour, the economic perspective would recognize that market forces may sometimes generate inappropriately low levels of investment in general (non-specialized) human capital, because employers who invest in training cannot be sure of appropriating the returns and because individuals may find it difficult to borrow against future earnings to finance their own training. In the case of specific or highly specialized human capital, the second factor may again make it difficult for individuals to finance the acquisition of such skills, at least through institutional training (hence, a major justification for public financing of higher education). Once such capital is acquired, individuals may find it difficult to obtain private insurance against the risk of the depreciation of this capital as a result of future changes in their economic environment and, by definition, cannot diversify away such risks nearly as easily as firms or shareholders.

The economic perspective would thus be unsympathetic to government assistance to firms or shareholders faced with costs of economic adjustment but somewhat readier to recognize a case for intervention to ease the adjustment costs of labour, principally by subsidizing the acquisition of new forms of human capital, for example, through retraining and relocation programs.

Ethical Perspectives

Ethical (or moral) perspectives on adjustment costs would, to some extent, tend in the same direction.[3] A particular form of argument from utilitarianism would stress that, assuming some degree of risk aversion by most members of the community, utilitarian policy makers may wish to control uncertainty costs to the extent that individuals entertain a special sense of grievance at being singled out by the collective as the victims of uncompensated losses. Thus, this form of the utilitarian framework might be especially concerned with unanticipated changes that frustrate long-standing economic expectations.

A Rawlsian social contract ethical perspective would stress that behind a veil of ignorance, where our individual lots in life and endowments are not known, we would all agree that no collective policy should be pursued that does not improve the lot of the least advantaged. In other words, we would all agree to a form of social insurance against the risk of finding ourselves in this plight.

On either ethical view, however, it will be noted that the welfare of individuals is central, and in particular the welfare of individuals who are not well able to protect themselves from unexpected changes in their economic environment. Firms and investors who can diversify against the risks of change will rarely be able to make out a strong ethical case for adjustment assistance. Displaced workers will more often be able to make out a stronger case. In this respect, the economic and ethical perspectives converge, although the latter may be more generous in compensating for some of the private costs of change (locationed fixities such as loss of value on homes, loss of social amenities and networks[4]) and not confine itself to responding to market imperfections in the formation of human capital, e.g., through retraining programs.

The Political Perspective

From a political perspective, this focus is unfortunately often likely to be substantially distorted. Geographic concentration of firms and workers in declining sectors will often lead to strong political pressures for intervention. Moreover, political considerations will often lead to the adoption of instruments of intervention that retard rather than facilitate the process of change. In particular, trade protection (tariff and non-tariff barriers to trade) has the political virtue of appeasing both investors and workers simultaneously, while spreading the costs of protection very widely over the economy and over time. Where these instruments are not available, political forces will often induce governments to adopt various forms of firm or industry-specific subsidies that sustain output and employment in declining sectors. These again have the political virtues of appeasing investors and workers simultaneously, and while the costs are more visible than those entailed in the use of trade protection instruments, these can partly be disguised through off-budget instruments such as loan guarantees, loans at below market interest rates, or tax expenditures.

On-budget expenditures on labour adjustment programs such as retraining, early retirement, severance payments, mobility allowances, in contrast, entail highly visible costs as well as a potentially politically costly acknowledgement that a particular sector cannot or will not be shielded from negative judgments about its future viability, i.e., that the industry is a loser and should be abandoned.

Thus, political forces are likely to lead to an almost complete inversion of the policy implications suggested by the economic and ethical perspectives. Instead of facilitating economic adjustment by easing the costs of adjustment faced by labour, policies are likely to be favoured that postpone or retard the adjustment process with concomitant reductions in national income. The operation of these political dynamics have been clearly evident in Canada in past policies towards the textile, clothing, footwear, shipbuilding, and Cape Breton coal mining industries, where the adjustment problems faced today are almost as large, if not larger, than at any time in the past despite massive assistance through trade protection and firm subsidies.

The nature and seriousness of the policy dilemma is well pointed up by an example. Jenkins concludes that for 1979 alone, the loss to the economy per job saved by the protection through tariffs and quotas of the Canadian textile and clothing industry was $34,500.[5] As Watson points out, since the average income of Canadian textile workers in the same year was $10,000, all those who would have lost their jobs if protection had been removed could have been paid two or even three times their real 1979 incomes annually for the rest of their lives, and there would still have been something left over for the consumer.[6] Robert Crandall has recently estimated that the cost to consumers of Voluntary Export Restraints in the U.S. auto industry between 1981 and 1985 was equivalent to $160,000 per year per job saved — more than four times the average annual compensation of auto workers.[7]

The question, therefore, becomes whether we can devise policies that facilitate rather than retard economic adjustment, while at the same time providing generous assistance to individuals most affected by change to enable them to adjust to such change. Economic and ethical considerations require this conjuncture of policies. The experience of Japan and West Germany in the postwar period suggests that a strong commitment to rapid adjustment is vital to a healthy economy, while the postwar experience of Britain suggests that the lack of such a commitment is a recipe for serious economic stagnation. However, the Japanese and especially the West German experiences also suggest the importance of well conceived adjustment policies to ease the costs of change, particularly in the case of labour. Can we endow our own political institutions with the capacity to generate similar conjuncture of policies? This issue must be addressed whether the future holds prospects of increased bilateral trade liberalization, increased multilateral trade liberalization or little change in the existing international trading regime. Substantial adjustment pressures (albeit of differing intensities) confront us in all of these scenarios.

Fashioning New Policy Approaches to Economic Adjustment

A concerted and enduring public policy focus on facilitating rapid economic adjustment and easing transition problems and concomitant adjustment costs clearly must be assigned a central role in any modern industrialized country's economic, social, and political priorities. It is too easy to be trapped by the tautological logic that during recessions no adjustment is possible, while once recovery takes place no adjustment is necessary.[8] Even in times of high unemployment, some industries may be growing, and suffering from lack of workers with appropriate skills. For example, a recent survey of 4,012 establishments in Canada found that "approximately half of the 1,354 respondents reported hiring difficulties during 1977 to 1979, and 43 per cent anticipated shortages hiring during the next five years."[9] Conversely, in periods of rapid economic growth and low overall unemployment, some industries may be declining, causing job displacement where workers with job-specific skills or facing losses associated with other locational fixities cannot readily be reabsorbed into the labour force.

In fashioning policies directed to declining sectors, a general difficulty facing policy makers in choosing appropriate instruments is making the initial judgment that a sector is in long-term decline. Picking losers may be no easier than picking winners. The Canadian experience bears out this difficulty. Does Canada lack any comparative advantage in shipbuilding, or are the difficulties being encountered by the industry a function of zero-sum subsidy behaviour by many foreign governments that now hopelessly obscures where our comparative advantage might lie in this sector? In other words, our industry may be internationally competitive in some areas if all nations with shipbuilding industries would agree to withdraw trade-distorting subsidies. If not, perhaps Canada should withdraw from the sector and accept these foreign subsidies. In the case of the Cape Breton coal mining industry, the widely accepted judgment at the end of the 1960s was that the industry was not viable and should be phased down. With the advent of OPEC, coal prices rose sharply and since that time the industry has in fact expanded. Coal prices have declined subsequently but, with more cautious prognoses for the future of nuclear energy and continuing uncertainty about price and supply conditions for Middle East oil, it is not as easy to make confident judgments about the economic future of this industry. In the case of textiles, U.S. exports have grown significantly in recent years and technological advances that substitute capital for labour suggest that at least some elements of this industry are or could become internationally competitive. In the cases of automobile and farm machinery manufacturing (two Canadian industries that have recently undergone severe economic difficulties), have they merely been facing a cyclical downturn in demand, with no long-run structural implications? Or have they lost their long-run international competitiveness? Difficult as these questions are for private sector decision makers intimately acquainted with an industry's problems and potential, they pose even more difficult judgments for public sector policy makers typically lacking in this familiarity and faced with special interest group pleadings that will exploit all prevailing ambiguities to their advantage. This would seem to suggest extreme caution in invoking adjustment policies that are designed to have fundamental long-run structural impacts on sectors that can only be defended by reference to highly debatable and uncertain premises. Rather, policies should be preferred that minimize the risk of these major systemic errors in judgment and instead increase flexibility, adaptability, and reversibility on a number of smaller margins where decentralized judgments by various affected economic agents about an industry's future prospects dominate over centralized public sector judgments on this issue.

Earlier in this section, it was suggested that political forces would tend to invert policy prescriptions suggested by economic and, to a lesser extent, ethical frameworks of analysis by yielding policies that first favour trade protection to preserve output and employment, then favour sectoral subsidies to maintain output and employment, and only then favour subsidies to labour to facilitate mobility. Short of a radical reordering of the political system that generates these policy impulses, it is assumed here that feasible policy alternatives to present policies entail marginal changes in the policy mix so as to reduce the degree of incongruence between policy outcomes dictated by good politics and those dictated by good economics and good ethics. I now turn to an examination of these policy alternatives.

Trade Policy

Given the substantial political attractions of trade protection despite its economic costs and the retardation of the adjustment process that it entails, it is unrealistic to propose the complete abandonment of trade protection instruments in import-impacted sectors, although falling global tariffs, sanctioned by multilateral treaty obligations, increasingly render extensive, long-term, import-substitution policies a tenuous option as a central ingredient of Canada's industrial policies.

However, where trade protection instruments are still available to the Canadian government, second-best policy options to abandonment, either unilaterally or in trade negotiations, might entail simply holding a tariff constant over time as foreign competitors' costs fall and imports increasingly override the tariff barriers and progressively erode the market shares of domestic industries, thus inducing more orderly and less disruptive contraction. Alternatively, as with the last round of multilateral trade negotiations, gently phased-in tariff reductions may mitigate the costs of adjustment, while allowing the gains from it to be realized over time (albeit with some reduction in these gains as a result of the more protracted transition). In terms of deflecting adjustment processes, the worst possible strategy is the invocation of long-term quotas, implying guaranteed market shares for domestic producers. Unfortunately, however, in sectors under severe import pressure, a policy of benign passivity is unlikely to be politically sustainable; hence demands for unilateral escape clause or safeguard action, anti-dumping duties or bilateral "voluntary" export quotas induced by implicit threats of unilateral action. These escape hatches available to domestic governments to countervail international trade commitments have been increasingly invoked both in Canada and elsewhere in recent years and again retard needed adjustments. Containing their deployment seems an important priority. One line of policy development might attempt to secure more tightly defined international agreements on their availability, perhaps by requiring that, as if a condition of their invocation, domestic governments simultaneously evolve an approved adjustment strategy for the affected sectors to provide for reduction of capacity and industry restructuring. One interesting suggestion recently advanced by Lawrence and Litan[10] is that the safeguard provisions of the GATT be revised to permit temporary protection of sectors under severe import pressure by the invocation of explicit tariffs targeted selectively at particular sources of imports but subject to a specified phase-out schedule and subject to a condition that revenues raised from such tariffs be allocated to adjustment assistance in the affected industries. Under this strategy, a government imposing such a tariff captures any scarcity rents induced by the tariff, not foreign exporters, while at the same time easing budgetary constraints on the provision of substantial levels of adjustment assistance.

Another line of policy development might be to implement institutional structures that improve information flows to policy makers about the reactions of affected constituencies. While taking politics out of government is not here being advocated, an expanded mandate for a body like the new Canadian Import Tribunal that provides that changes in effective levels of trade protection through invocation of safeguard measures, "voluntary" quotas, etc., cannot be implemented by government (presently simply by cabinet order-in-council in Canada) without first remitting the matter to the tribunal for investigation, public hearings, and a full public report assessing costs and benefits of the proposed action, and for recommendations, including alternative non-trade protection policies that might be preferable. The government would be free to accept, reject, or modify these recommendations, but against a political back-drop of an extensive public inquiry and published findings and recommendations. It is important that the agency given this mandate have a general economic focus (like the tribunal) and not a specialized industrial mission (like the Textile and Clothing Board) if "clientele" effects are to be mitigated. The United States International Trade Commission and the Australian Industry Assistance Commission embody some of the foregoing institutional characteristics. To offset producer pressures for protection, subsidizing consumer interest group participation in proceedings of such a board would seem to be a desirable additional institutional feature. More generally, further reforms of campaign financing laws and political party subsidy policies designed to reduce the dependence of political parties on financial contributions from producer interests would seem to militate in the same direction. In short, changing (if only marginally) the political dynamics surrounding protectionist policies by reducing information and participation costs for major but thinly spread cost bearers and by reducing political dependence on the resources of concentrated producer interests may increase the political costs of invoking such policies.

Firm Subsidies

If the deployment of trade protection instruments is legally more tightly constrained and rendered politically less expedient or more costly by heightening the visibility of decisions surrounding them, politicians are then likely to face political pressures to substitute the next most politically attractive instrument for preserving industry output and employment, namely sectoral or firm subsidies. Again, these undermine, or at least attenuate, the adjustment process. From an economic perspective, they entail most of the same economic costs as a tariff (a subsidy can always be devised to replicate the effects of a tariff), and in well-functioning capital markets, there are few convincing market failure arguments that justify industrial subsidies in declining sectors. One of the more seductive arguments is that state assistance to facilitate capital modernization may be necessary to render an industry internationally competitive. However, it is important to recognize that obsolete plant is often the result of the loss of international competitiveness, not the cause of it. Firms which are able only to cover variable costs are constrained to allow their fixed assets to run down and thus their long-term capacity. If an adequate return could be made on new fixed assets, presumably the capital market would provide the funds required to make this investment. A government judgment that such an investment will yield long-run competitiveness and profitability typically will be a variance with this private capital market judgment and should, for this reason, be viewed with circumspection.

Even in job maintenance terms, industrial subsidies are suspect.[11] For such a relationship to hold, it is necessary to assume that a subsidy has created jobs marginal to the recipient firm (i.e., jobs that would not have been created by the firm in the absence of the subsidy). Even if this is true, a firm-specific subsidy will not increase employment in the industry of which it is part unless the jobs are marginal to the industry (i.e., without the subsidy, other firms in the industry would not have increased their output and employment to absorb the share of the failing firm). Even if the subsidy creates jobs that are both marginal to the firm and marginal to the industry, are they marginal to the economy at large? Subsidies, by definition, have to be withdrawn from resources that would otherwise be employed elsewhere in the economy, and there is no reason to assume that the net employment effects of a subsidy will in fact be positive, notwithstanding that the political visibility of the benefits may be greater than the political visibility of the costs. Moreover, firm-specific subsidies to troubled firms in declining sectors often tend to preserve the most marginal and least efficient firms in the industry; here, job maintenance is directly antithetical to efficient restructuring.

If political pressures nevertheless dictate firm-directed subsidies in declining sectors, assisting the strongest firms, not the weakest firms, would seem a superior strategy, for example, by bearing some of the costs associated with mergers, consolidations, orderly reduction of physical capacity, etc. Recent bail-outs of failing firms in Canada have missed such opportunities.[12] Three separate farm machinery companies in financial distress have received substantial aid from the federal government (Massey-Ferguson, Cooperative Implements, White Farm), despite serious excess capacity at the firm and industry levels. No attempts at facilitating mergers and capacity rationalization seem to have been made. A major trucking company (Maislin Trucking) was bailed out (but ultimately failed), despite excess capacity in the industry and despite possibilities of inducing a merger with other long-haul carriers with similar route networks. The bail-out of the Atlantic fish processing companies, while industry-wide in its focus, still acquiesced in the maintenance of inefficient branch processing plants.

While the economic arguments for government subsidies to firms to induce rationalization or exit from a sector are generally not compelling, if one takes as given that firm-directed subsidies are politically unavoidable, the absence of conditions on assistance to induce efficient contraction and rationalization may entail substantial problems in determining which firms to subsidize and for how long, as well as substantially increasing political vulnerability to subsequent demands for subsidies. The political costs of either appearing to acknowledge an initial mistake in terminating a stream of assistance or of being perceived as the agent primarily responsible for the social fall-outs of firm failure if support is terminated, may expose the government to opportunism on a severe scale. In other words, it seems imperative that if support is to be provided, it takes a form that minimizes the prospects of recurrent demands for assistance through insisting on (orderly) contraction and rationalization as terms of the initial grant of assistance.

A danger to be noted with the proposed policy focus is that identified earlier of the government making an erroneous judgment about the future of an industry and inducing major structural changes in the industry predicated on that judgment. This danger might be reduced by leaving the initiative for formulating restructuring proposals, within the policy framework suggested, with the industry in question, rather than imposing a centrally conceived blueprint on it. Moreover, as the British and, to a lesser extent, French experiences indicate, inducing mergers and consolidations without also inducing reductions in capacity and enhanced residual productivity courts the danger of assembling elaborate corporate umbrellas that mask the perpetuation of inefficient multi-branch operations which may continue to require subsidies. Orderly contraction and the reinforcement of points of strength in the industry, viewed as a whole, become the focus of policy, not government-financed operating subsidies or modernization programs that attempt to maintain existing industry capacity. The use of a buffer body, as in the case of the Canadian Industrial Renewal Board, to implement policies with this industry-wide focus may allow politicians to "distance" themselves from political interests demanding other forms of subsidy, and thus reduce the risks of erosion of the policy objectives, although "clientele" effects with a specialized industry board involve significant countervailing risks that an initial mandate, framed as proposed, will be perverted over time (as is arguably illustrated by the history of the Cape Breton Development Corporation).

A further policy refinement would be to discourage the use of low visibility subsidy instruments—a tighter GATT Non-Tariff Barrier Code on government procurement;

compelling the costing of off-budget subsidies such as loan guarantees, loans at below-market interest rates and tax expenditures and inclusion of these costs in government expenditure budgets and spending envelopes at the time that the assistance is provided so as to increase visibility and accountability. Again, at a more general level, reform of campaign financing laws so as to further reduce political dependence on the financial resources of concentrated producer interests may be important.

Labour Adjustment Policies

If these policy shifts were to be feasible, political attention would then necessarily be directed to a greater extent to addressing the adjustment costs faced by labour, which is where both economic and ethical frameworks of analysis suggest that focus should be placed. This general orientation was accepted by the Macdonald royal commission in its proposals for a Transitional Adjustment Assistance Program (TAAP).[13]

In this context, two tiers of proposals might be contemplated. The first tier would address adjustment costs faced by unemployed workers generally and provide much more generous assistance than at present to individuals undertaking institutional and on-the-job training and more generous relocation allowances. In financing this increased policy emphasis on training, retraining, and mobility, it would seem desirable to consider, as in West Germany and Japan, making receipt of unemployment benefits conditional on participation in retraining programs after an abridged period, for example, 16 weeks, of unconditional benefits. The presumption would be that unsuccessful job search for this period of time implies a need for different or upgraded skills. Thus, a significant portion of Unemployment Insurance Commission expenditures would be redirected to underwriting the costs of job retraining. While it might be argued that either unconditional lump sum and/or periodic payments to displaced workers will allow them to make decisions about future employment options or retraining in the light of the best labour market information than can be made available, the social costs of unemployment are not fully internalized to the workers, at least in the case of periodic payments. In the case of lump sum payments, a serious moral hazard problem arises in cases where the lump sum has been expended without retraining, relocation, or re-employment and governments then face politically difficult decisions as to whether to deny further forms of assistance. As in the case of firm-specific subsidies, it seems imperative that assistance be conditioned on the recipient adopting some course of action that minimizes the prospects of recurrent demands for relief.

In terms of improving existing retraining policies, Saunders makes a number of useful suggestions:[14]

First, Canada Employment Centres, maintained by the federal Department of Employment and Immigration, have highly incomplete information about job vacancies across the country and are consequently limited in their ability to match workers facing lay-offs with jobs in other sectors. By way of responding to imperfect information about labour markets, Saunders proposes that employers or at least larger employers be required to register all job vacancies with Canada Employment Centres. Alternatively, if this requirement is viewed as imposing excessive costs on employers, Canada Employment Centres might collectively be charged with the responsibility of maintaining an up-to-date information bank of all job vacancies advertised anywhere in Canada. In addition, more disaggregated and more regular Labour Force Survey data for specific occupations as well as more systematic, medium-term forecasting of skill shortages would enable better matching of workers facing the prospect of lay-offs with institutional or on-the-job retraining programs that are responsive to those shortages.

Second, existing institutional retraining programs that purport to respond to market failure in the investment of human capital, have been criticized – they are often of too short a duration to provide significant higher skills training; too few places for qualified and interested candidates are available; living allowances for trainees are inadequate and student loans are not applicable to such programs; federal-provincial financing arrangements give a largely exclusive right of participation in these programs to provincial educational institutions and mostly exclude private sector training institutions, thus precluding more diversified judgments about future employment opportunities.

Third, geographic mobility assistance currently covers only part of the direct costs of a move and provides insufficient assistance in advance of the move. Again, effective mobility assistance grants are responsive to information imperfections in labour markets and difficulties of borrowing against human capital.

Fourth, early retirement schemes for older workers (e.g., enriched Unemployment Insurance Commission benefits for workers between the ages of 60 and 65), while available at present in the textile, clothing, footwear and tanning industries, may warrant consideration more generally to increase on-the-job training and employment opportunities for younger and potentially more productive workers.

Fifth, wage subsidies currently payable to employers who agree to provide on-the-job training to employees, including those previously unemployed, probably should be varied counter-cyclically to provide adequate incentives to participate in such programs. An extension of the wage subsidy concept would be to provide portable wage subsidies of limited duration (e.g., two years) to unemployed workers, perhaps conditional on receipt of on-the-job training from employers. In this way, expanding sectors are assisted at the same time as the exit of resources from contracting sectors is encouraged. At present, institutional retraining programs dominate on-the-job retraining programs in terms of public expenditures and numbers of participants. It may well be that this policy emphasis should be reversed, in part again to diversify judgments about future employment opportunities and in part to provide greater opportunities for more applied job experience.

Finally, the lack of portability of private pension plan entitlements, in cases where the employer's contributions have not been vested, may be a significant deterrent to job mobility and may justify concerted federal-provincial action to develop uniform and more permissive rules on vesting, although it must be acknowledged that some tension exists with a firm's incentives to provide general on-the-job training if returns on such investments cannot be fully captured by the firm. Public subsidies to some firms for on-the-job training may partly offset these disincentive effects.

All of these policies are designed to facilitate the re-employment of human capital from declining to expanding sectors by easing the transition cost involved in such shifts. In this respect, they stand in contrast to general Unemployment Insurance programs or sector-specific extended unemployment benefits policies (such as those obtaining under Canada's textile adjustment programs or the United States Trade Adjustment Assistance program), which in many cases appear to retard rather than promote the adjustment process.

The net effect of these proposals would be to integrate much more fully social policy with economic policy, which Japanese, German, Scandinavian and, to a lesser extent, French experiences all suggest are pivotal to an effective adjustment strategy. Politically, it is difficult to see major impediments to these shifts in policy. The costs as well as the benefits are likely to be widely dispersed and, if retraining is linked to receipt of unemployment benefits, budgetary implications are reduced while reassurance is provided to cost-bearers that these expenditures are not simply welfare under another name.

However, this first tier of proposals is general in nature and is directed to all unemployed workers. What the proposals do not address is the large private costs that may be incurred by workers and related interests dependent on declining industries in depressed communities. These costs may be quite substantial and may have expenditure implications that are politically unattractive, given the availability of other instruments (trade protection, industrial subsidies) that attenuate or conceal the costs of assistance while also, of course, attenuating the gains from rapid industrial adjustment. Here, political and economic considerations might best be reconciled by focusing resources on communities where the economic costs of adjustment are likely to be highest and where, consequently, the political costs of not intervening in the adjustment process are also likely to be highest. In the second tier of proposals, these communities would be designated for special assistance where the policy goal would be to facilitate adjustment by generously subsidizing exit costs. In these cases, in addition to the first tier of proposals, generous severance packages for older workers, compensation for loss of resale value on houses and loss of social amenities, and compensation to the residual elements of the community to offset higher per capita public services (through assistance to municipalities) also would seem to be dictated—principally for political but to some extent ethical reasons, even though economic rationales for intervention might not directly justify such policies.

Under these proposals, by concentrating resources on severely distressed communities to induce members to forego the stay option and exercise the exit option, the budgetary implications can be contained. The federal government's Industry and Labour Adjustment Program (ILAP), recently terminated, has some of these features. Under this program, 10 communities and two industrial sectors were designated as distressed. However, the program was temporary in nature, was modestly financed, focused excessively on providing financial assistance to firms to stay or relocate in designated communities rather than on adjustment assistance to individuals and, with respect to the latter, focused excessively on attempting to create mostly temporary employment opportunities in existing communities. In short, the program appeared to embrace and confuse both cyclical and structural concerns. While the program exhibited serious shortcomings, it suggests the beginnings of productive new policy directions. However, it must be emphasized that such a program must be permanent in nature. Adopting policies only in recessions when alternative resource deployment options are severely constrained is likely to be much less effective and more costly than adjustment policies directed to declining sectors in a generally more buoyant economic environment. Focusing on problems of adjustment at the bottom of the business cycle is much less constructive than addressing them at other points in the business cycle. Recent preoccupation with, and popular writing about, problems of structural adjustment in North America, while responsive to political currents of concern in a deep recessionary environment, reflects this distorted policy focus. The Japanese Structurally Depressed Industries Law, which provides for industry-wide, government-approached (and sometimes subsidized) adjustment plans entailing mergers, reductions in capacity, buy-outs of marginal firms, scrappage of excess physical plan, and worker retraining in designated distressed sectors, is a prominent contrasting example of the recognition of the need for a longer-term perspective on facilitating adjustment in declining sectors. Dramatic reductions in capacity and substantial restructuring and consolidation have been achieved in industries such as aluminum, ship-building, and coal mining, in relatively short time frames. It is acknowledged, of course, that a primary focus on labour adjustment policies in a period of low economic growth and high unemployment is unlikely to prove politically acceptable or even economically very effective; hence, one would expect to observe pressures for continued reliance in this environment on trade protection and industrial subsidies to preserve existing jobs. But an acknowledgement of the difficulties of fashioning effective adjustment strategies in a sluggish economy should not be allowed to obscure the fact that these adjustment-retarding policies have also been employed in declining sectors in Canada in much more buoyant times when difficulties of adjustment were much less acute, or to obscure the importance of re-ordering our adjustment responses in the future as a stronger economy mitigates these difficulties.

A potential problem with these second tier labour adjustment proposals is one common to the other policy instruments already reviewed (trade protection and industrial subsidies), that is, that they are predicated on government judgments that communities or sectors are in long-term decline. If, for example, five years ago the automobile industry and communities like Windsor had been designated as distressed and a major exodus of labour induced by the foregoing policies, this in retrospect would appear to have been a serious mistake. This, of course, suggests extreme caution in invoking radical exit-oriented policies on the basis of short-run evidence of industrial difficulties. However, even with such caution, mistakes may still be made, but what differentiates these labour adjustment policies from either trade protection or industrial subsidies is that the risks of error are much more widely diversified in the sense that individual workers are free to accept or reject compensatory offers as they see fit in the light of their own judgments of future industry prospects and their own willingness to accept wage concessions or profit (risk) sharing renumeration arrangements that reduce real wages to levels closer to opportunity costs. If they elect to relocate, new employment decisions will be diversified across the economy and are unlikely to prove systematically misconceived, as trade protection or industrial subsidy policies may prove to be; adjunct policies to the latter of attempting to "hot-house" new industries into depressed communities run the added danger (amply borne out by Canadian experience e.g., Labrador Linerboard, Deuterium, Clairtone, Bricklin, Churchill Forest Products) of attempting to save losers by substituting winners. Moreover, in the case of all of these industry-oriented and regional policies, reversibility is often politically constrained because of continuing and concentrated community dependencies, unlike the dispersed consequences of mistaken labour adjustment policies and low political costs of market-led reversibility. This is an extremely important dynamic consideration in the choice of adjustment strategies.

Institutional Reform

While importing institutional structures that seem to exhibit desirable economic properties in their home context would seem a highly speculative exercise in terms of likely effects in the recipient country, and would, in any event, probably face strong political resistance from incumbents in existing structures threatened with deplacement or depreciation, some simple lessons might be gleaned that are of relevance to the economic policy-making process in Canada in better concerting industrial policies. Comparative experience, while far from unambiguous in these respects, suggests that strong peak or encompassing interest groups in the private sector, principally business and labour, may be likely to internalize more fully the costs and benefits of proposed policies than narrow special interest groups.[15] This experience also tends to suggest that a central government with a strong and organizationally well-integrated and closely concerted industrial policy role, and an expert and semi-autonomous bureaucracy with major industrial policy formulation and implementation responsibilities, may be important institutional strengths.[16] On the other hand, problems of political accountability with strong centralized private sector interest groups and a powerful semi-autonomous bureaucracy, and the risk of serious systemic error in policy in a highly integrated policy-making process, also suggest dangers in unqualified acceptance of these propositions. Rather, marginal or more measured changes in institutional structures that are responsive to the most dysfunctional features of present arrangements may be more realistic policy options.

Diffusion of policy-making and implementation responsibilities within the Canadian federal government across numerous departments and agencies with different roles in the industrial policy fields is sharply at variance with much more concerted decision-making structures evident in Japan, West Germany and France. Whether centralization within a more tightly defined departmental structure (Japan) or stronger central direction and coordination through high-level inter-ministerial committees (France) would be more responsive to this deficiency is unclear. However, when to the diffusion of focus within the federal government is added the diffusion of responsibility in the industrial policy field between the federal and provincial governments (which often diffuse responsibility further within their own structures), government policy making almost necessarily becomes *ad hoc*, reactive, and inconsistent, with special interest groups able to pursue numerous avenues to government influence, enlisting "clientele" institutions of government at either level in their support.

With respect to federal-provincial relations, apart from ambitious and, perhaps, unattainable agendas of reform whose economic impacts may in any event be debatable (such as fundamental reform of the Senate), some obvious comments seem suggested both by collaborative or consultative structures elsewhere and by elementary lessons from game theory. In seeking cooperative accords between federal and provincial governments in industrial policy (as with other areas of policy), comparative experience and basic precepts of game theory suggest that institutional arrangements that emphasize constrained agendas of issues, constrained numbers of players, repeat players with long-term involvements in the issues, and a regular cycle of interactions, are more likely to achieve cooperative outcomes than arrangements lacking these features. Federal-provincial structures that focus on negotiating accords on, for example, certain well-defined classes of interprovincial barriers to trade, that meet regularly and privately, that involve senior representatives of government with some permanency of tenure and with some professional or technocratic expertise in the subject area that tempers transitory considerations of political expediency that might otherwise dominate decision making, surely hold out more promise for more coherent development of economic policy in a federal-provincial framework than current structures. In the same vein, bilateral agreements that might concert adjustment policies for a given sector, reduce the bargaining costs otherwise entailed in multilateral relations.

While federal-provincial relations have come to dominate so much of policy making in Canada (probably largely unavoidably, given our constitutional structure and regional diversity), this has equally undoubtedly come at a cost. These relations emphasize what Simeon calls vertical or territorial diversions within the country and conflicts over the spatial or geographic allocations of resources.[17]

In several major OECD countries (e.g., West Germany, the Scandinavian countries) much more attention is devoted than in Canada to reconciling horizontal rather than vertical divisions, particularly among producer interests, especially labour and capital. While corporatism, tripartitism, or social contract theories in the mould of the German and Scandinavian models may not be readily reproducible in Canada, some much more systematic form of interaction between the national government and national labour and business interests in the economic policy-making field, beyond the present process of *ad hoc* and separate consultation, seems highly desirable. A deliberative structure of this kind may tend to internalize the costs of favoured policies to a greater extent than narrow special interest groups are likely to and to a greater extent than political parties *per se* where voters and interest groups typically lack the organized structure of regular interactions among repeat players in the formulation of policy preferences to ensure cooperative outcomes or the development of information networks required to evaluate fully the likely impact on their interests of alternative policies. Producers—capital and labour—are, of course, keenly interested in how the gains and pains of adjustment are to be shared, but they also share a common well-defined interest in increasing the net wealth to be shared. Following closely the simple game theory precepts noted above (i.e., constrained agendas, limited number of players, repeat players, regular interactions), some institutional structures where representatives of the national government can meet on a regular basis with national representatives of labour and business to share information about the present state of the economy, forecasts of future trends, difficulties being encountered in particular sectors, and implications of alternative policy options, may have economic advantages. Such a consultative structure is likely to provide the federal government with perspectives on policy making in the industrial policy field unlikely to be revealed in federal-provincial government relations with their more diffused focuses, and to assist it to identify and, over time, perhaps help share some margins for policy development that address not only the sharing of existing economic wealth but also the enhancement of our future economic well-being. It must be emphasized that such a structure must be national in its perspective and avoid the narrow industry-specific and regional focuses entailed in the Tier 1 and Tier 2 industry review committees set up by the Department of Industry, Trade and Commerce in the 1970s, where management and labour from the sectors concerned simply produced wish lists of government favours for their sectors. The British experience with mini-triparite bodies (sectoral working parties) set up under the aegis of the National Economic Development Council appears to have been similarly unproductive. This is not to say that a **national** deliberative structure of government, business and labour could not profitably consult with particular business and labour interests when reviewing sector-specific problems, but this must be distinguished from abdicating policy-formulation initiatives to such interests. Whatever the structure, the government cannot afford to be ambivalent in its general policy orientation if these deliberative mechanisms are to retain a constructive and coherent focus.

Conclusion

Avoiding policies that create excessive state dependencies relative to underlying economic forces (e.g., through regional and industrial policies), and where dependencies have arisen as a result of major shifts in underlying economic forces, adopting policies that subsidize the dissipation of those dependencies rather than their perpetuation (e.g., firm and labour adjustment policies that encourage reallocation of resources), are central to this focus. The concept of conditionality is crucial to this orientation. The proposals here advanced have advocated conditionalizing trade protection measures, industrial subsidies (if these two policies cannot be avoided), and labour assistance programs, to ensure that the beneficiaries adopt some course of action that will change their economic status and thus reduce their dependence on future state support. In addition, the importance of diversification has been stressed in the range of judgments brought to bear on alternative economic opportunities, so that excessive reliance on monolithic (and possibly mistaken) judgments by the state as to appropriate strategies for the redeployment of redundant capital and labour is avoided. Finally, it must be re-emphasized that the effectiveness of a country's adjustment policies must be judged by how **rapidly** they enable adjustment to changes in underlying economic forces, not how successful they are in **postponing** the process of adjustment. Many, if not most, of Canada's so-called "adjustment" policies to date have only been successful if judged against the latter criterion. But in an era of increasing international competitiveness and rapid technological change, dynamic growth strategies require dynamic adjustment policies. The economic and ultimately political costs of antithetical policies are likely to be much larger in the future than they have been in the past.

Notes

1. *Challenges and Choices* (Ottawa: Supply and Services, 1986), p. 27.

2. Joseph Schumpeter, *Capitalism, Socialism and Democracy* (Cambridge, Mass., Harvard University Press, 1975), p. 87.

3. See John Quinn and Michael Trebilcock, "Compensation, Transition Cost and Regulatory Change," University of Toronto Law Journal, 32, 1982, pp. 117-75.

4. Christopher Green, *Industrial Policy: The Fixities Hypothesis.* Policy Studies Series (Toronto: Ontario Economic Council, 1984).

5. Glenn P. Jenkins, *Costs and Consequences of the New Protectionism: The Case of Canada's Clothing Sector.* Policy Studies Series (Ottawa: North-South Institute, 1980).

6. William G. Watson, *A Primer on the Economics of Industrial Policy* (Toronto: Ontario Economic Council, 1983), p. 85.

7. Robert W. Crandall, "Import Quotas and the Automobile Industry: The Costs of Protectionism," The Brookings Review, Summer, 1984, pp. 8-16.

8. See Thomas J. Courchene, Comments, in Douglas D. Purvis (ed.) *'Economic' Adjustment and Public Policy in Canada* (Kingston: Queen's University, John Deutsch Institute for the Study of Economic Policy, 1984).

9. Ronald Saunders, *Aid to Workers in Declining Industries.* Policy Studies Series (Toronto: Ontario Economic Council, 1984), p. 1.

10. See Robert Z. Lawrence and Robert E. Litan, "Living with the Trade Deficit: Adjustment Strategies to Preserve Free Trade," The Brookings Review, Fall, 1985, pp. 3-13.

11. See Dan Usher, "The Benefits and Costs of Firm-Specific Investment Grants," (Kingston: Queen's University, mimeo, 1981).

12. See M.J. Trebilcock, M. Chandler, M. Gunderson, P. Halpern, and J. Quinn, *The Political Economy of Business Bailouts.* Research Studies (Toronto: Ontario Economic Council, 1986).

13. Michael Trebilcock, *The Political Economy of Economic Adjustment* (Ottawa, Research Study No. 8, 1986 for the Royal Commission on the Economic Union and Development Prospects for Canada, 1986), vol. 2, pp. 616-619.

14. Saunders, *Aid to Workers ...*

15.   See Mancur Olson, *The Rise and Decline of Nations: Economic Growth, Stagflation and Social Rigidities* (New Haven: Yale University Press, 1982).

16.   See Kenneth Dyson and Stephen Wilks eds., *Industrial Crisis: A Comparative Study of the State and Industry*, (Oxford: Martin Robertson, 1983) esp. concluding chapter, pp. 245-272.

17.   Richard Simeon, "Intergovernmental Relations and the Challenges to Canadian Federalism," Canadian Public Administration, 23, 1980, pp. 14-32.

The Role of Management in the
Adjustment to Freer Trade

Donald J. Daly

In this paper I deal with the role of management in the process of adjustment to free trade with special emphasis on management in the private sector. My function is not to give a technical discussion to professional economists, but rather to summarize and synthesize what has been done previously and published in books, articles, and research studies done for the Royal Commission on the Economic Union and Development Prospects for Canada. However, I do not know of any other topic in the field of economics that has had as much study in Canada over the past three decades than the topic of the costs of tariffs, the gains from freer trade, the options for achieving tariff reductions, the responses to the tariff reductions which have already taken place, etc. I can see no justification for the comment by Premier Peterson of the province of Ontario that no studies have been done on free trade. However, there has been less study on the managerial aspects than on other topics on the economic side.

This paper will cover four broad topics:

- Where do we start from?

- The past adjustments to tariff reductions

- The role of management in the adjustment process

- The nature of future adjustments

We can learn quite a bit about the types of adjustments that will have to occur in response to further reductions in tariff and non-tariff barriers between Canada and the United States because we have already had a significant amount of tariff reduction since this whole process started in the late 1930s with the administration of Prime Minister

Mackenzie King and the Liberal government of that time. During the postwar period there has been a series of negotiations under the General Agreement on Tariffs and Trade on a multilateral basis, and the Canada-United States automotive free trade agreement. These reductions have lowered the nominal tariff rate in Canada to about one sixth currently from what it had been in the 1940s.

We should be aware, however, that when we are looking at some of the major changes and adjustments that have occurred over the last three or four decades, that tariff reductions are only one of a large number of major economic developments that have occurred over the same period. Examples of other major adjustments would include a protracted and pronounced period of inflation, significant shifts in the distribution of economic and political power (including the relative decline of the United States and the United Kingdom, and the increased relative importance of Japan and the European Economic Community), the major increases and then declines in petroleum prices since early in the 1970s, and the widespread adoption of floating exchange rates among the major industrialized countries. These uncertainties and fluctuations in the world economy have not prevented a major increase in the volume of world trade since, say, 1950. Trade in manufactured products in particular has become an increasing share of world trade. Thus, when we are trying to identify the responses to past tariff reductions in Canada, we have to recognize that a number of other important economic developments were occurring simultaneously.

Where did we start from?

There are a number of important characteristics of the Canadian economy in relation to the rest of the world that have had an important impact on the whole process of adjustment. We will mention a number of these which are particularly important in affecting developments since.

One of the major features in the Canadian economy historically has been the emphasis on natural resources in our economic development and in the structure of our exports. Canada continues to be the best endowed of all the major industrialized countries in terms of mineral resources, water resources, forestry and arable agricultural land. However, these are not a major part of the employment and income for the Canadian economy to the same extent now as they had been earlier in the present century. Part of the reason for this is that world trade in natural resource products has been a falling share of world trade since before the First World War. One of our key historic areas of comparative advantage has been in an area of declining demand on a relative basis.

A second important characteristic of the Canadian economy at the end of the Second World War is that the whole position of manufacturing in the Canadian economy was heavily influenced by the existence of important tariff and non-tariff barriers to trade in Canada and the other industrialized countries. The existence of tariff and non-tariff barriers to trade in other countries limited our potential sales of manufactured products to them. However, our own tariff barriers provided a degree of protection to domestic producers that encouraged such developments as considerable product diversity (the range of products and models produced in a typical plant), a size of plant that was sometimes too small by world standards to achieve low cost per unit, and the high costs that these factors led to. Such high costs within Canada would have led to restraints on exports of manufactured products even if tariff and non-tariff barriers had not existed in other countries. These differences can be illustrated by the fact that in 1950 the level of output per hour in Canadian manufacturing was only about half the level then prevailing in the United States, but Canada was still the second highest of all the major industrialized countries at that time.[1]

These lower productivity levels were partly matched by lower levels of total compensation per hour in Canadian manufacturing at that time relative to the United States. However, unit labour costs (based on total compensation including fringe benefits) were about 20 per cent higher than in the United States and higher than the other major industrialized countries at that time. We were able to attain a fair amount of exports of manufactured products during those years primarily because of the widespread pressure of demand against capacity on a world basis, and many countries imported from Canada because of the availability of such products here and in spite of our high cost tendencies.

There were, of course, considerable diversities within Canadian manufacturing, and some parts of manufacturing were fully competitive internationally, but these were more than offset by the much larger number of firms and plants with low productivity and high cost levels.

One important contrast to be emphasized is the differences between Canadian-owned and U.S.-owned plants and firms. There was not much difference in productivity levels between large Canadian plants and large U.S.-owned plants in Canada, a point that had been well established by A.E. Safarian's study.[2] However, later research has established the point that Canadian-owned plants and firms have considerably lower levels of output per person than in the subsidiaries, after standardizing for industry and size.[3] In other words, the productivity problems were initially more pronounced in the Canadian-owned firms, where the levels of value added per production worker in Canada were only half the foreign-owned firms for plants with fewer than 50 employees. For plants between 50 and 400 employees the levels of value added in the Canadian-owned plants were only two thirds or three fourths of the foreign-owned plants.[4]

Past Adjustments to Freer Trade

A number of important changes have occurred in Canadian manufacturing, primarily in response to the reductions in tariff and non-tariff barriers that have taken place. The productivity gap between Canadian and United States manufacturing that was almost 50 per cent in 1950 has been reduced to between 25 and 30 per cent over the last decade. Thus the gap has been reduced to almost half of what it had been more than 30 years ago. This has come about primarily because the increases in output per hour were more rapid in Canada than the United States fairly steadily from 1950 to about 1974, with little significant narrowing since then.

Important new developments have taken place between Japan and Europe relative to North America. Most other industrialized countries have had fairly consistently more rapid increases in output per hour than in North America. To some extent this reflects the lower initial starting position for those other countries, but Belgium, France, Germany, Sweden and Japan have now begun to exceed Canada in levels of output per hour. Thus, Canada has moved from a position of the highest country after the United States in 1950 to the third from the bottom of the major industrialized countries by the middle of the 1980s. A further important point should be noted with respect to Japan. Japan has levels of output per hour in the large plants that are about 50 per cent above the country's national average, while the smaller plants are about half the national average. The larger Japanese plants currently have levels of output per hour that are about 30 or 40 per cent above levels in comparable industries in Canada, and they have continued to grow more rapidly there than in North America. This is particularly important when the large Japanese plants dominate the export market.

This narrowing in the productivity gap between Canadian and U.S. manufacturing has been associated with both an increase in the average plant size in Canada and a greater specialization than previously. The net effect has been an increase of about 40 per cent in both the average production run and the average plant size, with related effects on productivity and costs per unit. This has led to an increased degree of specialization, which has been reflected in an increased two-way flow of trade in manufactured products, usually referred to as intra-industry trade.

This increased specialization has been reflected in an increase in the two-way flow of trade in manufactured products as reflected in the trade statistics. There has also been an increase in the ratio of purchased materials to value added from the Census of Manufacturing, and also in the coefficients in the input-output tables for Canada.[5]

A recently published special survey of manufacturing firms has provided new evidence on the reductions in unit costs with a tripling of output. A matched sample of Canadian-owned and subsidiary firms producing the identical product were surveyed for their costs initially, and what would prevail with a tripling in output. Widespread reductions in costs were reported for purchased materials, labour, factory cost, overhead, marketing costs, etc. The following table shows the average reductions reported in four major product groups.

Two points can be noted about this result that reflect significant economies of scale. (It was not possible from the information provided to be able to identify the extent to which these reductions were associated with product specific and plant specific economies of scale). One point is the significant variation from one industry to the other, with significant reductions in the electrical and electronics group on the one hand and quite small reductions in the chemical and plastics groups on the other. A second point is that it would not have been possible to anticipate which industries had small and which ones had large economies of scale. These companies were all below about 400 employees in size, and it would have been impossible to obtain any of this information from existing data available within the government. Such new material is expensive to collect, which is one of the reasons why so little of it is available.

Table 1
Unit Cost Reductions with a Tripling of Output,
Four Manufacturing Product Groups

	Percentage Reduction in Unit Cost
Auto parts	21
Electrical and electronics	32
Chemicals and plastics	9
Machinery and equipment and miscellaneous	14
Average	19

Source: D.J. Daly and D.C. MacCharles, *Canadian Manufactured Exports: Constraints and Opportunities*, (Montreal: Institute for Research on Public Policy, 1986), p. 54.

The Role of Management in the Adjustment Process

The previous section has summarized the main themes from the work that has been done on the adjustment process within Canadian manufacturing over the postwar period. All of the changes required conscious and deliberate decisions by company management to make the types of changes summarized in response to the changes in the environment which were under way.

This can be seen most clearly in the management characteristics of the small Canadian-owned companies, which had initially started off with levels of output per employee well below the larger plants and firms within Canada and the comparable industries in the United States. The survey indicated that an important number of these small firms had been able to specialize, to identify a niche in the world market that had been overlooked by the large firms in a large country, and export a significant proportion of their total output. A common characteristic of the successful companies was that their managers tended to be very entrepreneurial, hard working, and frequently had some initial technical expertise in the type of product they were manufacturing. A second common characteristic was that they had identified an overlooked niche in the world market that matched their areas of interest and expertise. A third common characteristic was that they had active programs of training and executive development within the firm.

On the other hand, a number of existing companies had continued with their previous high degree of product diversity, producing primarily for the domestic market. A number of these were experiencing financial troubles, and some had gone out of business or there had been changes in management before the interviews were completed. Clearly the differences in management and openness to change were important factors in the contrasting company experience, even though the changes in environment were broadly similar in the differing firms.

Information had also been obtained on the performance of the foreign-owned subsidiaries in Canada. The previous predictions on what would happen to subsidiaries with tariff reductions had been contradictory. One prediction had been that with freer trade the subsidiaries would make the biggest gains. Such subsidiaries did have many potential advantages that would have been likely to facilitate increased exports. For example, they started off with higher productivity than in the smaller plants and firms; they had access to new technology and management practices from their parents, and had access to markets abroad through the marketing channels of the parents. On the other hand, a quite contradictory interpretation had suggested that the subsidiaries would withdraw from the Canadian market and the market would then be supplied by the foreign parent, and the Canadian subsidiary would become only a warehouse through which the Canadian domestic market would be supplied.[6]

The evidence from the survey on which this paper is partly based suggests that neither of these extreme predictions is emerging. The subsidiaries are not apparently moving into the export market as rapidly as the Canadian-owned firms. This may partly come about because the subsidiaries had already been more specialized and more profitable than the Canadian-owned ones. It is also much more difficult to introduce change as one part of a much larger organization. For example, after Canadian General Electric had decided to move in the direction of increased specialization for the Canadian plants, it still took three or four years of hard work by senior executives to implement all the changes in a major way.

The subsidiaries that were exporting were primarily doing it as part of a broader program developed in co-operation with the parent. World product mandates have received a lot of public attention in Canada, but the proportion of subsidiaries that have moved in this direction are in the minority.

The initiative for moves toward increased specialization normally came from the subsidiary, and plans were developed which were then discussed with and approved by the parent. Most of the parent companies which had been interviewed were quite sympathetic to moves in this direction and very few examples were encountered of limitations by the parents on exports from the subsidiary into the markets previously filled by other plants of the parent company. A number of the parents would have welcomed more initiatives from the subsidiary to move in this direction and, in at least one case, the initiative for change had come from the parent. There was no evidence that the closing down of Canadian plants was taking place or planned.

On the other hand, it would appear from other data that the large direct investment that had taken place in Canadian manufacturing during the 1950s and

1960s had slowed down significantly. However, this change need not necessarily have come about just because of the changes in tariff rates. Other factors in the domestic environment were far more important in leading to a much less attractive situation for investment in Canadian manufacturing in the 1980s than previously. These factors included slow increases in output and productivity, a high rate of domestic inflation, high interest rates, low rates of return to investment in Canadian manufacturing, a hostile framework for labour-management relations and a perceived adverse environment for government-business relations (at the time that the survey was taken). These factors had also all been mentioned by the Canadian-owned firms, some of which had already established subsidiaries elsewhere, and a number were also seriously considering that possibility.[7] Both the Canadian-owned and the subsidiaries emphasized that these changes were primarily a reflection of the above changes rather than changes associated with freer trade.

Openness to change on the part of senior corporate management is an important element in the whole adjustment process. Previous work on management has indicated that younger managers tend to be more open to change than older managers (although there are some exceptions). Higher levels of formal education also tend to make people more open to new ideas. What can we say about differences between Canadian and U.S. managers in these respects?

There are several differences in educational patterns between Canada and the United States that have been documented from census data and special surveys of management. Canada has a lower proportion of the existing labour force with university degrees and this is also reflected in differences in management. Canada also has a substantially lower proportion of those between 18 and 25 who are taking graduate and undergraduate degrees in commerce and business administration. The proportion taking these courses in the United States continues to run four to five times larger than in Canada.

The evidence also indicates that managers are promoted into middle and senior levels of management much later in their working life than in the United States. Both of these characteristics would tend to lead to less openness to change in Canada than in the United States.

One other area has been emphasized by sociologists and political scientists as factors in the slow adoption of new scientific and managerial ideas. They emphasize the high social values placed in Canada on continuity and gradual change, compared to the openness to change emphasized in the United States. The United States takes pride in rapid change, and their managerial selection and promotion tends to emphasize performance, rather than family status and seniority with the company.[8]

An additional interpretation (which is not inconsistent with the one in the previous paragraph) is associated with the research by Mancur Olson. He emphasizes that the economic and social upheavals in continental Western Europe and Japan since the Second World War have led to the emergence of new business and financial leadership and increased international competition from those countries. This has been reflected in more innovative leadership and faster adoption of new technology. The absence of radical shake-up in the U.S. economic and social structure may have contributed to the extent of erosion of the economic and political leadership that the United States had at the end of the Second World War. A similar absence of a radical shake-up in leadership has been present in the two other members of the Anglo-Saxon Club of slow-growing countries, namely, Canada and the United Kingdom.[9] One of the big questions for the 1980s and 1990s is whether the increased international competition from Japan and some of the newly industrialized countries in the Pacific Rim will lead to a successful industrial renaissance in the United States.

Nature of Future Adjustments

What can one say about the extent of further adjustments and the ease with which such adjustments will take place?

Some observers have suggested that the changes under way will eventually lead to a significant amount of deindustrialization in Canadian manufacturing, with the expectation that essentially all manufactured products would be produced elsewhere and imported into Canada. If one were to measure this by absolute declines in manufacturing, this has not yet occurred in Canada (apart from the 1981-1982 severe recession). On the whole, declines in man-hours worked in manufacturing have already taken place to a far greater extent in Europe than in Canada.

Furthermore, I do not expect to see a major selling out or closing down of foreign-owned plants and firms within Canada. Their levels of costs and productivity are already closer to those of the parents, and further specialization, adoption of new technology and increased sales to other companies in the home country of the parent and elsewhere can be expected.

It would appear that important further adjustments are likely to be heavily concentrated in the Canadian-owned small companies. This is the area in which dynamic changes have already begun, but it is also clear that further adjustments are likely. However, the special tabulation of data on value added per employee by industry, by size and by ownership, was last done for 1974, and we have no comprehensive information since that time. Rein Peterson's study of small business was also based on the data for the 1970s, and the evidence suggests a substantial growth in employment in small plants has taken place over the last decade in Canada as well as in the other major industrialized countries.

Further adjustments are also necessary in a number of what have become to be called "sunset industries." These would include such industries as clothing, textiles, boots and shoes etc., reflecting the labour-intensive products which are increasingly being provided from the low-wage, rapidly growing countries in the Pacific Rim. These industries are experiencing problems in both North America and Europe, but adjustments in these industries have frequently been slowed by higher effective tariff rates and non-tariff barriers in the industrialized countries. Although these industries have experienced increased competition in the industrialized countries of North America and Europe, it is often overlooked that the major industrialized countries have net trade surpluses in manufactured products with the developing countries. Import competition is concentrated in a relatively narrow line of highly visible products, with less public awareness of the significant net sales in the other direction.

The evidence on which this paper is based would suggest that the adjustments can be made and can be made relatively easily in the Canadian-owned firms if management is willing to initiate the necessary changes and they have taken time to achieve consensus on this within the firm and with union leadership and membership (where unions are present). It is not just a matter of a once-and-for-all change, but a continual adjustment as the companies in other countries are not standing still.

It is not just a matter of increasing productivity and adopting new technology more quickly. In addition, a major part of these productivity gains would have to be passed to the buyers of manufactured products within Canada and internationally for a number of years ahead. The evidence for Canada would suggest that real wages in Canadian manufacturing are now approaching U.S. levels, while the levels of output per hour are between 25 and 30 per cent below the United States. (To analyze the demand for labour by firms, there might be some advantages in having data on real wages from the point of view of the firm, but such data are not available on any comprehensive basis. Furthermore, I am not aware of any changes in Canada relative to the United States over the last decade that would make the consumer price index an inappropriate guide for the changes between the two countries.) This change is necessary both to obtain an increased share of the rapidly growing world market for manufactured products, and to continue to maintain a share of the Canadian domestic market.

The contrasts with the Japanese experience in this respect are enlightening. Output per hour in Japanese manufacturing has more than doubled over the last decade. However, real wages per hour in Japanese manufacturing have increased only about 20 or 25 per cent. A major part of the productivity gain has been passed to the buyers of manufactured products both within Japan and internationally. This has permitted Japan to obtain an enlarged share of the world market for manufactured products, and maintain a low unemployment rate.

Canadian management will have to give more consideration to the whole question of pricing and the division of productivity gains between buyers and workers. There can be a good deal of labour-management friction for this proposal to be implemented, but a continuation of the current situation would perpetuate the plant closures, corporate bankruptcies and high unemployment which has been a characteristic of the business cycle expansion that began in December 1982.

Notes

1.   D.J. Daly and D.C. MacCharles, *On Real Wage Unemployment.* Focus #18 (Vancouver: The Fraser Institute, 1986), Appendix A, p. 61-77.

2.   A.E. Safarian, *Foreign Ownership of Canadian Industry*, (Toronto: McGraw-Hill, 1966).

3.   D.C. MacCharles, *The Cost of Administrative Organizations in Canadian Secondary Manufacturing Industries*, (Toronto: University of Toronto Dissertation, Department of Political Economy, 1978).

4.   D.J. Daly and D.C. MacCharles, *Canadian Manufactured Exports: Constraints and Opportunities*, (Montreal: The Institute for Research on Public Policy, 1986), p. 20.

5.   D.J. Daly, "Rationalization and Specialization in Canadian Manufacturing," in Donald G. McFetridge, *Canadian Industry in Transition*, (Toronto, University of Toronto Press, Volume 2, Ch. 4 of the Royal Commission on the Economic Union and Development Prospects for Canada, 1986), p. 197.

6.   Jack Baranson had prepared a study for the Ontario government which was released in the fall of 1985 which emphasized this interpretation. This study was just not up to the calibre of Dr. Baranson's previous work, primarily because it assumed that all the productivity and cost problems which had developed inside an environment of tariff and non-tariff barriers to trade would continue unchanged after those barriers had largely been eliminated. This ignored the Canadian work which has been done in recent decades emphasizing modern cost theory and the Ricardian theory of comparative advantage which predicted a narrowing in productivity and cost differences with freer trade.

7.   D.J. Daly and D.C. MacCharles, *On Real Wage Unemployment*. Focus #18 (Vancouver: The Fraser Institute, 1986), Appendix B pp. 79-109.

8.   D.J. Daly, "Canadian Management: Past Recruitment Practices and Future Training Needs." In Max von Zur-Muehlen, ed., *Highlights and Background Studies*, (Ottawa: Canadian Federation of Deans of Management and Administrative Studies, 1979), pp. 178-200.

9.   Authors who have emphasized this interpretation would include Seymour M. Lipsett, Robert H. Presthus, Arthur Lower, John Porter and Wallace Clement. For the full list of citations, see Footnote 27 in D.J. Daly, "Technology Transfer and Canada's Competitive Performance." In Robert M. Stern and others, eds., *Current Issues in Trade and Investment in Service Industries: U.S.-Canadian Bilateral and Multilateral Perspectives*, (Toronto: University of Toronto Press, 1986). For a discussion of social change (and its absence) on economic growth see Mancur Olson, *The Rise and Decline of Nations: Economic Growth, Stagflation and Social Rigidities*. (New Haven, Conn.: Yale University Press, 1982).

Further Results Concerning the Canada-U.S. Productivity Gap: A Comment on Donald Daly's Paper

John Baldwin

Professor Daly is to be congratulated for single-mindedly pursuing a topic for some years that is important for any discussion of free trade. Since his pioneering work for the Economic Council of Canada in 1968, he has provided us with considerable information on the plant scale disadvantages suffered by the Canadian manufacturing sector. His recent work extends this in an important direction.

What I should like to stress here is the complementarity between his work and studies which have been pursued at the Economic Council by Paul Gorecki and myself. These studies use a very different set of data. Daly has collected extensive evidence from interview evidence. We have relied upon an extensive data base that has been developed from the Census of Manufactures with the aid of Statistics Canada. Before I summarize our work, let me say a brief word about the questions that both we and Daly have attempted to answer.

While there has been previous work done on plant-scale disadvantages and the U.S./Canada productivity gap, a number of questions remain only partially answered. First, the importance and size of the plant-scale disadvantages have not been well established. Estimation of the importance of the disadvantages requires knowledge of the cost or production function. Industry production functions require establishment data for estimation purposes. To overcome the previous deficiency in this area, we have used Canadian Census of Manufactures establishment data to estimate individual production functions at the four-digit Standard Industrial Classification (SIC) level of aggregation.

61

We also attempt to augment our knowledge of the extent of plant-scale disadvantages by developing data on plant size for a large sample of Canadian industries — 167 — at the four-digit SIC level of aggregation and by matching them to comparable U.S. industry data.

The existing information on the extent to which plants are excessively diversified is as unsatisfactory as that on plant scale. In order to further our information here, we developed measures of plant diversity using information on the number of products produced in each plant that is available on the Census of Manufactures questionnaire but has not previously been used in quantitative analyses.

Previous productivity studies of Canadian industry are also unsatisfactory. Few focus on productivity differences at a relatively disaggregated level. Even fewer link plant-scale disadvantages to productivity disadvantages. We do both.

The Results on Plant Specialization

It is often claimed that the Canadian manufacturing sector is disadvantaged because plant production runs are too short; this occurs because of the small Canadian market, tariff protection, and lack of competition. We used our measure of plant diversity to investigate this issue. We found that, as industries have grown during the 1970s and trade increased, plants have tended to become more specialized. In cross-sectional regressions with plant diversity as the dependent variable, we found that larger plant size was associated with greater product diversity, but the rate of increase in product diversity slows as average plant size increases. Thus plants add product lines to exploit plant-scale economies but the advantages of doing so are limited. In this case, growth of market size brought about by trade liberalization should eventually solve the product diversity problem. In our regressions, we found that falling tariffs over the 1970s were associated with increased length of production runs.

The Canada/U.S. Relative Plant-Scale Results

Concern has been voiced that tariff protection exacerbates Canadian plant-scale disadvantages and that trade liberalization would reduce this.

Our findings were that, on average, across 125 comparable Canadian and U.S. manufacturing industries, we suffered a 30 per cent size disadvantage in our largest plants. Our statistical analysis of the determinants of plant size found market size to be the most important determinant of our disadvantage. Trade liberalization by more fully opening U.S. markets to Canadian producers would be expected to reduce plant size disadvantage.

We also found that higher Canadian tariffs led to smaller Canadian plant sizes compared with those of U.S. plants, but only where tariffs were high and combined with high industry concentration. A decrease in tariffs resulted in an increase in the relative plant scale. Exports in those industries in which Canada has a comparative advantage were associated with the building of plants closer to the Minimum Efficient Scale (MES).

The Results on Relative Canada/U.S. Efficiency

We also compared Canada/U.S. efficiency by developing measures of total factor productivity that made use of our estimated industry production functions. When no account is taken of different plant size, the calculated measure indicated Canada had a level of efficiency of about 70 per cent of that of the United States. Our scale-corrected measure of relative efficiency accounts for about one third of the difference in the conventionally measured productivity gap between Canadian and U.S. manufacturing sectors. Thus scale effects are important, but there is a residual efficiency gap that still remains after plant-scale differences and the importance of scale economies are taken into account.

In conclusion, our work finds support for many of the propositions about the problems in the manufacturing sector. Moreover, it suggests that in the past changes in tariffs and increases in trade have had a beneficial effect. The work by Daly and ourselves, coming at the problem with very different methodological approaches, reaches much the same conclusion. It is this type of independent corroboration that is required if we are to have confidence in the prescription of economists — and which is all too often lacking in the profession.

64   *KNOCKING ON THE BACK DOOR*

Bibliography

Baldwin, J.R. and P.K. Gorecki. 1985. "The Determinants of Small Plant Market Share in Canadian Manufacturing Industries in the 1970s," *Review of Economics and Statistics* 67, 1.

_____ 1986. "The Relationship Between Plant Scale and Product Diversity in Canadian Manufacturing Industries," *Journal of Industrial Economics* 34, 373-388.

_____ 1986. "The Relationship Between Trade and Tariff Patterns and the Efficiency of the Canadian Manufacturing Sector in the 1970s: A Summary." In *Canada-United States Free Trade*, Vol. 11 of the research studies prepared for the Royal Commission on the Economic Union and Development Prospects for Canada, Toronto: University of Toronto Press.

_____ 1986. "Canada-U.S. Productivity Differences in the Manufacturing Sector: 1970-79." In *Canadian Industry in Transition*, Vol. 2 of the research studies prepared for the Royal Commission on the Economic Union and Development Prospects for Canada, Toronto: University of Toronto Press.

_____ 1986. *The Role of Scale in Canada/U.S. Productivity Differences in the Canadian Manufacturing Sector in the 1970s*, Vol. 6 of the research reports prepared for the Royal Commission on the Economic Union and Development Prospects for Canada, Toronto: University of Toronto Press.

_____ 1987. "Trade, Tariffs, and Relative Plant Scale in Canadian Manufacturing Industries: 1970-79," Recherches Economiques de Louvain, March.

Daly, D.J., B.A. Keys and E.J. Spence. 1968. *Scale and Specialization in Canadian Manufacturing*, Economic Council Staff Study 21, Ottawa: Queen's Printer.

Sovereignty and Other
Non-Economic Issues

Non-Economic Implications of a Comprehensive Canada-U.S. Free Trade Agreement

Denis Stairs *

From a purely economic perspective, the case in Canada for negotiating a comprehensive free trade agreement with the United States has been based essentially on three arguments. The first, reflecting an anxiety generated by the increasingly protectionist inclinations of the American Congress, stresses the need to provide long-term security for Canada's present access to the one external market that is crucial to the health of the Canadian economy as a whole. The second, founded largely on the expectation that a comprehensive agreement would provide, among other things, for the removal by the United States of important non-tariff barriers to Canadian exports, emphasizes the economies of scale benefits that would accrue to previously disadvantaged Canadian producers, who would be able for the first time to exploit a continental marketplace inhabited by more than a quarter of a billion consumers. The third, expressed more readily in the senior common rooms of academic economists and in the quiet corridors of the federal Department of Finance than in the public pronouncements of government representatives, is that a bilateral free trade arrangement would expose the Canadian industrial structure to the healthful invigoration of a "cold shower." In short, it would discipline the Canadian economy by subjecting it to powerful American competition. In this process, the weak and the marginal among Canadian economic enterprises, if they could not adapt, would be destroyed, but the survivors would be capable of operating far

* This is a slightly revised version of a paper originally prepared for a collection published through the Canadian Studies Program of the David M. Kennedy Center for International Studies at Brigham Young University. I am very grateful to the program's coordinator, Professor Earl H. Fry, for his kindness in agreeing that it appear, with only minor changes, in the present volume as well. Extracts of this paper have also appeared in *International Perspectives*.

more successfully in the North American market than before and possibly — by extension — elsewhere in the world as well.

The counter-arguments on the other side rest partly on suggestions that a formal treaty, being subject to abrogation, would not in itself provide the security to which Canada aspires, and that, in the current American climate, there is little prospect of negotiating a measure of access greater than what is already available. More significantly, opponents of the initiative argue that the "cold shower" would be more than the Canadian economy could stand. The resulting dislocations, they maintain, would be so extensive as to overwhelm such "adjustment policies" — blunt instruments at the best of times — as might be introduced to contain and repair the damage. The danger applies not merely to Canadian enterprises that would be unable to withstand American competition, but also to the branch plants of American multinationals, since with free access to the Canadian market from the United States, many of these might be tempted to dismantle their Canadian operations and "rationalize" their production south of the border.

The economic argument is difficult to settle, partly because the participants in the debate often speak with specific vested interests in view, and partly because — in the aggregate — no one really knows what the precise economic consequences would be, or where they would be felt. The available research on the probable impact in particular sectors is very limited, and much of it can be challenged on methodological grounds. Even at the macro level, the predictive work of professional economists is usually based on theoretical models which rest in turn on assumptions that can be called into question. Hence the rhetoric of the discussion has been sprinkled with references to "leaps of faith" and "leaps in the dark," and not even the government has claimed that its initiative is without risk.[1]

But it is not the purpose of this paper to assess the economic case. Instead, the objective is to consider some of the implications for Canada of a bilateral free trade agreement when the question is examined essentially from a non-economic point of view. It is obvious, of course, that the non-economic consequences, like the economic ones, would depend very heavily on the precise terms of the treaty in which the agreement was enshrined. It is quite possible either that no agreement will be reached at all, or that it will be concluded in relation to so narrow a range of sectors that the ancillary effects will have only marginal importance. For the purpose of the present discussion, however, it is assumed that the treaty is genuinely "comprehensive" — that it covers a wide and substantial range of goods and services, that it provides for the removal of a significant collection of non-tariff barriers on both sides of the border, and that its list of exemptions is relatively short.

It may be useful to begin by placing the matter briefly in its historical context.[2]

The Bilateral Trade Debate: Earlier Rounds

It is a commonly held view of Canadians that their country has been created and maintained in explicit defiance of the requirements of economic rationality as determined by the combined forces of North American geography and the continental marketplace. There is much to be said for this interpretation of Canadian history. But in fact there have always been some Canadians who have argued that, if our pockets could only be kept full, our political, social and cultural identities could safely be left to take care of themselves. If we prospered economically, we would have the means with which to prosper politically, socially and culturally as well. In the middle of the nineteenth century, for example, after the British had repealed the Corn Laws, and had moved in the direction of free trade at the expense of the system of colonial preferences that had previously given Canadian products an advantage in British markets, Canadian authorities were quick to pursue access to the U.S. market as an alternative. One of the arguments that was mounted in support of the reciprocal free trade agreement that resulted in 1854 (confined though it was to natural products – fish, timber, coal and agricultural commodities notably among them[3]) was that it would help to undermine the case for political annexation to the United States as a solution to Canada's economic problems. If Canadians could maintain their economic wealth, in short, full political amalgamation with the United States would seem neither necessary nor attractive. A policy of reciprocal free trade, that many were later to oppose on the ground that it would eventually lead to the political integration of the two countries, was thus perceived at first as a necessary defence of Canada's independence.

The 1854 Reciprocity Treaty was abandoned at American request in 1866, and it is sometimes forgotten that in the early years of Confederation Canadian governments vigorously pursued its renewal. They failed, and the prime minister, Sir John A. Macdonald, mounted his so-called "National Policy" in 1879 almost as a second-best solution. At the beginning, moreover, he defended the policy partly on the ground that one of the principal advantages of the new structure of protective tariffs that it included was that it would lead the Americans eventually to the realization that reciprocal free trade with Canada was actually in their own best interest, and would therefore ultimately make possible a resurrection of the reciprocity agreement. Macdonald's adoption, therefore, of the view that free trade with the United States would actually **threaten** Canada's independence (and with it the cherished Canadian connection with Great Britain) came only with his successful election campaign in 1891, when the opposition Liberals were advocating the negotiation of an unrestricted Canada-U.S. reciprocity arrangement, and hence offered an irresistible target for political attack on nationalist grounds.

Even in 1911, when the Liberal government of Sir Wilfrid Laurier announced that a new reciprocity agreement had been successfully negotiated with the Americans, the opposition that ensued came first from interests that were vested more in economics than in politics. It was led, that is, by business leaders – mainly from central Canada – who feared that the new arrangement, which again applied only to natural products, would soon be extended to manufactured goods as well, and thereby deprive them of their beloved protective tariffs. The electoral battle that ensued, being exposed to public view, was naturally fought on higher ground. The maintenance of the British Empire (widely viewed by Canadians as a force for good), and the survival, as one of its more important parts, of a Canada that was independent of the United States, were portrayed as the principal stakes at issue. But in retrospect, some, at least, of the architects of these high-blown arguments appear to have been transparently self-serving.

Even if the political arguments were inspired at their source more by economic advantage than by political conviction, they struck a responsive chord in the electorate. The Liberals were turfed out of office, and reciprocity was turfed out with them. The result thus reflected in large measure the more general and persistent Canadian fear that economic integration with the United States would soon be followed by political, social, and cultural integration as well.

It was this same preoccupation that caused Prime Minister Mackenzie King in 1948 to reject an ambitious proposal for a Canada-U.S. customs union, which had been engineered by Canadian and American officials in negotiations over the previous winter. It was also, of course, the source of the concern later expressed by Walter Gordon and others over the heavy volume of American direct investment in the Canadian economy, and their sense that the extensive foreign ownership of Canadian enterprises not only diminished the effectiveness of Canada's economic operations, but deprived the country of much of its autonomy and independence as well.[4]

More specifically, the "nationalists" argued on the economic side that Canadian subsidiaries of foreign firms were reluctant to compete with their parent corporations in export markets abroad; that Canada's "branch plant" industrial structure undermined its ability to make full use of economies of scale; that multinational corporations tended to concentrate their research and development activities in their home base, with the result that their subsidiaries encouraged much less product innovation than they might otherwise have done; that they also tended, in periods of excess capacity, to export their unemployment to their branch plants abroad, and that their internal transfer-pricing arrangements allowed them to manipulate their accounts in such a way as to incur their profits in the most favourable tax jurisdiction. The result, it was said, was that the Canadian government was often deprived of corporate income tax revenues to which it would otherwise be entitled, and that it also came under pressure, over time, to align its tax policies — and even its labour policies — with those of the United States.

From the more directly "political" point of view, it was suggested that the strong American presence in the Canadian economy constrained the government's conduct of its foreign policy (through the impact, for example, of the American "Trading with the Enemy" Act on the willingness of subsidiaries to export their products to markets in "communist" countries); that it created economic obstacles in the way of indigenous cultural expression (as in the commonly cited cases of television broadcasting and book, magazine and motion picture distribution); that it substantially moulded Canadian fashions and tastes; that it profoundly influenced attitudes to work and leisure; and so forth.

The Policy Response

In responding to these various and persistent anxieties over Canada's economic relationship with the United States, Canadian governments through the years have mobilized an impressive array of policy instruments. In the economic field, these have included not merely the usual devices in support of economic growth – east-west rail and road construction, domestic airline development, tax incentives for indigenous investors, industrial subsidies of various kinds, and the like – but also restrictions designed to inhibit, or at least to regulate, external penetration. Among these have been protective tariffs and non-tariff barriers in the case of trade, and – until recently – the screening activities of the Foreign Investment Review Agency in the case of investment.[5] In certain key sectors, like banking, the constraints imposed on foreign participation have been more direct, and have left relatively little room for argument or manoeuvre.

In the cultural field, restrictive policies are usually less congenial, if only because they collide with liberal principles bearing on freedom of communication and artistic expression, and on the unencumbered flow of information and ideas. There are exceptions, of course. Some of them are indirect, as in the case of Canadian content regulations applied to television and radio broadcasting. Others are direct, as exemplified by the attempts of immigration authorities to inhibit the appointment of foreign academics to the staffs of Canadian universities.[6] But the preferred policies in the cultural area take the form of artificial pump-primings of the national-building sort. The obvious examples include the Canadian Broadcasting Corporation, the National Film Board, the granting operations of agencies like the Canada Council (in the arts) and the Social Sciences and Humanities Research Council (in scholarship), the Canadian Film Development Corporation, the National Arts Centre in Ottawa, and the National Museums of Canada, along with programs for providing subsidies to Canadian book publishers, tax incentives aimed at encouraging private donations to cultural causes, and a host of others.

It should be noted that these various strategies tend to be either defensive or constructive in character, rather than externally aggressive. That is, they are designed either to prevent further new penetrations by American interests, or to give artificial support to indigenous alternatives. Only rarely have Canadian governments attempted actually to remove or roll back an established American presence. This is partly because operations that were already in place tend to have staunch defenders on both sides of the border, and partly because they are able to claim a special legitimacy by virtue of their having been tolerated before. Attempts to alter the *status quo* have been perceived almost as acts of aggression and, for that reason, tend to be especially unwelcome in the United States. The few available examples illustrate the point. One of them was the controversy generated by the Canadian decision to remove tax benefits for businesses advertising in *TIME* magazine – a measure obviously aimed at encouraging them to advertise in *Maclean's* and other Canadian periodicals instead – and to deprive *TIME* of what many regarded as its "privileged" position in the Canadian market. Another was the bitter American response some years ago to the decision of the provincial government of Saskatchewan to assume control of an American-owned corporation operating in the potash industry. And still another was the universally hostile reaction in the United States to the now-dismantled National Energy Program.

In the field of external affairs and foreign policy, Canadian governments have tried to compensate for the disparity of power in the Canada-U.S. relationship, first, by attempting to diversify Canada's connections abroad, and second, by trying to operate as much as possible in multilateral arenas rather than on a purely bilateral basis. The diversification strategy reflects the proposition that it is unwise to put all one's eggs in the same basket. The multilateral strategy rests on the thought that there is safety in numbers. The first has been most graphically illustrated in recent times by the negotiation in the middle 1970s of a so-called "contractual link" with the European Community.[7] The second has been reflected most clearly and persistently in Canada's support for the United Nations and its various specialized agencies, as well as in the government's repeated attempts to expand and promote the consultative practices of the North Atlantic alliance. Needless to say, the strategies do not always work, and some would argue that they are now less effective than they used to be. But they have been persistent and recurring features of the conduct of Canada's external affairs, particularly in the period since 1945, and they are driven above all by the need to cope with "Uncle Sam."

Historically, therefore, it is clear that Canadians in general have found it difficult to separate their economic relationship with the United States from their concern to preserve their autonomy and independence in other areas of public policy and to protect what they have perceived – often only dimly – as distinctive features of their society. Canadian governments, moreover, have deployed a substantial array of policy instruments in their attempts to respond to these preoccupations. In so doing, they have had, in some measure, to defy the iron laws of economics and resist the natural pull of continental economic forces.

Economics and Politics in the Current Debate

Given this historical background, one of the surprising features of the present debate in Canada is the degree to which it has focused on the economic aspects of the issue, to the neglect of traditional concerns about its implications for the country's political, social and cultural life at home, and for the conduct of its foreign policy abroad. It would appear, in effect, that those who support the bilateral initiative are in pursuit of economic gains (for the first time in Canadian history) without serious reference to non-economic costs. Implicitly, therefore, and sometimes explicitly too, they have accepted the primacy of economics over other values. Their ranks include not merely the prime minister and the governing political party, which seems almost completely to have abandoned its traditional nation-building role (or, at least, its conception of how that role can be most effectively played), but also, and far more important, the technocrats and bureaucrats by whom the government is most obviously advised, and those sectors of the academic, journalistic and business communities by which it is most heavily influenced.

This is not to say that non-economic arguments are never heard, for some of them obviously are (and with increasing frequency as the debate wears on), but it is to suggest that, for the first time in Canadian history, they are not being considered seriously and on their merits by those who are responsible for the making of Canadian public policy. They are received, that is, not so much as considerations that must be carefully weighed in the balance and taken soberly into account, but as the untutored expressions of the immature and the naive – an inconvenience emanating from a domestic political environment in which the exercise of reason is threatened by irrational myths and ignorant fears. That being so, they amount to obstacles against which tactical campaigns must be mounted, rather than concerns that responsible public policy may need to reflect.

This is, of course, a sweeping assertion, and sweeping assertions are never entirely true. But impressive supporting evidence can nonetheless be found, and it may be useful to consider some of it here, beginning with the changes that have taken place over the last decade or so in official expressions of government positions and policies.

For this purpose, the obvious point of departure is the special white paper on Canadian-American relations that was issued by the Department of External Affairs in the autumn of 1972 under the title "Canada-U.S. Relations: Options for the Future."[8] Almost entirely preoccupied with the question of continental "integration," the paper examined the problem from the military, political, economic and cultural points of view. Drawing attention to the pervasiveness of the American presence in almost every aspect of Canadian life, it identified three broad options for Canadian policy.

The first option was to try "to maintain more or less our present relationship with the United States with a minimum of policy adjustment." This was rejected — largely because there was "a risk," as the paper observed, "that in pursuing a purely pragmatic course, we may find ourselves drawn more closely into the U.S. orbit."

The second option was to "move deliberately toward closer integration with the United States." This option, too, was rejected. The paper's authors, observing that a "free trade area or a customs union arrangement with the United States would, to all intents and purposes, be irreversible for Canada once embarked upon," noted that the idea had "been rejected in the past because it was judged to be inconsistent with Canada's desire to preserve a maximum degree of independence, not because it lacked economic sense in terms of Canadian living standards and the stability of the Canadian economy." Their own conclusion was the "probable economic costs and benefits ... would require careful calculation," but that the "more fundamental issues ... (were) clearly political," and it was "a moot question whether (the) option, or any part of it, is politically tenable in the present or any foreseeable climate of Canadian public opinion."

The acceptable option, therefore, was the third. Ottawa wags called it the "ham in the sandwich." It was described as "comprehensive, long-term strategy to develop and strengthen the Canadian economy and other aspects of our national life and, in the process, to reduce the present Canadian vulnerability."

This was a little, perhaps, like having one's sandwich and eating it, too. It could be argued, after all, that to suggest that Canada should develop its economy while promoting its independence was to state the problem rather than the solution. But what in fact it meant was a strategy of diversification in economic activity abroad, of which the "contractual link" with the European Community was to become the chief example, combined with traditional national-building policies in economic, cultural and other fields at home. The entire thrust of the paper reflected, above all, the view that the relationship with the United States could not reasonably be considered in economic terms alone but also had to take into account an interlocking array of political, economic, social, cultural and foreign policy interests.

This performance can be usefully contrasted with the discussion paper entitled *Canadian Trade Policy for the 1980s*, issued by the Department of External Affairs 11 years later, in 1983.[9] The paper was a sophisticated review of Canada's trading position in an increasingly competitive international environment. While generally favouring a multilateral approach to trade liberalization — that is, an approach through the General Agreement on Tariffs and Trade — and while stopping short of advocating a policy of complete bilateral free trade with the United States, it suggested the negotiation of limited Canada-U.S. free trade arrangements on a sector-by-sector basis. In rejecting bilateral free trade across the board, the paper made brief mention of the political sovereignty factor, but the issue was not further developed in the discussion, and the cultural aspects of the problem were not considered at all.

The department's position — now reflective of settled cabinet policy — was taken one step further in its December 1985 booklet, entitled *Canadian Trade Negotiations: Introduction, Selected Documents, Further Reading.*[10] The texts that are included in the collection are focused almost entirely on the economic objectives of the Canada-U.S. discussions, and little attention is given to political or other issues. The booklet includes a June 1985 departmental analysis in which there is a brief mention of "political sovereignty implications," but these are assessed in beneficial terms. A move toward freer trade, the authors argue, "should strengthen the economic fabric of the country; it would reduce regional differences on the conduct of trade policy; and it should reinforce a growing sense of national confidence." They go on to suggest that "a bilateral treaty could be a better guarantor of our sovereignty than the gradual uncontrolled drift toward integration now taking place. The possible adverse consequences can be managed by pursuing deliberate policies of strengthening cultural and other fields of endeavour which would bolster our national identity." The authors, in effect, reach conclusions that are the precise antithesis of the arguments advanced by their predecessors in 1972, and their position is echoed in a speech by the secretary of state for external affairs, Joe Clark, which is reprinted elsewhere in the volume under the title "Trade Negotiations and Cultural Industries".[11]

In assessing these evolutions, it may be pertinent to note that by 1983 the Department of External Affairs had been amalgamated with the trade divisions of the old Department of Industry, Trade and Commerce. It is possible, therefore, that the change in the department's policy can be explained in part by the change in its bureaucratic composition, as well as by the more obvious turnover in the country's political leadership. At the same time, it should be understood that this organizational reform was not itself a mere "accident," but was deliberately aimed at harnessing the conduct of "foreign policy" to economic objectives.

In fairness, too, it should be noted that the 1983 and 1985 publications were directed specifically to trade policy, and not to the analysis of Canada-U.S. relations in general. The point, however, is that in 1972 it would have been thought totally inappropriate — and certainly unhelpful — to analyze the problem of Canada's trading relationship with the United States without also taking fully into account a variety of other political, social, cultural and foreign policy interests. In short, the policy problem would not have been **conceived**, much less resolved, in economic terms alone.

This may have the appearance of making too much of too little. Government position papers, after all, come and go — like academic enthusiasms — in easy accommodation of passing fads. But there are other indicators — apart from the negotiations themselves — to suggest that the change may be more deeply rooted than this interpretation would allow. Bilateral free trade with the United States has also been supported by the Economic Council of Canada and by the Senate Committee on Foreign Affairs. It was one of the most central recommendations of the massive report of the Royal Commission on the Economic Union and Development Prospects for Canada (the Macdonald commission),[12] and the commissioners found strong support for bilateral negotiations in the testimony of many of those who presented briefs at their public hearings. All of the provinces except Ontario have been broadly supportive of the free trade initiative, and even the Ontario government is cross-pressured by an economic constituency that is clearly divided on the issue. Business community organizations, like the Canadian Manufacturers' Association (until recently a strongly protectionist voice) and the Canadian Federation of Independent Business, have also tended to favour the negotiations. In the press, there have been occasional expressions of caution and concern, but relatively little of the comment has focused on the non-economic aspects of the debate.[13]

It could be argued, of course, that these indicators reflect only a temporary phenomenon, and that the pendulum will eventually swing the other way. But there are reasons for suggesting that this will not happen. Four of them appear to be particularly important.

The first results from the obvious fact that, in spite of the various counter-measures that Canadian governments have deployed, the country has already become so closely integrated with the United States that the process appears now to be an irreversible "force of history." Some 30 per cent of Canada's Gross National Product (GNP) enters into foreign trade, and more than 75 per cent of total Canadian exports go to the American market. Similarly, more than 70 per cent of imports are purchased from American sources. The proportion has been increasing steadily, and in the manufacturing sector it has been encouraged, in particular, by the growth of intra-corporate exchange — that is, by trade between Canadian subsidiaries and their American parents. Tariff walls have been dropping, in any case, as a result of multilateral agreements negotiated through the GATT.

On the cultural side, it is true, there have been very substantial displays of indigenous Canadian prowess in the literary and performing arts, but this has been much less noticeable in the related, but more commercially-dependent, field of popular entertainment.[14] The flood of American books, magazines, films, and television programs — to say nothing of fashions and fads — continues unabated. In some areas, advances in communications technology have reached the point at which government regulation becomes managerially impossible even if regarded as socially desirable. The Liberal government's abandonment not long ago of the attempt to regulate the private use of devices for receiving satellite transmissions of American television programs provides an obvious case in point. The initiatives of the Canadian Radio-television and Telecommunications Commission in trying to moderate the flow into Canada of American radio and television programming have been no more effective than were the efforts of the RCMP in attempting to prevent rum-running along the Atlantic coast during prohibition—and for many of the same reasons. Even the reports and interpretation of the international news that Canadians read, hear and see come largely from American sources.

These realities seem now to be producing two reactions, and they reinforce one another. The first is pragmatic. It is represented by the conclusion that the attempt by government authorities to resist the integrative process through the use of countervailing public policy instruments is ultimately futile because it is impracticable. It is better, in short, to align with the inevitable than to wage a war that cannot be won.

The second reaction is at once more subtle and more significant. It is reflected in the view that resistance is not merely ineffectual, but also, to some extent, improper or illegitimate. This is partly, of course, a matter of allowing the secular principles of western liberalism to take over, and to assert that it is not the proper function of government to attempt, in **these** areas at least, to inhibit or otherwise influence the spontaneous evolution of our political, social and cultural values. These are questions for individuals in society to determine, and not for governments to mould. But the argument may also reflect the pervasive success of the assimilative process itself, so that liberal postulates of this sort are being invoked, not because Canadian policy makers and "attentive publics" are more enthusiastic liberals now than they were before, but because they no longer see anything fundamentally worrying in what has been happening to their society. If this is true, it effectively means that Canada's cultural integration with the United States has passed the point of no return. It has ceased, that is, to be perceived as a legitimate issue on the national agenda.

It may be worth pointing out in passing that this phenomenon is not peculiar to Canada, and it can be argued that Canadians are merely experiencing a process that is common to most of the western industrialized countries and, increasingly, to much of the rest of the world as well. National cultures, in this view, are disappearing everywhere before the onslaught of a kind of universal pluralism. As Anthony Westell, during the course of an elaborate defence of the free trade option, has put it,

> the concept of national identity rooted in a national culture is being washed away by the technologies of transportation and communication that are producing not the uniform man in a homogenized society, but variety and diversity in an international society. To be a Canadian citizen does not signify a way of life, or a set of values beyond attachment to the community and loyalty to the national state. So the fear that closer association with the United States will erode a Canadian identity in the making or abort a Canadian culture about to be born is unfounded.[15]

In short (and as Marshall McLuhan might have predicted), the world is becoming more homogeneously heterogeneous, and none of us—Canadians perhaps least of all—can escape the process.

If many Canadians have given up on their founding national purpose, therefore, it may be partly because they no longer believe that continental integration **can** be resisted, and partly because they have lost the will to think that it **should** be resisted. But they may have given it up for a second reason as well—economic panic. For, with some exceptions, Canadian economists and public administrators have become more and more concerned that, in an increasingly regionalized world, Canada has no other place to go. The negotiation of the "contractual link" with the European Community may have been a triumph of Canadian diplomacy, but it was a lamentable failure as an instrument of foreign economic policy. It has become increasingly difficult, in fact, to find overseas markets for Canada's manufactured goods, and exports of raw materials and natural resources (as an inhabitant of British Columbia will attest) are subject to unseemly ups and downs. Having no easy access to either industrialized Europe or industrialized Asia, and having discovered that for the foreseeable future there is little prospect of solving the problem through trade with the so-called "Third World" (to say nothing of the newly industrialized countries (NICs)), it seems natural to turn to the United States as the only accessible market of sufficient size to encourage the exploitation of economies of scale, and hence the production of value-added goods at internationally competitive prices. That being so, there is a strong feeling in Ottawa and elsewhere that every effort should be made to ensure that Canada's access to the U.S. market is not only expanded, but permanently secured, so that Canadian producers will be exempted from such future rounds of American protectionism as may eventually find unwelcome expression in Congress. Economists are practitioners of the dismal science, and the alternative they describe is appropriately gloomy: a contracting Canadian economy, plagued with inefficient industries, rising prices, high levels of structural unemployment, and public services substantially reduced as a result of declining government revenues. Economic integration with the United States thus comes to be a virtue driven by necessity. And necessary virtues, unlike optional ones, are difficult to resist.

Attitudes may have changed, thirdly, because the distribution of pertinent political forces **within** Canada has been altered in such a way as to make the change politically more acceptable. Historically, the lines of battle on the free trade question have reflected the regional interests of different parts of the country, with the natural resource and agricultural economy of the West being in conflict with the industrial and manufacturing economy of Central Canada. Now, however, the national economy as a whole has become more diversified and complex, and even within particular economic sectors there are differences of interest, and hence of opinion. The result is that support for the free trade option has become more general, and the opposition more diffused. Ontario, at the manufacturing core, still hesitates, but its position is ambiguous, and it is not clear whether its reservations are genuinely and deeply held, or are only being expressed on the one hand to test the waters, and on the other to establish bargaining leverage for concessions from the federal negotiating authorities. In any case, the government in Ottawa is in a position to pursue the initiative with much less fear than ever before that it will arouse significant concentrations of opposition that are congruent with particular regions of the country. The issue, in short, is now much less likely than in earlier decades to generate cleavages that coincide with important provincial boundaries.

Finally, there is evidence of a growing conviction among decision makers in Ottawa, as well as among their most attentive publics, that the political and cultural arguments against economic integration with the United States are not, in any event, propositions that can be "proved" in accordance with the normal methodological canons of social science, and hence are not persuasive. This, of course, is not an entirely new factor in the debate. The connection between economic relations abroad on the one hand, and political behaviour, public policy and cultural values at home on the other, has always been difficult to demonstrate by empirical means. The cause-and-effect linkages are too indirect, and the behaviours and values at issue are too intangible for the matter to be resolved by simple inspection of the facts, no matter how sophisticated the research methods employed. Political science is a weaker discipline than economics, or it has a more difficult agenda. Either way, it seems unable here to give clear answers. The result is that opinions on the general impact of continental economic relations are reached through subtle combinations of interest, preference, and judgment, and not by reference to irrefutable fact — which presumably helps to explain why the disagreements persist, and the issues involved have so frequently been debated with more rhetorical heat than substantive evidence. The difference in the present round of debate, however, is that the other forces involved are lending unprecedented weight to the integrationist position, and, perhaps for the first time in Canadian history, are shifting the onus of proof from the supporters to the opponents.[16] The predicament of the latter is that they cannot provide a satisfactorily persuasive case if they are required to pass quantitative empirical tests. The economists, by contrast, at least **look** as if they can.[17]

The Stakes at Issue

The central question obviously remains: does it really matter?

The answer clearly depends in part on the perspective and values of the analyst, and even then a "judgment call" is required. Individuals, therefore, who start from the same premises often reach different conclusions. It may be useful, nonetheless, to identify some of the more important of the non-economic concerns, and to attempt in each case to assess the significance of the argument. For purposes of exposition, it will be convenient to consider first the arguments that can be safely dismissed, and second the ones that thoughtful Canadians will want to take seriously into account.

There is no reason, first of all, to conclude that a bilateral free trade agreement would lead — even by slow degrees — to Canada's political integration with the United States in the formal, or institutional, sense of the term. That is, there is no reason to expect that it would eventually culminate in the unification of the two countries. For a variety of reasons, Canadians would vigorously resist any such development, and there is no cause to think that the Americans would press the case. In any event, both parties would have obtained most of what they wanted without this further step being required.

Secondly — and with qualifications to be discussed below — it seems unlikely that a bilateral free trade regime would have a significant impact on at least the **fundamentals** of Canada's political culture. This is partly because the two countries are driven, at the level of political philosophy, by the same basic values and are organized politically on similar premises. They are like-minded, that is, in their commitment to the liberal democratic state, as governed by representative political institutions. To the extent, moreover, that there are differences in their political styles and practices, these are deeply embedded in their respective institutional arrangements, and it seems improbable that these will be dislodged (unless, for some unforeseeable reason, Canadians choose to abandon their parliamentary system of responsible government in favour of the American system of checks and balances). There is nothing, certainly, in any of the proposals for continental free trade to suggest that this will happen.

Thirdly, it seems unlikely that a bilateral free trade arrangement, in itself, will have a truly significant impact on Canadian cultural activities or popular entertainments. This is not because patterns of trade are unimportant as determinants of the cultural process, but because the citadel — if ever there was one — has already been taken. Pump-priming of indigenous cultural activities could still be maintained (although probably not without occasional American protest), but there is little reason to think that the influx of American "products" in cultural fields would be more overwhelming under free bilateral trade than it is now. The problem here — if "problem" it be — is rooted in other forces.

The argument, finally, that free trade will lead to an erosion of the amiable gentilities of Canadian society also seems not to be entirely persuasive, although here it is more difficult to be certain. It is, of course, a cliche of Canadian commentators to observe that theirs is a more ordered and restrained, and less ruthlessly competitive community than the American; that Canada prefers industrious beavers to soaring eagles, "peace, order, and good government" to "life, liberty, and the pursuit of happiness," and the RCMP to Billy the Kid. The vitality of America is expressed in its creative accomplishments and in the exuberance of its economic life. Canadians are duller. On the other hand, they can safely walk the streets of their cities at night.[18]

These, obviously, are stereotypical images. It is hard to know what to make of them. But to the extent that they reflect a genuine contrast between the two societies, it is not clear that it will be eroded, at least in the short run, by a slight expansion of continental trade.

There are other areas, however, in which the side-effects of a comprehensive free trade agreement could be very substantial and, from the Canadian point of view, not altogether welcome. Three possibilities — or **types** of possibility — come most obviously to mind.

The first of these is that a bilateral agreement will tend to reduce Canada's freedom of manoeuvre in a large number of areas of public policy that are not directly related to trade *per se*, and lead in time to a "harmonization" of Canadian policies with those of the United States. This will happen, not because of the specific provisions of the treaty itself (although these could be a harmonizing factor, too), but because of the impact of two simultaneous political processes, one on the Canadian side of the border, and the other on the American.

On the Canadian side, the process will result from the fact that any policy within Canada that has the effect of increasing the costs of Canadian producers relative to those of the United States will be strongly resisted by the industries concerned. These will argue, in effect, that if they are to have a reasonable chance of surviving the powerful competition of their American rivals, they must have an even start at the gate, and cannot be unfairly disadvantaged by government policy. This is a phenomenon that can be detected even now, but it will intensify—and certainly it will be more difficult for governments to resist—if it is legitimized by an agreement founded on the principle that all enterprises should have equal opportunity in the marketplace. Where Canadian corporate taxes are higher than the American, for example, Canadian producers can be expected to demand that they be appropriately reduced.

The same phenomenon can be expected to arise in relation to regulatory controls. If, for example, Canadian labour codes, safety requirements, product standards, or environmental regulations are, in certain areas, more stringent than the American, and hence more expensive to implement, Canadian production costs will be correspondingly higher, and Canadian firms will be quick to demand relief. The consequence over time is almost certain to be a harmonization of Canadian policy with American in a host of fields. In some areas, depending on one's point of view, this may be seen as an advance. In others, it will not. But in either event, the government's freedom of fiscal and regulatory manoeuvre will have been eroded.

Constraints on Canadian policy can also be expected to result from political forces generated on the American side of the border, although this time in the opposite direction. That is, American producers will object to any Canadian policy that has the effect, not of **increasing** Canadian production costs, but of **reducing** them. The most obvious examples are government subsidies and other incentives designed to promote regional and industrial development (including the development of so-called "cultural industries"). There is evidence already, however, of this argument being mounted against policies that in Canada have a much wider social import—notably unemployment insurance, and other ingredients of the so-called social security "net." With a free trade regime visibly in place, American industries that were feeling the pain of Canadian competition could be expected to cry "Foul" with even more than their present vigour.[19]

In anticipation of such problems, Canadian negotiators will obviously try to protect their future freedom of domestic manoeuvre by bargaining for specific exemptions from the general provisions of the treaty, and much will depend on the terms of the eventual agreement. Even in the case of regional and industrial subsidies, moreover, the problem will presumably arise only in cases where part of the production is destined for the American market. Nonetheless, the potential implications for the autonomy of Canadian public policy are real and extensive, and it should come as no surprise if Canadians, in their public discussions, begin to take them seriously into account. Even now, there is a realization in some quarters that the negotiations with the United States have as much to do with "deregulation" as with trade *per se*. That, of course, gives them a significance which goes to the very heart of contemporary political debates in the Western World — debates bearing on the perennial question of the proper role in society of the state.

There is a second group of considerations arising from the possible impact of a Canada-U.S. free trade agreement on **perceptions** of Canada, both at home and abroad. In external affairs, for example, it is possible that the declaration of a Canada-U.S. free trade area would persuade governments elsewhere in the world of what many of them suspect already — that, for practical purposes, Canada's interests in international politics are the same as those of the United States, and that Canadian foreign policy can be routinely expected to support the American cause. Perceptions of this kind — even now a problem for the Canadian foreign service — could seriously limit Ottawa's freedom of diplomatic manoeuvre, and make it more difficult for its voice to be heard.

Within the United States itself, moreover, the creation of a free trade regime could lead to very similar expectations, with the result that Canadian deviations from American policy would be viewed as surprising acts of betrayal, and hence would be more vigorously resented than they are at present. Canadian governments, aware of these realities, might therefore become increasingly reluctant to adopt independent positions on international issues. This is already the case, for example, in relation to Latin America. While precise measurement in such matters is difficult, under free trade the problem could become worse (when viewed, at least, from the Canadian vantage point). For Ottawa, moreover, the political consequences of this dilemma could be intensified were American policies to become especially unpopular in Canada — as they were, for example, during the Vietnam War. Federal authorities would then have the always difficult choice of irritating the Americans or irritating their constituents.

More important still, it seems probable that a public announcement that Canada and the United States had established a bilateral free trade area would have an enormous impact on the perceptions of Canadians themselves. Psychologically, in effect, they would be "throwing in the towel" after more than 200 years of trying, against the opposition of overwhelming economic forces, to establish and maintain a political and social community clearly distinguishable from that of the United States. In other words, it would place Canadians — psychologically — inside the American "world view," and in so doing it would well erode such slender will to meaningful national survival as they still possess. This does not mean that they would give up their formal sovereignty — for reasons already discussed, that would hardly be necessary. It means only that they might give up the attempt to **use** their sovereignty in significantly differentiated ways.

The third serious possibility, closely related to the other two, is that the implementation of a free trade agreement would have the effect, very broadly, of changing the prevailing "public philosophy" in Canada in such a way as to make it very similar to that of the United States. This is partly a matter of "deregulation," and of the particular version of modern liberalism that deregulation represents. But, more broadly, it refers to the way in which the role of the state in society is conceived, and the priority that is given to economic over other values. In such matters, easy generalizations are often misleading, but one way of illustrating the difference is to observe that, in the United States, there is a general assumption in economic matters that labour should move to where the jobs are, while in Canada the expectation is that the jobs will move to where the labour is (and that the government will take remedial action if they do not). This is an economically inefficient principle. Nonetheless, it has always been argued in Canada that it is a socially, culturally, and politically desirable foundation upon which to base public policy. It has been regarded, in effect, as a conception dictated by the kind of country Canada is, by the way in which its population is geographically distributed, and by the history and environment that its inhabitants have experienced. While there may be a strong argument in economics for saying that Cape Breton, for example, should be allowed to turn into a nearly deserted national park, it is (Canadians have traditionally held) insufficient as a foundation for public policy precisely because it comes from economics alone, and neglects other community values. If a free trade agreement, by exposing Canadians to both the philosophy and the reality of American economic competition, alters these assumptions, it will have transformed the character of the country itself.[20]

Notes

1.   A brief governmental assessment of the state of extant knowledge of the probable implications of a bilateral agreement can be found in a June 1985 Department of External Affairs paper entitled "Canada-United States Trade Negotiations: The Elements Involved." The paper is reproduced in Canada Department of External Affairs, *Canadian Trade Negotiations: Introduction, Selected Documents, Further Reading* (Ottawa: Supply and Services, Canada, 1986). See especially pp. 29-33.

2.   An extensive summary of the history in Canada of debates over Canadian-American trading relations is J.L. Granatstein's "Free Trade Between Canada and the United States: The Issue That Will Not Go Away," in Denis Stairs and Gilbert R. Winham, *The Politics of Canada's Economic Relationship with the United States* (Toronto: University of Toronto Press in cooperation with the Royal Commission on the Economic Union and Development Prospects for Canada, and the Canadian Government Publishing Centre, Supply and Services Canada, 1985), pp. 11-54.

3.   The limited character of the 1854 agreement is emphasized in Bruce W. Wilkinson's "Canada and Sectoral Free Trade," in Lee H. Radebauh and Earl H. Fry, eds., *Canada/U.S. Trade Relations: Problems and Prospects* (Provo, Utah: Brigham Young University David M. Kennedy Center for International Studies, 1985), pp. 18-19.

4.   The literature of what was often described as "economic nationalism" eventually became very extensive. Walter L. Gordon's views at the time can be found, of course, in his *A Choice for Canada: Independence or Colonial Status* (Toronto: McClelland and Stewart, 1966). One of the most influential treatments was Kari Levitt's *Silent Surrender: The Multinational Corporation in Canada* (Toronto: Macmillan, 1970). A representative selection of articles can be examined in Abraham Rotstein and Gary Lax, eds., *Independence: The Canadian Challenge* (Toronto: The Committee for an Independent Canada, 1972).

5. There is, of course, an irony in the fact that protective tariffs were originally established to inhibit U.S. penetration of Canadian markets, but ultimately had the effect of encouraging penetration in another form – that is, by means of direct investment. Those who opposed the disease thus find themselves now opposed also to what many would regard as the cure. Paradox, however, lends interest to politics.

6. Cynics might argue that this had more to do with protecting academic jobs than with protecting indigenous culture. In its original form, however, the debate was clearly founded on cultural arguments. See, for example, Robin Mathews and James Steele, eds., *The Struggle for Canadian Universities* (Toronto: new press, 1969).

7. The link had little practical effect. See, for example, Robert Boardman, "Initiatives and Outcomes: The European Community and Canada's 'Third Option'," *Journal of European Integration*, Vol. 3, No. 1 (September 1979), pp. 5-28.

8. The paper appeared over the signature of Mitchell Sharp, then secretary of state for external affairs, and was published as a special issue of *International Perspectives*, September/October 1972.

9. See External Affairs, *Canadian Trade Policy for the 1980s: A Discussion Paper* (Ottawa: Minister of Supply and Services Canada, 1983). The paper was accompanied by a more substantial volume entitled, *A Review of Canadian Trade Policy: A Background Document to Canadian Trade Policy for the 1980s* (Ottawa: Supply and Services, 1983).

10. *Canadian Trade Negotiations: Introduction, . . .*

11. It is particularly instructive to compare pp. 15-17 of the 1972 paper *International Trade Perspectives*, with pp. 32-33 and 83-87 of the December 1985 paper, *Canadian Trade Negotiations . . .*

12. See *Report of the Royal Commission on the Economic Union and Development Prospects for Canada*, 3 vols. (Ottawa: Minister of Supply and Services, 1985). Volume I is particularly relevant.

13. This may be a reflection in part of deliberate government strategy. The political leadership has attempted to focus the debate as much as possible on the economic aspects of the issue, recognizing that on other grounds the case for its initiative is more vulnerable to attack. Nonetheless, as the public debate has progressed, representatives of the performing arts community, among others, have come increasingly to express their alarm, and even in the media there are exceptions to the general rule. *The Toronto Star* is perhaps the most notable example.

14. Canadians tend, of course, to see popular entertainment as an expression of community culture. Americans, by contrast, appear often to regard it as no more than a business. An interesting discussion of the implications of this difference in

attitude can be found in an address by Pierre Juneau, president of the Canadian Broadcasting Corporation, to the Canada-U.S. Seminar Series at the Harvard University Center for International Affairs. Originally delivered on April 1, 1986, the address is entitled "Canadian and U.S. Attitudes to Culture: Some Comparative Observations."

15. Anthony Westell, "Economic Integration with the U.S.A.," *International Perspectives* (November/December 1984), *passim*. As an indicator of the growing popularity of Westell's argument in public policy circles, it should be noted that his article is described as "seminal" in the report of the Macdonald commission, which quotes it at some length (p. 299). It is also quoted on two occasions in the Department of External Affairs booklet on *Canadian Trade Negotiations* (pp. 36 and 81).

16. It is thus no coincidence that the Department of External Affairs finds it appropriate to include in its booklet on *Canadian Trade Negotiations* the following passage from a November 18, 1985, editorial in *The Globe and Mail*: "It is often alleged that those supporting liberalized trade 'have not done their homework.' In reality, that is far more true of those who oppose free trade. Among the critics, therefore, rhetoric, passion and a maudlin nationalism sometimes fill the gap or conceal a defence of economic privilege. That does not pay the issue anything like its due. Who are the real 'nationalists' in the free trade debate, and who are the defenders of special interests? Who has done the research, and who appeals to generalized fears? A debate exists; its quality is the problem." (See *Canadian Trade Negotiations*, p. 9).

17. The Department of External Affairs appears, however, to recognize the limitations of the economic argument. See, again, *ibid.*, pp. 31-32.

18. Contrasts of this kind are developed at length in Pierre Berton's *Why We Act Like Canadians: A Personal Exploration of Our National Character* (Toronto: McClelland and Stewart, 1982).

19. This may seem like a somewhat one-sided analysis, but, of course, the disparity in the size of the two countries ensures that the "harmonizing" will occur far more extensively in Canada than in the United States.

20. This **could**, of course, have an effect on what were described earlier as "the amiable gentilities of Canadian society."

Canadian Sovereignty and the Free Trade Debate

Glen Williams

If sovereignty can be determined at least in part by a nation's ability to chart its policy directions without the need to submit to external political, economic or social forces, then the best of our political economists have long held rather pessimistic views on Canadian sovereignty. Harold Innis wrote after World War II that Canada had moved from "colony to nation to colony."[1] More recently, Leo Panitch remarked that "in Canada's voyage from colony to nation to neo-colony, we seem to have exchanged the "shadowy and unreal" independence offered within the British Empire for the "shadowy and unreal" independence tolerated by the Americans."[2] Canadian sovereignty, for the political economists, is always bounded and rendered meaningful by the external structural relationships which attend the unique manner of our integration within empire.

Within the study of Canadian political science generally and Canadian foreign policy in particular, the powerful implications of these observations have been scarcely explored. Canadian sovereignty has largely been viewed as a quantifiable variable; the Canadian state has more or less of it according to the manner in which specific circumstances or challenges, like the free trade debate, manifest themselves over time. At one extreme, Canada has been presented as a fully independent modern nation-state (or binational state) much like any other western liberal democracy and, accordingly, the significance of the structural relationship of empire for assessing Canadian sovereignty is minimized or ignored.[3] At another extreme, it has been argued that the weight of foreign domination is so great that Canada enjoys scarcely any meaningful degree of sovereignty.[4]

While this latter opinion might appear to hold something in common with the Innisian perspective of "colony to nation to colony," this is only because Innis's views on

85

this question have been so often misinterpreted. Although Innis wrote that our economic history had been "dominated by the discrepancy between the centre and margin of western civilization"[5] and catalogued important economic disadvantages associated with our marginal status, on the whole he believed that our "colonial" association with the centre had promoted Canada's economic and political development. Conditioned by the shifting demands of more advanced industrial centres for our resource products, the pace of this economic development was vulnerable to violent swings as the world economy expanded and contracted. However, this vulnerability was not an indicator of exploitation or underdevelopment but was simply the essence of the **regional relationships** between the "new countries," like Canada, and the more established centres of empire, Great Britain and the United States, within "western civilization." Unquestionably, because the "new countries," characterized by staple export specialization and relative industrial backwardness, followed the pace and pattern of industrial development set in more advanced centres, the regional relationship was asymmetrical. But in economic development, as measured by productivity and living standards, and in political development, as measured by liberal democracy, the centre and margins of western civilization were largely equivalent.

Innis's technique of viewing Canadian development through the lens of its lesser, but nonetheless associate, status within the British and American empires has had a significant influence on tendencies within the revival of Canadian political economy surfacing in the 1970s and 1980s. My own work on Canadian industrial policy, for example, puts forward the thesis that it was an initial location within the British Empire which accounted for the peculiar import substitution **character** of Canadian manufacturing, while its later organization as a regional extension of U.S. industrial production rendered its modern branch plant **form**.[6] From our vantage point in the late 1980s, it is possible to argue that the Canadian economy as a whole may now be better understood in many respects as a geographically large zone **within** the U.S. economy rather than as a distinct national economy. Although this position may at first appear extreme, it is merely the logical conclusion of an analysis based on the consideration of factors such as the three quarters of Canada's import and export trade that is accounted for by the Americans and the nearly one half ownership share of our productive apparatus that they now enjoy. Under these conditions, and given the relative size of the economies, it would be odd indeed if industrial and resource production in Canada failed to dance to rhythms written south of the border. In recent years, the integration of the two economies has been enhanced by the GATT agreements on tariff reduction. These have already brought us to a kind of *de facto* free trade with the United States. By 1987, 95 per cent of Canadian goods are scheduled to enter the U.S. with duties of 5 per cent or less and 91 per cent of U.S. exports to Canada will be in equivalent position in our market.

The Regional Relations of Empire

Presiding over the northern extension of a continental economy organized by American interests, the Canadian state system's political autonomy can only be fathomed within the nexus of empire. In the 1909 creation of the Department of External Affairs, it was the primacy of the British colonial office in the conduct of our inter-imperial and foreign relations which defined Canada's international business as "external" rather than "foreign." As Glazebrook suggested, "foreign and imperial relations were, to some extent, the same."[7] Innis observed with respect to Canadian foreign policy that "autonomy following the Statute of Westminster (1931) has been a device by which we can co-operate with the United States as we formerly did with Great Britain."[8] Today, two thirds of our bilateral relations are conducted with the United States[9], thereby leading our foreign relations, in their essence, to continue to manifest themselves as imperial relations.

Far-reaching constraints on the ability of the federal and provincial states to challenge the power of America in Canada result from the primacy of the continental relationship in economic policy making. While the formal autonomy of the Canadian state can seldom be directly challenged, perceived hostile nationalist challenges to the continentalist status quo can often be forestalled, muted, or repudiated at a later point after concerted campaigns of pressure by U.S. multinationals and the U.S. government. These campaigns need never step outside the normal decision rules of Canadian liberal democracy but can simply utilize all the many points of political access and leverage available within a multi-party, executive-dominated, federal system. In making their representations, Canadian branches of multinationals are typically accorded the same legitimate "corporate citizen" status by state elites as domestically-owned firms.[10] As the fate of the early 1980s Trudeau government initiatives on the Foreign Investment Review Act (FIRA) and the National Energy Program (NEP) vividly illustrate, key to the success or failure of American pressure campaigns is the degree to which factions within the executive class of our bureaucracy, the cabinet, and the leadership of our political parties resonate within their own decision forums the multinationals' arguments for a continentalist vision of the Canadian national interest.[11] Key, as well, is the manner in which the maintenance or cultivation of the global continental relationship can hold even nationalist Canadian policy makers hostage on specific issue disputes.

One 1975 survey of some 300 members of our foreign policy elites captured very nicely the anti-matter universe of Canadian state autonomy within empire. Nearly two thirds saw the United States as Canada's best friend and one half defined Canada as a "partner" in North America, suggesting that on most issues in international affairs Canadian and American interests are essentially the same. And yet, 52 per cent felt that the continental economy "significantly limited" Canadian autonomy in domestic affairs and only 28 per cent believed that, compared to most other countries, Canada acts independently in international relations.[12]

Just as the effective expression of American political interests within the Canadian state rests on the mainly continentalist definitions of the Canadian national interest found amongst our governmental decision makers, so ultimately the domination of continentalist persuasions within the state elite is rooted in the pattern of mass opinions within Canadian civil society.[13] Seventy per cent of Canadians in the 1980s viewed the United States as Canada's best friend, and one half between 1977 and 1986 expressed "very great" or "considerable" confidence in the ability of the U.S. to deal wisely with world problems.[14] Only one quarter of Canadians were prepared to agree that we should withdraw from NATO and NORAD and adopt neutrality when asked in the mid-1970s and again in the mid-1980s.[15]   At least a plurality of Canadian public opinion usually backs controversial U.S. foreign policy initiatives such as Star Wars research in Canada or the 1986 bombing of Libya.[16]

While most Canadians tend to follow the U.S. lead in the grand issues of imperial foreign policy, they have been less certain, in some periods, that American economic interests always coincide with those of Canada.   During the 1970s, for example, two thirds thought there was sufficient U.S. capital invested in Canada and approximately one half were prepared to countenance schemes to buy back majority control of U.S. companies in Canada **even if this were to reduce living standards**.   During this peak of nationalist sentiment, it should nonetheless be noted, popular misgivings about continental economic integration were far from universal, with approximately one third disapproving a buy-back.   As well, during the 1980s, public opinion on these questions became considerably softer following a concerted campaign by business leaders in conjunction with provincial and Progressive Conservative party politicians to link the economic recession of the early 1980s to the before mentioned NEP and FIRA initiatives of the Liberal party.[17]

Within this unique historically defined nexus of empire, then, what can be understood as the meaning of Canadian sovereignty? When autonomy is bounded by the essential unity of imperial and foreign relations, what breathes life into the symbols and institutional structures of Canadian nationhood? In striving to address these questions we must remember that the instability that attends being both inside and outside of the U.S. political economy has, of necessity, meant an increasing reliance on governmental institutions as points of balance.   Defined functionally, then, sovereignty refers primarily to the maintenance of the capacity of the Canadian federal and provincial states to focus, mediate, protect and develop the regional position of the Canadian socio-economic formation within the continental political economy.   While this may be very distant from classical definitions of sovereignty, it can afford us a far clearer vantage point from which to view the peculiar vista of Canadian foreign policy.

The Canadian state system has given considerable advantage to Canadian elites in protecting and developing their regional position within the greater American economy.   Although the Canadian social formation is not, of course, electorally represented in the U.S. political system, Canada's federal and provincial state system has nonetheless developed considerable means for the "external" political expression of our regional interests through both direct representation and negotiation. As well, more indirect support is, from time to time, conveyed to indigenous forces within U.S. politics whose positions are seen as coincident with our own.[18] Two prerequisites underlie an effective long-term articulation of Canadian interests within North America. First, the relative autonomy of the Canadian state system from the direct demands of U.S. governments and multinationals must be safeguarded in order that our distinct regional interests can emerge in the play of domestic forces through our political institutions. As well, a reservoir of nationalism in civil society must be preserved both to preclude outright political annexation and to mobilize, when necessary, as leverage in continental bargaining.

The 1985 Free Trade Initiative

Using this framework, which focuses on the role of the Canadian state in providing for regional representation within empire, we can transcend the conventional manner in which the question of sovereignty and free trade is most often debated between "continentalist" and "nationalist" economists: the former arguing that free trade will increase the potential for the exercise of Canadian sovereignty because it will strengthen economic growth and therefore give the state more resources on which to ground independent action, the latter arguing that free trade means greater economic dependence on the United States and therefore a more limited ability for Canada to act autonomously. Insofar as these perspectives both view sovereignty as a quantitative issue-specific variable rather than a qualitative historical-developmental relation, they miss much of the significance of the current debate.

As noted earlier, Canada and the United States achieved a kind of *de facto* free trade under the GATT regime of tariff liberalization by the late 1980s. The dismantling of the old National Policy system of tariff protection began in the late 1930s and proceeded at a quickened pace after the mid-1960s. Because of the volatility and intensity of emotions that this issue had stirred in the national politics of all of the five decades between 1880 and 1930, the inexorable movement toward continental free trade was presented by various Canadian governments as a disjointed and technical series of incremental tariff adjustments. The fear of the electoral consequences of repoliticizing this issue, a possible rerun of the 1911 "no truck nor trade with the Yankees" reciprocity campaign, largely accounts for why there has been so little public debate about the repudiation of the heritage of the National Policy and a continentalist reorientation of Canada's trade and industrial policy.

In this context, what must be explained is the emergence of the free trade issue in the mid-1980s at the conclusion of the long process of tariff liberalization which has already created something very close to a free trade area between the two countries. I have argued elsewhere that a specific conjuncture of three actors was responsible for the re-entry of free trade into the Canadian political atmosphere: (1) the search for a simple, practical and ideologically acceptable formula to address Canada's complex economic difficulties, (2) the rise of protectionism within the U.S. political system which threatened to disrupt a Canadian production regime already significantly reorganized on the basis of assumed low tariff access to American markets, and (3) the struggle for partisan electoral advantage.[19] Let us briefly review these factors.

Of all the many weaknesses in the Canadian economy, the most obvious are those displayed in our manufacturing sector. Of all the many ills of our manufacturing sector, none is more debilitating than our failure in world markets. And nowhere is this failure more clearly demonstrated than in our appalling balance of trade in end manufactures: a deficit of $87.6 billion in the 1970s and $118.1 billion in the first six-and-a-half years of the 1980s. The figures for the 1980s would be worse if not for the $17 billion surplus posted between 1982 and 1985 in the Auto Pact, a traditional deficit item in this account now enjoying a measure of success due to the lower labour costs in Canada which accompany our devalued dollar.[20] These trade deficits generate very high stakes in the Canadian economy as a whole. Many tens of thousands of jobs could almost certainly have been created if Canada had exported enough end manufactures to wipe out the staggering fifth of a trillion dollar deficit we have been accumulating in this category since 1970.

Authorities representing almost all persuasions concede the ineptitude of our manufacturers in the world economy. Prime Minister Mulroney has observed "we do not have a very good track record. Our products have not been of the highest quality. Our deliveries have been lacking in reliability. Our expertise has been in large measure borrowed. Our technology has been purchased. What the hell makes us so special?"[21] Conrad Black, as one of our foremost capitalists, surely must have been in a position to know when he recently concluded that "Canada's performance in secondary industry has been, on balance, mediocre. There have been some uplifting exceptions such as Spar, Bombardier and Magna, but generally Canadian manufacturing is ... largely auto-related, branch-plant, heavily protected, or very marginal."[22]

Although general agreement on the dimensions of the problem can be discovered, two radically different approaches to its solution have confronted each other through recent decades in bitter and prolonged debate. Simplifying somewhat, a "continentalist" school argues that the National Policy legacy of tariff protection has made Canadian industry inefficient and uncompetitive and that Canada-U.S. free trade would rationalize our manufacturing. On the other side, a "nationalist" school blames foreign investment and the branch-plant nature of Canadian industrial production. It proposes a state-directed industrial strategy to regulate an improvement in the performance of the branch plants.[23]

Since the 1950s, the continentalist school has been dominant within the federal state, although the nationalist school did make some headway during the 1970s. Nationalist influence reached its summit in 1980 with the introduction of the National Energy Program and the suggestion that minimum export and research and development performance standards might be imposed on foreign-owned manufacturing subsidiaries through FIRA. The subsequent no-holds-barred public campaign by business elites in conjunction with provincial and Progressive Conservative party politicians rejecting the NEP and FIRA initiatives was to rejuvenate the continentalist free trade position within the state and, as well, to catapult it forcefully onto the public stage. Free trade, after all, was a non-interventionist, market-oriented alternative which also promised a cure-all solution to Canada's chronic economic difficulties. Chambers of Commerce across the country were evangelized by professional economist missionaries, fanning out from the universities and business think tanks. In failing to note that Canada's manufacturing difficulties had persisted in spite of our steady march toward free trade with the United States under the GATT, these missionaries seemed inanely oblivious to the great irony of their crusade.

Powerful and more sophisticated business interests were also beginning to rally around the free trade banner during 1984 and 1985. These interests encompassed both resource-based industries, which had long depended upon unimpeded access to U.S. markets for the sale of their products, and manufacturing industries, which had seized on the staged Canada-U.S. tariff liberalization under the GATT as a chance to meet intense foreign competition in the domestic market by reorganizing their production on a continental basis along the lines suggested by the Auto Pact. While less knowledgeable entrepreneurs looked forward to an awesome expansion of their markets as promised to them by the continentalist missionaries, these more established business elites were looking backward to secure their investments in continental production from an emerging protectionist threat within the U.S. political system. While some advocated the initiation of Canada-U.S. free trade negotiations as a tactic to exempt Canada from protectionist measures as long as the talks were in progress, others were more concerned with developing permanent mechanisms which could stabilize the access they already enjoyed in U.S. markets.[24]

From several directions, then, representatives from small, medium and large Canadian businesses began to impress upon the newly elected Conservative government their desire for free trade negotiations. However favourably the Tory party leadership generally looks on the logic of business representations, free trade has been such a historically divisive issue that, in other circumstances, it might have given them pause. However, it was an issue which also appealed to two important strands within the party[25] — the traditional western free trade electorate and the neo-conservatives who favoured it both because free trade smacks of free enterprise and because an agreement would bring Canada closer to Reagan's America. And, most important, it was an issue which Conservative leaders believed could be manipulated to serve their partisan electoral advantage. Internal studies had suggested that free trade could be sold to the public as a demonstration of Tory "decisiveness and consistency" in formulating an "economic renewal program."[26] After an undistinguished first year in office marked by bank failures, rancid tuna, and petty scandals, the Tory leadership was certainly primed for a major policy initiative like free trade which could be used to try to demonstrate that their ship of state was not hopelessly adrift in a deep Ottawa fog.

The Free Trade Negotiations and Imperial Relations

Following our spelling out of the three factors which came together in 1985 to propel Canada-U.S. free trade onto the political stage, it should now be apparent that much of the public "debate" has progressed in a fundamentally historical fashion. Its "sides" are locked in arguments more appropriate to the 1950s or early 1960s, before the subsequent GATT-sponsored continental trade liberalization had gathered steam. We are neither gaining entry to paradise nor being pushed over Niagara Falls. Rather, in the face of pressing 1980s' threats to Canada's economic stability posed by intermittent recession, high unemployment, international trade challenges from Japan, Europe and the newly industrialized countries, and the rise of protectionist forces in the United States, the free trade talks are essentially an attempt to adjust the balance point in the continental relationship so that the already existing network of commercial associations can be safeguarded. In the light of our earlier discussion of the Canadian state system's role in focusing, mediating, protecting and developing the regional position of the Canadian socio-economic formation within the continental political economy, then, it is misleading to see the negotiations as either a threat to, or an advance for, Canadian sovereignty. Instead, they stand as an excellent illustration of how our autonomy is manifested in the management and reproduction of regional relations within empire as the continental capitalist accumulation process expands and transforms itself over time.

Canada's state and economic elites had hoped that they could use the free trade negotiations as a cattle prod to keep U.S. protectionist forces at a comfortable distance. One can only imagine their growing sense of horror as the talks turned into a lightning rod attracting the ire of those Americans with an interest in braking the import of Canadian products. In Canada, too, the issue of free trade, once politicized, transmitted a nasty jolting electric surge to its sponsors. The Tories, in particular, found the issue difficult to manage because it manifested itself along four inescapably central dimensions of national political conflict: labour and social distribution, federal-provincial, industrial policy, and partisan.[27] The effect was at once discontinuous and cumulative: as soon as a fire appeared to be dampened in one dimension, it would jump to begin anew in another. And, while the negotiations proceeded, the intermittent countervail victories won by American protectionists exacerbated the difficulties the Mulroney government faced in getting the public to view its management of Canada-U.S. trade issues in a positive light.

The setbacks the talks experienced in both national political arenas made it seem increasingly likely that they would either collapse or result in a mainly symbolic agreement which provided for non-binding statements and/or mechanisms to enshrine sentiments of free and fair trade between the two countries. The logic behind this conclusion stands greatly reinforced by reports from insiders which portray the negotiations as singularly weak on the specifics of a deal — "a minuet in which two partners dance with each other but do not touch."[28] The model for a treaty emphasizing principle over substance might be found in the U.S.-Israel free trade agreement which allows for the continued application of countervail and anti-dumping duties subject only to submission of disputes to a non-binding advisory commission.[29] U.S. Ambassador Thomas Niles has recently suggested that it "was somewhat unrealistic under present circumstances" to believe that "we won't have any more anti-dumping and countervailing duty cases" and that his government would likely only agree to establish a non-binding procedure for settling trade disputes.[30]

As soon as it became clear that the negotiations were unlikely by themselves to provide for the kind of stable trading environment sought by the business and political elites who had initiated them, our state system came under increasing pressure to bargain and administer incremental, sector by sector, accommodations directly with hostile U.S. producers. Major steel companies and the Steelworkers' Union, for example, began to press the federal government to set up a system of export permits to rein in maverick firms who failed to honour a program of voluntary export restraints.[31] In the softwood lumber sector, the British Columbia government was the first to blink. It suggested that its low stumpage fees, the basis of a countervail action by U.S. producers, could be "reviewed." This raised the ire of the lumber companies who were moving on their own to discuss the imposition of federal export quotas or an export tax. "A tariff is temporary but stumpage charges are forever," one company president reasoned.[32] Nevertheless, subsequent meetings of provincial, federal, company and union officials resulted in an Ottawa proposal that U.S. producers abandon their countervail action in return for promises by British Columbia, Alberta, Ontario, and Quebec to add about 10 per cent to the export price of Canadian lumber by collecting an additional $400 million annually in new forest management fees. Even though this initiative was to fail, it precisely corresponds to our functional model of Canadian state sovereignty which stresses its role in mediating the ever-fluid continental relationship. In her defence of Ottawa's "end run" on the free trade negotiations in the softwood case, Pat Carney, minister of state for international trade, places our thesis in stark relief.

> The Canadian position is aimed at saving thousands and thousands of jobs in our biggest industry. We are taking that position with the firm support of the provinces, the firm backing of the industry involved, and with the support of the labour union involved . . . . We have had this case before us for about five or six years, creating a lot of uncertainty, a lot of harassment, affecting investment decisions and worrying a lot of people in Canada. What we have done, with the support of the provinces, the industry, the labour union, and the U.S. administration, which is also trying to seek a pragmatic response to this problem, is to resolve (sic) the problem on a permanent basis and to protect this industry and these jobs from continual harassment.[33]

Dominion from Sea to Sea

U.S. chief trade negotiator Peter Murphy has warned that "very meaningful concessions" must be offered by Canada if it hopes to make any progress in shielding itself from countervailing import duties.[34] However, in the face of the previously described contemporary threats to our economic stability, if the Canadian state system is to maintain its capacity to represent effectively the regional position of the Canadian socio-economic formation within the continental political economy, its scope for manoeuvre in making "meaningful concessions" is severely constrained in four critical areas: the exchange rate, procurement policy, regional development programs, and cultural policy. A brief review of each of these areas will make clear their centrality in the present definition of Canada's regional position within North America. Any serious attempt to place them on the table would almost certainly destabilize the 1980s continental balance in ways unfavourable to Canada's political and economic elites.

Exchange Rate: In the era before tariff liberalization, we had a lever to induce and to hold foreign and domestic capital investment in Canadian manufacturing-access to our market. Now, as production is increasingly rationalized on a continental basis under the GATT, Canada has to compete with all of the other regions within the U.S. economy for our share of plant locations. This is not a competition for which we are particularly well prepared. Neither our market size nor our geographic location is especially advantageous. In addition, our peculiar import substitution industrial heritage has left us with few special skills, technologies, or innovative industrial sectors not available elsewhere. The post-1945 continentalist free trade faith has always been predicated on the assumption that manufacturing in Canada would be based on the exploitation of our somewhat lower wage levels.[35] In the 1980s, successive devaluations of the Canadian dollar have successfully been used as a device to maintain considerable manufacturing capacity in Canada by cheapening our labour relative to U.S. labour. The Canadian automotive sector in particular has experienced the benefits of the devalued Canadian dollar with average wages in 1985 of US$14.15 as compared to US$19.94 for American auto workers.36 Put simply, any significant rise in the exchange rate would leave in tatters the Canadian investments already made in continental rationalization.

Procurement: Plant location is also influenced by the formal and informal federal and provincial government markets for industrial products. Although Canada as a whole can be seen as a region within the U.S. economy, our sub-regional and provincial markets provide extremely important sources of demand upon which to base manufacturing and distribution facilities. In 1979, 44 per cent of the total output of Canadian goods was initially marketed within the province of origin, while 27 per cent was shipped to other provinces and 29 per cent was exported. Newfoundland was the only province in which the value of export sales (51 per cent) exceeded the value of Canadian sales.37 The federal and provincial states, working on their own and through municipalities, Crown corporations, hospitals, and boards of education maintain a vast arsenal of weapons to stimulate production (and distribute patronage) within their jurisdictions. As the 1985 Macdonald commission explained:

> A preferential purchasing policy may be implicit or explicit, a matter of practice or of law. The usual methods of preferential procurement involve selective or single tender instead of public tender; inadequate publicity or information on bidding, through the use of local source lists; short time limits for the submission of bids; performance requirements tailored to what local business can provide; residence requirements for vendors; and preferential margins for local suppliers.38

Multinational firms have, of course, adapted themselves to these practices through their creation of production facilities in Canada. One 1983 study of plant location decisions within the Canadian computer industry abounds with illustrations. For example, some firms cite specific government contracts or initiatives as key. "In the late 1960s," one company stated, "IT&C (the old federal Department of Industry, Trade and Commerce) advised us that if we wanted to be a government supplier, we had to locate production in Canada. Since that date we have set up a plant and a research centre." Other firms demonstrate a more global vision in coming to terms with the regional political realities of the Canadian market within continental production.

> . . . Canada has no specific advantage for manufacturing since the local base is not good enough. Over 90 per cent of the input for the production of a computer would have to be imported. Thirty-five per cent of the production would have to be for the export market . . . . However, we are committed to putting production here in order to protect our share of the Canadian market. You can look at this decision as being an insurance policy because it provides political leverage.39

Regional Development: In every list of "off the table" items presented by the Conservative government since the trade negotiations were announced, regional assistance programs have received prominent mention. Yet these include precisely those social and industrial items most often identified as "subsidies" by the Americans in countervail actions. How can we account for Ottawa's firm stand on this question? It is true that Article 36 of the Constitution Act of 1982 entrenches a commitment to further economic development by reducing regional disparities and to provide comparable levels of public services to all Canadians. It is also true that regional assistance programs cut across all of the dimensions of national political conflict that we previously identified as being central to the free trade debate — labour and social distribution, federal-provincial, industrial policy, and partisan. Accordingly, any attempt to deal directly with regional development issues would almost certainly unleash a firestorm of opposition which would consume all the Tories in its path.

However, neither of these factors can sufficiently account for Conservative intransigence in the face of persistent U.S. pressure. The inviolability of these programs can only be properly understood within the perspective of the role of our state system in the organization of a Canadian regional interest within the U.S. economy. Canada's pattern of economic expansion within successive empires has resulted in a patchwork quilt of unevenly developed local economies. Insofar as Canadian regional assistance programs manifest themselves in the payment of both the social and industrial costs of uneven development, they provide a necessary point of national focus and integration to bind together the provinces. They allow our political and economic elites to present Canada as a region within the continent and not simply as a northern series of balkanized economies tied to contiguous U.S. regions.

Culture: The "cultural industries" of broadcasting, publishing and entertainment have so far been conspicuously zealous in damping public enthusiasm for the free trade negotiations.[40] This seems in keeping with the special role these institutions must play in preserving what we suggested at an earlier point in our discussion to be a necessary reservoir of nationalism in Canadian civil society. Workers in this industry are naturally apprehensive that the already fragile base of the distinct Canadian nationality and identity on which their livelihoods depend will be further eroded by the heightened continental integration they fear is represented by free trade. For their part, some of this sector's most prominent owners and managers have placed the Tories on notice by warning that "the culture and communications industries are simply too different and too crucial to the survival of the Canadian identity to be included as part of an overall free trade agreement."[41] Cultural nationalism, for this latter group, is very often restrictively interpreted as the right to use the border as a voodoo zombie able to conjure for them lavish profits through the occult practice of their own unique brand of import substitution — importing U.S. content and substituting Canadian advertising for American.[42] Nevertheless, in demanding that the Canadian state protect their turf, they are merely illustrating the manner in which regional positions within continental production are defined and developed by our economic and political elites.

Notes

1. H.A. Innis, "Great Britain, the United States and Canada," in *Essays in Canadian Economic History*, (Toronto: University of Toronto Press, 1956.)

2. Leo Panitch, "The Role and Nature of the Canadian State," in *The Canadian State: Political Economy and Political Power*, L. Panitch, (ed.) (Toronto: University of Toronto Press, 1979) p. 18.

3. See, for example, D.B. Dewitt and J.J. Kirton, *Canada as a Principal Power: A Study in Foreign Policy and International Relations.* (Toronto: John Wiley, 1983); J. Eayrs, "Defining a new place for Canada in the hierarchy of world power," *International Perspectives*, November/December 1981; and, P.V. Lyon and B.W. Tomlin, *Canada as an International Actor.* (Toronto: Macmillan, 1979), Chapter 4.

4. Influential Tory presentations of this perspective have been provided by D.G. Creighton, *Canada's First Century, 1867-1967.* (Toronto: Macmillan, 1970) and G. Grant, *Lament for a Nation: The Defeat of Canadian Nationalism,* (Toronto: McClelland and Stewart, 1965). For a discussion and critique of the dependency position within the new Canadian political economy see my "Centre-Margin, Dependency, and the State in the New Canadian Political Economy," paper delivered to the Annual Meeting of the Canadian Political Science Association, June 1986.

5. H.A. Innis, *The Fur Trade in Canada*, revised edition. (Toronto: University of Toronto Press, 1970), p. 385.

6. G. Williams, *Not for Export: Toward a Political Economy of Canada's Arrested Industrialization*, Updated Edition. (Toronto: McClelland and Stewart, 1986).

7. G.P. deT. Glazebrook, *A History of Canadian External Relations.* (Toronto: Oxford University Press, 1950), p. 229. Reg Whitaker notes that in this period "the **nation** and the **state** were not coterminous concepts in Canadian discourse. The concept of cultural nationality and the concept of political or state sovereignty were distinct and analytically separate. Moreover, the idea of differing cultural nations coexisting under a wider political sovereignty—whether French and English within Confederation, or Canada within a wide empire, or the moral federation of the English-speaking peoples—was at the root of most thinking about the national question." See his "Images of the state," in *The Canadian State*, ed. L. Panitch, pp. 48-49.

8. Innis, "Great Britain, the United States and Canada," pp. 405-406.

9. Lyon and Tomlin, *Canada as an International Actor*, p. 71.

10. An excellent illustration of the significance of this point can be found in the response by Pat Carney, minister of state for international trade, to a recent question in the House of Commons from NDP Trade critic Steven Langdon. Noting that the U.S. government had refused to allow U.S. branch plants of Canadian companies to sit on their free trade talks advisory committees for "national security" reasons, Langdon wondered why the Canadian government had appointed at least 15 representatives of U.S. subsidiaries to sit on our trade advisory committees. Carney observed that "we have appointed representatives to our trade committees because we want to ensure the broadest possible consultation with all sectors of Canadian industries, Canadian provinces, and Canadians generally on the issues before the negotiators to ensure a free trade agreement which meets the concerns of all Canadians ... I and the Government

approve of the process of consultation on a national issue which affects all Canadians."

11. For relevant discussions of these policies see S. Clarkson, *Canada and the Reagan Challenge.* (Toronto: Lorimer, 1982); G.B. Doern and G. Toner, *The Politics of Energy: The Development and Implementation of the NEP.* (Toronto: Methuen, 1985); and, Williams, *Not For Export,* Chapter 8.

12. Lyon and Tomlin, *Canada as an International Actor,* p. 85.

13. As Leo Panitch points out, "it is not the state that primarily sustains American imperialism within Canadian society. The imperial relation is secured and maintained more fundamentally within civil society itself. . . ." See his "Dependency and Class in Canadian Political Economy," *Studies in Political Economy,* Autumn 1981, p. 26.

14. Canadian Institute of Public Opinion, *The Gallup Report,* July 4, 1985, and March 6, 1986.

15. *Ibid.,* June 19, 1976, and May 26, 1986. For a very general overview of post-1945 Canadian public attitudes on East-West security and nuclear weapons issues which shows "on such a fundamental dimension as support for Canada's Western alignment there has been little, if any, perceptible change," see D. Munton, "Public opinion and the media in Canada from Cold War to detente to new Cold War," *International Journal,* Winter 1983-84, p. 208.

16. *Ibid.,* July 8, 1985, and June 5, 1986. For an interesting discussion of how the "prevalent view of the highly critical Canadian public" on the U.S. pursuit of the Vietnam war was "somewhat exaggerated," see J.H. Sigler and D. Goresky, "Public Opinion on United States-Canadian Relations," *International Organization,* v. 28, #4, Autumn 1974, pp. 661-664.

17. M. Molot and G. Williams, "The Political Economy of Continentalism," in *Canadian Politics in the 1980s,* Second Edition, Whittington and Williams, (eds.) (Toronto: Methuen, 1984), pp. 92-93.

18. Highly suggestive hypotheses on such lobbying emerge from A. Rotstein, "Foreign policy and the Canadian business community," *International Journal,* v. 39, #1, Winter 1983-84, pp. 136-145. He argues that Canadian business, "passive and reticent in relation to its own survival," has failed to represent the "national interest" in Washington when compared to "business communities in other countries which tend to identify more closely with broad national policies." The Canadian state has had to step in "to fill the vacuum" in representing our national interest in the U.S. Thus, Canadian business "relies heavily on the state to carry responsibilities that advance its own interests while reserving the right to denigrate and undermine the state from the sidelines. It is a complex but uninviting prospect."

19. See, "Symbols, Economic Logic and Political Conflict in the Canada-U.S.A. Free-Trade Negotiations," *Queen's Quarterly*, v. 9, #4, Winter 1985, pp. 659-678 and Williams, *Not For Export*, Chapter 9.

20. Computed from Statistics Canada, *Summary of External Trade*, various years, and *Statistics Canada, Daily*, March 28, 1985, and March 25, 1986.

21. *Fortune*, March 4, 1985, p. 116.

22. Conrad Black. "The Menace Posed by a Yuppie-ridden Lumpenproletariat," in *Report on Business Magazine*, v. 3, #4, October 1986, p. 118.

23. For a review of some of the more important figures in the development of the continentalist and nationalist schools, see Williams, *Not For Export*, Chapter 7.

24. Canada, Special Joint Committee of the Senate and the House of Commons on Canada's International Relations, *Minutes of Proceedings and Evidence*, August 8, 1985, p. 17:62, and July 17, 1985, p. 4:34.

25. For an insightful discussion of the factions represented within the modern Conservative Party, see M.J. Brodie and J. Jenson, "The Party System," in *Canadian Politics in the 1980s*.

26. Prime Minister's Office, "Canada-U.S. New Bilateral Trade Initiative Communications Strategy," 1985, (draft document).

27. These dimensions are outlined in my "Symbols, Economic Logic and Political Conflict."

28. *Globe and Mail*, November 12, 1986, p. B6.

29. "Agreement on the Establishment of a Free Trade Area between the Government of the United States of America and the Government of Israel," *Journal of Palestine Studies*, Winter 1986, pp. 119-131. See especially Articles 17 and 19.

30. *Globe and Mail*, November 8, 1986, p. A5.

31. *Globe and Mail*, September 11, 1986, p. B2.

32. *Globe and Mail*, September 9, 1986, p. B4.

33. Canada, House of Commons, *Debates*, October 3, 1986, p. 29.

34. *Globe and Mail*, November 15, 1986, p. A5.

35. See, for example, H. Johnson, *The Canadian Quandary*, (Toronto: McGraw-Hill, 1963.)

36. *Globe and Mail*, December 11, 1985, p. B4.

37. Canada, *Report of the Royal Commission on the Economic Union and Development Prospects for Canada*, Volume 3, p. 104.

38. *Ibid.*, p. 118.

39. K.C. Dhawan and L. Kryzanowski, *High Technology Plant Location Decisions: U.S.-Based Multinationals in the Canadian Computer Industry.* (Montreal: Concordia University, Faculty of Commerce and Administration, November 1983) pp. 78, 87.

40. See, for example, Rober Fulford, "Continental Drift," *Saturday Night*, v. 101, #11, November 1986, pp. 7-11.

41. *Toronto Star*, September 17, 1986, pp. A1, A12. This group included John Bassett, chairman of Baton Broadcasting; Donald Campbell, chairman of Maclean-Hunter; Phillippe de Gaspe Beaubien, chairman of Telemedia; and, Pierre Juneau, president of the CBC.

42. For a discussion of the CTV network in this light, see *Globe and Mail*, November 14, 1986, pp. B1-B2.

Negotiating Freer Trade

The Process of Negotiating Canada-U.S. Free Trade: An Interim Assessment

Gilbert R. Winham

The Canada-U.S. free trade negotiation was formally proposed by Canada nearly two years ago. The negotiation was effectively joined by the United States in April 1986, when the Senate Finance Committee narrowly approved "fast-track" procedures that would allow the United States to negotiate. The conclusion of the negotiation is expected to be around December 1987, in order that it might end before the U.S. presidential campaign gets under way in 1988. The negotiation has now run out much of its projected time span, and therefore an assessment is in order. Any such assessment will have to take account of a continuing atmosphere of pessimism about the negotiation, in which even the prime minister has been occasionally reported to have serious doubts about Canada's ability to conclude a trade agreement with the United States.[1]

Any interim assessment of the negotiation should proceed from certain fundamental principles about the negotiation process. For a negotiation to succeed, the parties must have a complementarity of interests sufficient to promote an acceptable *quid pro quo*; they must put into place negotiating structures that are able to mobilize support from those areas of government or society that have the power to thwart an agreement; and they must be presented with the substance of the negotiation at a time when their domestic institutions are prepared to take up the issues involved. On all these dimensions, namely, interests, negotiating structures and timing, the prospects for the Canada-U.S. free trade negotiation are problematic.

Interests

Canada's initiative to negotiate free trade with the United States (or "reciprocity" as it has been known in Canada) is not a new phenomenon. Because of the difficulties of establishing a healthy national economy in Canada, successive Canadian governments and parties since 1854 have come around to the idea of creating a broad-ranging reciprocity agreement with the United States. One characteristic of these efforts is that they have usually been stimulated by hard times in Canada. The current initiative is no exception. Canada's economy has traditionally been oriented towards the international economy, and resource-based products have been the staple of its exports. Today resource-based industries are in trouble, and a number of voices (including the Macdonald commission and the minister of finance) have said that Canadians cannot expect these industries to be the economic backbone of the country of the future. The emphasis in the future will have to be put on the manufacturing sector, and increased productivity will have to be achieved if Canadians are to retain their economic standard of living.

The concern for improving Canada's manufacturing performance led easily to a concern for increased international markets, since Canada's economy alone does not provide the economies of scale needed for future growth. The natural result was an increased interest in the U.S. market, which takes nearly 80 per cent of Canada's exports. Canada's interests were expressed in what are by now three familiar arguments in favour of free trade, namely: to increase market access in the United States; to improve the security of access that already exists; and to increase the competitiveness of Canadian exports to the United States and elsewhere. If achieved, these interests (or goals, if one prefers) would help to redirect and revitalize the whole economy.

Often lost in the strategic discussions over trade policy are the more enduring interests of Canada in seeking a free trade agreement with the United States. Historically, governments in Canada have played a large role in the economy, due in part to the importance of natural resources and transportation in Canada. The role of government in the economy is now being sharply questioned in Canada, as well as in other developed countries. The arguments for less government were laid out clearly in the report of the Macdonald commission, and over and over it emphasized this theme as follows: "The stimulation of competition is key to economic growth and productivity improvement"; and "... we Canadians must significantly increase our reliance on market forces"; and "... we recognize (free trade) as proposing a fundamental change in the relationship of the state to the market."[2] What is genuinely intriguing is that, although the commission was ultimately proposing something similar to domestic deregulation, it chose a foreign policy, namely trade policy, as the main instrument by which to achieve its purpose. The commission stated: "The National Policy of 1879 (of high tariff protection) has played itself out," and "Free trade is the main instrument of this commission's approach to industrial policy." The fact that the Macdonald commission turned to an international solution (and indeed to the United States) to solve what is essentially a domestic problem is consistent with the traditional external focus of Canada's political economy.

The report of the Macdonald commission was embraced by the Mulroney government because it reflected the philosophy and broader concerns of the government.[3] Likewise, the main policy recommendation of the Macdonald commission (*vis-à-vis* Canada-U.S. free trade) has become the major economic policy of the Mulroney government, precisely because it is a means to accomplish a reduction of the scope of government and revitalization of the private sector in Canada. In short the Mulroney government is seeking to use a negotiation with the United States as a stimulus for domestic reform, which is increasingly a use to which international negotiation is being put these days. If one wanted an analogy from the current GATT multilateral trade negotiation to what Canada is doing bilaterally, it would be in the willingness of the European Community (but not necessarily the French government) to negotiate agricultural export subsidies in a new GATT round.

On the U.S. side, there is no equivalent grand design for the negotiation. The bilateral negotiation with Canada probably was a useful bargaining chip for the United States in its effort to get other governments (especially in the European Community) to agree to new multilateral trade negotiations, but now that the latter has officially started, this rationale is less important. There has been some suggestion that the United States might use the bilateral negotiation as a testing ground for new issues like services or intellectual property, but it is questionable whether the tight timetable for the bilateral negotiation will allow for that much innovation. What is left of the U.S. position is that of responding to another nation's proposal for a trade negotiation, and it has responded in a cautious manner of calculating costs against benefits. The United States is not in a position to appreciate Canada's need to use a trade negotiation to deregulate its economy, nor is it likely to give compensating benefits for this purpose. In terms of its more profound interests, what Canada wants from the bilateral negotiation, it could achieve unilaterally, and this fact will be as well known to the Americans as it should be to the Canadians. Thus, there is an imbalance in the negotiation at its more profound levels that does not augur well for the overall endeavour.

There is also an imbalance of interest in the specific issues that might be tabled in a bilateral negotiation. Usually, in assessing a negotiation, one calculates in which issues each nation might be the principal demandeur. It is hard to avoid the conclusion — using commonly accepted trade calculations — that the positions of the two nations are not even. On most issues the United States appears to have far more to receive that it has to give. For example, on tariffs, the average Canadian tariff on dutiable U.S. imports is about 9 per cent, while the U.S. equivalent on Canadian imports is about 1-2 per cent. Clearly, tariff-free trade would work out substantially in favour of the United States. On services and intellectual property, the United States is a major exporter, and if these issues were included in the negotiation, it is probable Canada would be in a position to give more concessions than it receives. On auto trade and the Auto Pact (which constitutes one third of Canada-U.S. trade), it is the United States that is expected to table demands. On trade-related investment issues, Canada is again on the defensive. The same is true for trade-related subsidy practices and as well many regulatory policies that affect trade, such as provincial liquor board practices and agricultural marketing boards. The one area where a self-balancing deal seems possible is on government procurement, for the practices are approximately equally wicked on both sides of the border, and while the United States has a market 10 times the size of Canada's, it also has 10 times the number of producers who could take advantage of liberalization on the Canadian side. The fact that a government procurement code was negotiated at the Tokyo Round between nations as unequal as Jamaica and the United States suggests a negotiation between Canada and the United States is quite possible.

Of all the issues that might be raised in the free trade negotiation, the only one on which Canada would unequivocally be the principal *demandeur*, is U.S. unfair trade remedies, or contingency protection as it is called in Canada. The Canadian side of this issue is that Canada has bought and paid for access to the United States market with its participation in previous GATT negotiations, but this access is unfairly threatened by a number of policies, such as countervailing and anti-dumping procedures, escape clause measures and unfair trading actions. These policies give U.S. industries which have lost out in the economic marketplace a chance to win back business from their Canadian competitors through a costly legal procedure that is conducted entirely within U.S. institutions. The fact that unfair trading remedies are usually initiated by U.S. industries only after Canadian trade has become well established creates the impression that it is a penalty for being successful. Not only is this an emotional issue, but it calls into question the fundamental wisdom of establishing closer trade ties with the United States. To get around contingency protection, one Canadian objective has been to negotiate "national treatment" for Canadian exports, whereby Canadian products would receive the same treatment in the United States as the products made there. A fallback objective has been to set up a bilateral intergovernmental institution that would adjudicate cases of unfair trading in a manner that gave Canadians more participation and influence over the process.

The U.S. response is that unfair trade remedies are directed against illegitimate foreign practices (usually the actions of foreign governments in promoting the interests of their producers), and that remedies are needed to ensure that competition through international trade with U.S. producers remains on an equal footing. The issue is particularly sensitive on the matter of government subsidies. The U.S. view is that Canadian governments subsidize their producers extensively, which is a view that would be hard to dispute after the Nielson report,[5] and that U.S. firms are entitled to countervailing duties to offset the effects of subsidies on traded goods. This view is firmly held in Congress, so firmly in fact that the legislation establishing the free trade agreement between the United States and Israel explicitly prohibited any devolution from existing U.S. fair trade legislation.[6] Behind this legal position, however, lies an even deeper concern. Americans operate a more litigious system than Canadians in order to promote the rights of the individual against the society, and this system finds its expression in the trade world in unfair trade legislation and in the hoary judicial practices of the International Trade Commission (ITC). The legislation and the judicial practices form a kind of safety valve, and without them it is questionable whether any support for trade liberalization would continue to exist in the United States. To the suggestion that the United States should extend "national treatment" for Canadian goods, the probable U.S. response would be that the Canadian practices which produce those goods are not "national." And to the suggestion that the United States should submit ITC practices to an international joint commission, the United States is likely to respond that the national subsidy practices of Canadian governments should first be submitted to a similar international forum.

To sum up, it is difficult to project an obvious solution to the Canada-U.S. free trade negotiation from the perspective of the interests of the two parties. A major interest on the Canadian side is to increase the competitiveness of the Canadian economy, but this goal is not easily achieved in a negotiation process where the *modus operandi* is the exchange of specific concessions. On most issues before the negotiation, as measured in traditional trade bargaining terms, Canada appears to have more to give than to get. In terms of Canada's specific interests as they have been enunciated in the past, which are to increase access to the U.S. market, to secure that access, and to increase the competitiveness of the Canadian economy, the following observations should be made: (1) Canada's access to the U.S. market is already very substantial in most sectors and, in any case, it is largely tariff free, (2) an increase in the competitive environment of Canadian business could be achieved by Canada unilaterally without any action by the United States, and (3) an increase in the security of Canadian access, particularly "national treatment" of Canadian goals, is probably beyond the scope of the negotiation because Americans care more about the principle of unfair trade remedies than they care about negotiating a free trade agreement with Canada. How a balanced and reciprocal package might be put together in this situation is hard to imagine. If an agreement is to be reached, it will have to be sold and accepted in Canada in terms of the broadest national interest, and not in terms of narrow calculation of specific concessions given and received.

Negotiating Structures

The Canada-U.S. free trade negotiation, like most modern trade negotiations, is a complicated affair which touches many bases in the respective national societies. To negotiate effectively, one must have a negotiating machine that can deal with the most powerful internal critics that are likely to be mobilized against the negotiation. In the United States, the most likely opposition to a Canada-U.S. deal appears to be in Congress. In Canada, a similar opposition will likely come from provincial governments. It is uncertain whether either side has worked out a means for dealing with its principal internal critics.

The U.S. negotiating team consists of a very small core group, with a much larger group of specialists that it can draw from the various agencies of the Washington bureaucracy. The structure is well coordinated through the use of regular inter-agency meetings, but the small size of the core group poses problems both of initiation and task loyalty. Initiative in bureaucratic endeavours is often a matter of having sufficient resources, and the small numbers attached to the free trade negotiation mean that the United States will be in a reactive mode rather than being able to initiate proposals that could advance the process. Task loyalty is a matter of which jobs bureaucrats are principally tasked to do, and in the United States it is clear there are not many bureaucratic reputations tied up with the Canada negotiation. What is worse, the U.S. structure—however good it is at pulling together talent from around Washington—is also a fine structure for promoting bureaucratic politicking, which can produce delays in an already tight time schedule. One example of bureaucratic politics may have already occurred in a report early in the negotiating that because of the insistence of the Treasury Department, services would be excluded from the bilateral negotiation.[7] This could be problematic in later negotiations, because Congress is expected to want a larger rather than a smaller deal, and one way of gathering support in Congress would be to include some of the new issues like services in an agreement.

At mid-point in the negotiation, it is too early to tell whether an effective relationship will be established between the negotiating team and Congress. Congress appears to be moving in the opposite direction from trade liberalization, which makes it difficult for the negotiators to even gain a hearing. Comparisons with the Tokyo Round are inevitable, and not particularly favourable for the negotiation with Canada. In the Tokyo Round an effective rapport was established between the Trade Representative's Office and Congress, without which it is doubtful Congress would have approved the accord. The Canada-U.S. negotiation has the capacity to raise even more complex legislative problems than did the Tokyo Round. Hence it would seem a similar rapport will have to be established if the negotiation is to succeed.

On the Canadian side, the main concern will be to maintain support of the provincial governments. For this negotiation, the business constituents have been organized into a series of sectoral advisory groups reminiscent of the sectoral advisory committees used by the United States in the Tokyo Round. This arrangement will probably facilitate the transmission of constituent opinion, but it is unlikely to be a major factor in the negotiation because it disproportionately represents a group that is already widely supportive of the negotiation.

It is inevitable that any major trade negotiation with the United States will involve the participation of the provinces, if for no other reason than that some issues — like government procurement — deal directly with the activities of provincial governments. It is also likely that the involvement of provincial governments in the negotiation will complicate the process and make it more rancorous, simply because they represent interests different from the federal government. However it is important that the inevitable differences be focused on meaningful issues of substance, and not on the less important issues of style and procedure. The conflict, as the theorists say, should be as productive as possible.

One problem is that the trade negotiation has been integrated into a model of federal-provincial relations drawn from past constitutional negotiations. This has created a tendency to negotiate the process of federal-provincial interaction in the absence of the substance of the negotiation. One example of this is the search for a ratification formula for a prospective Canada-U.S. trade agreement. In the context of a negotiated agreement, it is probable that the ratification debate is a red herring, because in the end it is the negotiating partner (that is, the United States) that decides whether its negotiating partner (that is, Canada) has sufficiently accepted a negotiated agreement to justify signing it itself. Of course, Canada will be in the same position with respect to a U.S. ratification.

For example, if the two nations were to negotiate a code that placed restrictions on subsidies in Canada and on countervailing duties in the United States, it is unlikely the United States would be expected to honour the agreement for exports of fish if Nova Scotia refused to abide by the agreement. Thus ratification is likely to be handled in the normal process of giving and taking compensating benefits and, if there is any lesson, it is that the governments in Canada should get on with the business of reaching or not reaching trade agreements, and not hang up on the symbolics of the ratification process. If any guarantees are needed, they would lie in the fact there is little likelihood the United States would find a trade deal with Canada attractive if it were known that provincial governments were opposed to the agreement and might therefore take actions to undermine it.[8]

A second aspect of "constitutional" thinking in the trade negotiation is found in the procedures established for bureaucratic cooperation between the federal and the provincial governments. Reportedly, there is substantial consultation between levels of government, particularly focusing around major scheduled meetings.[9] Furthermore, a senior position has been established in the Trade Negotiation Office (TNO) with responsibility for federal-provincial relations. The danger with this structure is that it tends to define conducting relations with provinces as a task for the TNO, with the subtle effect that it separates provincial bureaucrats from the remaining real work of the TNO.

What Canada might find attractive by analogy is the operation of the European Community (EC) in trade negotiations, for the EC has a structure that bears some similarity to the Canadian federal structure. In the EC, national trade bureaucrats are integrated into EC structures and work alongside commission staff (notably in the 113 committees) on the basis of their specialized skill or competence. In this manner bureaucratic differences often tend to be resolved and a more task-oriented cooperation is built up between the EC commission and member governments. A similar process in Canada might help to coordinate the federal and provincial governments at the working level, with favourable impact on bridging the inevitable differences that will arise at the political level.

In the last analysis, the free trade negotiation is very much over the nature of bureaucratic programs in Canada. While it is by no means certain that federal and provincial bureaucrats will easily agree on these matters, what is much more likely is that there will be last ditch opposition in some provincial bureaucracies if far-reaching agreements are negotiated without effective provincial participation. It is probably better for the internal disputes to flow freely throughout the negotiation process, than to try to resolve all federal and provincial disagreements through some heroic effort at the eleventh hour.

Timing

On the matter of timing, it is obvious that the free trade negotiation is not well placed on the political timetable of the United States. There is essentially only a window of about 15 months available to negotiate an agreement. Particularly in Congress, the focus has been on issues like tax reform rather than the international economy, and when attention turns to the latter, the U.S. trade deficit is the overwhelming concern. Legislators mainly want to know how other nations (including Canada) will help to solve the trade deficit problem. All of this has raised doubts in Canada about the will of the United States to negotiate. However, lest Canadians become too embittered about apparent American indifference, it might be wise to recall that some of the current difficulties lie with the slowness with which the Canadian government moved to announce its interest in a trade negotiation. Over two years ago Ottawa was being told there was a "window of opportunity" to negotiate bilateral trade with the United States, and that if it did not act quickly the chances of success would fade rapidly. This prediction now seems uncomfortably accurate.

The Canada-U.S. negotiation has had the misfortune to be conducted at a time when the United States has run a record trade deficit, which has increased the protectionist mood in Congress. This mood is profoundly discouraging to U.S. negotiators, because it has the effect of shutting off access to Congress. Even more problematic, it subtly reduces the scope of the negotiation. For example, sensitivities about a possible attack on unfair trade remedies have run so high in Congress that U.S. negotiators have been reluctant even to raise the subject, especially in the bureaucratically visible inter-agency process in Washington. This means the burden of initiative gets shifted to the Canadian side, which is frustrating since this is one area where Canadians might have expected some American efforts at resolving a long standing series of irritants.

On the Canadian side there is no real problem of timing, but the difficulties on the American side may take their toll on Canadian willingness to continue with the negotiation. From Ottawa's perspective, bilateral free trade is a politically risky strategy. If it begins to look as though it will not be acceptable to the United States, it is unlikely that political momentum could be sustained on the Canadian side. On issues where they can act unilaterally, political leaders can gain points with the public for acting in a resolute and decisive manner, even if they take policies that are not always popular. However, it is very difficult to be resolute and decisive about a negotiation if the other side is apparently disinterested. In this sense, the Canadian commitment to the negotiation may be fairly fragile and easily shaken by a perception of American indifference.

Conclusion

The conclusion of this paper is that the Canada-U.S. free trade negotiation is a deeply troubled affair. There is a serious risk, probably about 50 per cent or greater, that the negotiation will end in failure. Should this occur, Canada as a nation will probably lose economically, the Mulroney government will lose politically, and relations with the United States will probably be worse than if the endeavour had not been initiated. The obvious question is how to proceed from here, in order to salvage as much as possible.

First, Canada should continue to play the hand for a comprehensive trade agreement as long as political momentum is remotely sustainable. There is already an enormous political "sunk cost" in the negotiation; furthermore, it would be difficult for Canada to terminate the negotiation without blaming the United States, which would likely carry a foreign policy cost. At the technical level, considerable thought should be invested on how an agreement that would serve Canada's broader interests of reducing government involvement in the economy, could nevertheless be defined as a balanced deal when measured in traditional trade bargaining terms (which is how the public will assess it). This is a presentational problem which presumably the Americans might be willing to help solve. As one example, it has been argued in this paper that a government procurement agreement would be self balancing, but if enough importance were to be conferred on the procurement market in the United States (i.e., "ten times that of Canada's"), then some Canadian tariffs, which Canada might want to lower anyway for its own reasons, might be thrown into the balance.

The essence of the presentational problem is how to make a series of adjustment policies that Canada could have taken unilaterally (and probably should have taken unilaterally) nevertheless appear as a balanced deal when undertaken as part of a bilateral negotiation. In this instance, negotiation may not have been the best tool to accomplish the purpose to which it is being put. The reason negotiation was chosen is that because of the immobility created by overlapping federal and provincial jurisdictions, Canada lacks the political will to act unilaterally on many economic issues without the incentives or threats that can be posed by an external actor. Then, too, after 40 years of GATT negotiations, it is impossible to conceive of taking liberalizing actions without seeking a reciprocal benefit from other countries. It is only natural to look at U.S. protectionism, particularly contingency protectionism, as a price that Canada might demand for taking actions Canada would have wanted to take in any case for its own reasons.

Second, technical planning for a scaled down negotiation should be conducted. It is probably impossible to achieve a comprehensive trade agreement (other than a very general agreement) in the time remaining, especially since any such agreement would place great demands on developing new concepts and data in the new issues like services, intellectual property and high tech trade. What is more manageable is that the bilateral negotiation should seek to make some further progress on the sorts of issues that were negotiated in the Tokyo Round, which in itself would be a considerable achievement. An entirely appropriate bilateral agreement might include tariffs, a dispute settlement process, codes on subsidies and countervailing duties, and government procurement. Such an agreement could achieve Canadian objectives. Only time will tell whether it would be acceptable to the U.S. Congress.

Third, the bilateral negotiation should be used to stimulate thinking about trade policy. One problem is that the free trade negotiation has been promoted also as a policy in itself, whereas negotiation is only a tool of policy, and not a very certain one at that. For example, if the negotiation fails, it may be necessary for the Canadian government to consider what it should do about its very large and unsecured trade dependency on the United States.

Fourth, and most important, the negotiation should be used to stimulate federal-provincial cooperation on issues like government procurement and production subsidies, which are as problematic to the internal Canadian marketplace as they are to international trade. It was argued earlier that some of the Canadian interests in negotiating trade with the United States could have been achieved by Canadians acting unilaterally. If the negotiation should fail, the machinery of the TNO might be the place to start to campaign to reduce internal barriers to trade between Canadian provinces, and to achieve a needed reduction in the amount of government regulation of the economy.

Notes

1. Geoffrey York, "U.S. politics may doom free trade, PM says," *Globe and Mail*, September 17, 1986, p. A1.

2. See *Report of the Royal Commission on the Economic Union and Development Prospects for Canada*, Volume One, 58-63.

3. See, for example, Department of External Affairs, *Competitiveness and Security: Directions for Canada's International Relations*, Ottawa: Supply and Services, 1985 and the *Report of the Task Force on Program Review* (Nielson Report), Ottawa: Supply and Services, 1986, 3.

4. See Gilbert R. Winham, *Canada-U.S. Sectoral Trade Study: The Impact of Free Trade*; a background paper prepared for the Royal Commission on the Economic Union and Development Prospects for Canada, Halifax: Centre for Foreign Policy Studies, Dalhousie University, 1986, 15.

5. The Nielson Report characterized federal and provincial tax incentives, grants and subsidies to Canadian business as "giving with both hands," 6.

6. Specifically, Section 406 of the U.S. Trade and Tariff Act of 1984 (Public Law 98-573 of October 30, 1984) stated that: "Neither the taking effect of any trade agreement provision entered into with Israel under section 102(b) (1), nor any proclamation issued to implement any such provision, may affect in any manner, or to any extent, the applications to any Israeli articles of section 232 of the Trade Expansion Act of 1962, . . . title II and chapter 1 of title III of the Trade Act of 1974, or any other provision of law under which relief from injury caused by import competition or by unfair import trade practices may be sought."

7. See Christopher Waddell, "Financial sector not open to negotiation, U.S. says," *Globe and Mail*, June 19, 1986, p. A1.

8. Incidentally, this is one of the more important lessons of the recent lumber countervail case. The reason why the U.S. government insisted on an unseemly monitoring of Canadian compliance with the bilateral agreement is because it

distrusts provincial governments (probably with good reason) to comply with agreements reached between the United States and the Government of Canada.

9.   See Hyman Solomon, "Broad mandate now for trade talks," *Globe and Mail*, June 14, 1986.

The Evolving Role of the Provinces in International Trade Negotiations

David Barrows and Mark Boudreau

Introduction

Historically, the provinces have exercised relatively little direct influence on the formulation or negotiation of national trade policy. However, a key issue arising in the context of the present Canada-United States trade talks and prompting much public discussion is the role of the provinces. As with Canada-U.S. trade itself, the issue is related to a larger theme in Canada—how to best develop and coordinate policy in our federal system.

During the postwar era, Canada and the United States achieved substantial success in reducing tariffs and simplifying customs procedures through multilateral negotiations conducted under the authority of the General Agreement on Tariffs and Trade (GATT). But, as tariff and related border measures have declined in economic importance, other forms of trade restriction have gained greater economic importance. Current Canada-U.S. trade relations mainly concern conflicts over so-called "non-tariff barriers" or NTBs.[1] Those faintly pejorative expressions are often applied to almost all tax and regulatory laws, no matter what the level of government, and may include all public expenditures which either stimulate exports or restrict imports.

Therefore, the present Canada-U.S. trade negotiations will go beyond the traditional issue of tariff reductions and will involve matters within provincial jurisdiction. The potential impacts from changes in tariffs and federal regulations and subsidies mean that the provinces must also be concerned about the trade policy thrusts of the federal government, whether or not the trade policy instruments involved are technically within the jurisdiction of the provinces. There should be little confusion over

115

the need for provincial participation in the negotiating process. The only question, therefore, is what form this participation will take.

The purpose of this paper is twofold. First, it will concentrate on what concrete proposals to ensure "full provincial participation" have been articulated and agreed upon, with a special emphasis on Ontario's position. Second, it will flag a number of outstanding issues, (i.e., national treatment, dispute settlement, etc.) that will have to be addressed before any free trade agreement negotiated between Canada and the United States can be implemented. As a starting point, this paper will review the role of the provinces in past multilateral trade negotiations.

Provincial Role in GATT

The question of provincial participation in trade negotiations is a relatively new issue in Canada. Since the birth of the General Agreement on Tariffs and Trade (GATT) in 1947, international negotiations have primarily been about the rates of duty applied to goods between countries.[2] As a result, international trade agreements entered into by Canada have not required provincial acquiescence or action.[3] Prior to the Tokyo Round, the GATT consultative process within Canada was primarily between the federal government and the private sector which had specific interests in the level of foreign tariffs affecting their access to export markets and the degree of import penetration of Canadian markets.

The Tokyo Round of GATT negotiations lasted from 1973 to 1979. During this period, the federal government moved rather significantly to involve provincial governments directly in multilateral negotiations. Two factors—one external, the other internal—prompted this move. The external factor was that what had been perceived as "purely domestic policies were for the first time caught up in GATT negotiations."[4] These included government procurement practices and domestic subsidies.[5] The internal factor was that, during the mid-1970s, the provinces adopted a more active role in representing regional interest and were intent on "putting their stamp on" national policies.[6]

During the early stages of the Tokyo Round, federal-provincial trade discussions were informal. As the negotiations proceeded the process was formalized by the establishment of the Office of Canadian Coordination for Trade Negotiations (CCTN) in 1977. The CCTN was an effort to streamline internal Canadian decision making in order to allow Canada to negotiate effectively externally. The CCTN's primary purpose was to receive input from all interested parties—provinces and the private sector—and to provide regular briefings to provincial representatives on the status of proposed agreements dealing with tariff and non-tariff issues.[7]

Although provincial participation added a step to the complexity of the GATT negotiating process for the Canadian government, its success has been documented in a number of statements. Melvin Clark has attributed Canada's success at the Tokyo Round to the mutual federal-provincial consensus on both policy and negotiation objectives.[8] Larry Grossman, the former Ontario minister of industry and tourism, after the conclusion of the Tokyo Round trade negotiation, noted "the very success of the consultative process to date has persuaded us that the federal government now must maintain the machinery of consultation ... as a permanent feature of trade policy development in Canada."[9] However, the CCTN was dissolved following the Tokyo Round. Denis Stairs and Gilbert Winham have suggested that this action "seemed at variance with its major trading partners, who tended to continue those negotiations and decision-making structures that had worked well during the Tokyo Round."[10]

At the time, Ontario supported the continuation of the CCTN. Had the CCTN continued, it may have prevented some of the federal-provincial misunderstandings surrounding Canada-U.S. trade irritants (i.e., liquor boards, trucking, etc.).

The Rise of Non-Tariff Barriers

Most existing tariff barriers are currently being reduced as a result of previous GATT negotiations (see Table 1). Prior to the Tokyo Round, for example, the average Canadian tariff on dutiable industrial products was approximately 15 per cent. By 1987, when the Tokyo Round tariff cuts have been completely phased in, this will fall to 8-9 per cent. However, non-tariff barriers (NTBs) have proliferated and various estimates now indicate that as much as 40 per cent of world trade is "managed" by NTBs.[11]

Table 1
Current Tariffs
Selected Industrial Countries
(per cent)

	Canada	U.S.	Japan	European Community
Finished manufactures	8.1	6.9	6.4	7.0
Semi-finished manufactures	6.6	6.1	6.3	6.2
Raw materials	2.6	1.8	1.4	1.6

Source: Jock Finlayson, "Getting Ready for GATT," in *International Perspectives*, p. 11.

During the Tokyo Round, important progress was made on NTBs. Canada became a party to six NTB codes of conduct designed to lessen the restrictive trade effects of a number of non-tariff measures.[12] However, the codes were not agreed to by all GATT members (most of the developing countries, which make up a majority of GATT members, have not adhered to the codes).

The forthcoming round of GATT will also be preoccupied to a significant extent with NTBs to trade. Some of the NTBs, which have begun to be identified as important in international trade negotiations, touch either directly or indirectly on areas of provincial concern. For example, long-standing policies to promote industrial, regional, or socio-cultural development have come under increasing scrutiny.

Government procurement preferences, both federal and provincial, have been identified as trade restrictive non-tariff barriers. In addition, the idea of negotiating some agreement on trade in services and also on trade-related investment measures will have an impact on many aspects of provincial regulation affecting business practices and the right of establishment.[13]

Provinces are clearly involved in a wide range of behaviour that influences trade flows, and may pursue policies which run counter to obligations undertaken by Ottawa either in the GATT or in other negotiating contexts. However, the provinces have very rarely sought directly to challenge federal responsibilities for foreign policy or international trade. Given the growing salience of NTBs in trade policy, the role and the impact of provinces in formulating national trade policy can only increase over time. Ontario's special trade adviser, Robert Latimer, has commented that "the historical distinction between trade and industrial policy has been losing its validity, if it ever had any." With this, the role and responsibility of the provinces, both directly and indirectly, are coming into play in international trade negotiations.[14]

Canada-U.S. Freer Trade Initiative

The Quebec Declaration established political momentum, at the highest level, to "chart all possible ways to reduce and eliminate existing barriers to trade" between Canada and the United States.[15] The joint declaration on trade, issued by Prime Minister Mulroney and President Reagan on March 18, 1985, the last day of the so-called Shamrock Summit, charged their trade ministers to identify specific negotiating proposals on, among other things: "National treatment ... with respect to government procurement and funding programs ... standardization, reduction or simplification of regulatory requirements ... reducing restrictions ... on petroleum imports and exports, and [by] maintaining and extending open access to each other's energy markets ... reduction in tariff barriers ... elimination or reduction of tariff and non-tariff barriers to trade in high-technology goods and related services ... cooperation to protect intellectual property rights (copyright)."[16] The broad agenda prompted Mitchell Sharp, commissioner of the Northern Pipeline Agency and a former federal cabinet minister to write, "This is not an ordinary, conventional trade negotiation of limited application. It raises issues of the most fundamental nature and has already provoked a national debate, not only about the economic effects of a free trade agreement in various parts of the country, but about the effects upon our political independence and our cultural institutions."[17]

Canada's Constitution gives the federal government exclusive authority to negotiate international agreements but not the power to implement agreements in areas of exclusive provincial jurisdiction.[18] Given the sweeping nature of the Canada-U.S.

trade negotiations, the role of the provinces in reaching a workable agreement is crucial. The federal government has recognized that the provinces not only have to be consulted, but their agreement must also be attained. This raises the question of whether a federal-provincial agreement is necessary before or after an international agreement is signed by the federal government. This, in turn, raises the question as to whether the provinces, in effect, have a veto over the negotiations.

At the opening of the First Ministers' Conference in Halifax in November 1985, Prime Minister Mulroney assured the premiers that the provinces would be full participants in bilateral trade negotiations with the United States. As a starting point, the federal government urged the provinces to take the subject of "full participation" one step at a time and the initial process was to initiate the preparatory work for the Canada-U.S. negotiation.

On the last day of the conference, Prime Minister Mulroney announced the following agreement:

> The Ministers agreed to the principle of full participation in the forthcoming trade negotiations between Canada and the United States, and in the GATT.

The Canada-U.S. negotiations were then in their preparatory phase. During that phase, the ministers agreed in the following 90 days to give effect to the principle of full provincial participation through, among other things:

- establishing a common basis of facts and analysis

- each province and the federal government and setting out their objectives for the negotiations

- establishing a grand view of the obstacles to the achievement of these objectives that may exist in the United States

The ministers agreed further that this preparatory work should include the determination of how best to give effect to the principle of full participation in subsequent phases of the negotiations, and that the work might be accomplished, among other ways, through holding further meetings at the level of ministers and first ministers if necessary."[19]

Ontario's Proposal for Full Participation

Because of the provinces' constitutional responsibilities and their interests in the development of the Canadian economy, the Ontario government tabled a proposal calling for the establishment of an organizational structure that would ensure a cooperative federal-provincial process to deal with international negotiations (see Chart 1).[20]

Despite different interpretations of the meaning of "full participation," it has continued to be Ontario's position that one central component should be the decision-making involvement of first ministers, that is, the premiers and the prime minister, at key points in the negotiation process. However, Ontario did not seek to be actively involved in the actual Canada-U.S. negotiations themselves. In a speech delivered to interprovincial trade ministers, Ontario's minister of industry, trade and technology, the Honourable Hugh P. O'Neil, stated, "This does not mean that there would be eleven negotiators at the table. Rather, Ontario sees the ten provinces in daily or even hourly contact with what is going on in the negotiating room. As particular logjams occurred, it would be the ultimate responsibility of first ministers to develop a consensus."[21]

Chart 1
Federal-Provincial Cooperative Process
Organizational Structure

Federal-provincial
ministerial committee

| Special committee on adjustment | Subcommittee of senior officials | Delegation: federal-provincial officials |

Sub-group on
Ratification and Implementation

- The ministerial committee could meet at the level of first ministers as appropriate, and would otherwise meet at the level of ministers designated by the federal and provincial governments as having primary responsibility.

- The subcommittee of senior officials would be chaired by Ambassador Reisman during the preparatory stage and by a federal coordinator during the negotiating period.

- The special committee on adjustment would include **representatives from the private sector.**

- Provincial officials could be seconded to the negotiating team as full members of the delegation. Federal and provincial officials would have the same ability to report to their own ministers.

Source: Proposal tabled by the Honourable David Peterson, "Ensuring Cooperation between Ontario and the Provinces for Trade," p. 2.

Ontario has also proposed that the federal-provincial cooperative process should cover the four phases of the negotiating process: Canadian preparatory work, Canada-U.S. exploratory discussions, Canada-U.S. negotiations and, finally, ratification and implementation (see Chart 2).

Chart 2
Federal-Provincial Cooperative Process

Phase I:
Preparatory work

Issues   Concerns   Objectives

*Recommendations
to governments
for approval

Phase II:
Canada-U.S.
Exploratory discussions

Submit proposals   Evaluate U.S.
to U.S.   proposals

*Approve negotiating
mandate by
governments

Phase III
Canada-U.S.
negotiations

Develop draft agreement
based on mandate

*Prepare recommendations
to governments
for approval

Phase IV
Ratify and implement

* Major decision points

Source: Proposal tabled by the Honourable David Peterson "Ensuring Cooperation between Ontario and the Provinces for Trade," p. 2.

During the preparatory phase, it was envisioned that the subcommittee of senior federal-provincial officials[22] would participate in the identification of Canadian issues, concerns and objectives in the Canada-U.S. trade negotiations. Their work would be supported by the special committee on adjustment.

Emanating from this process would be the development of recommendations which would guide the Canadian delegation in exploratory discussions with its U.S. counterpart. These recommendations would then be referred to the federal-provincial ministerial committee, and ultimately to a meeting of first ministers for approval. Concurrently, the sub-group on ratification and implementation would begin their work with an examination of the legal and constitutional issues involved in implementing a Canada-U.S. trade agreement.

As the negotiation proceeded into the exploratory phase, any items submitted by the U.S. delegation would be referred to both the subcommittee and the ministerial committee for examination and comment.

From these discussions   negotiating mandate would be agreed to by first ministers and the prime minister.

Once the negotiations were under way, the ministerial committee and/or the subcommittee would meet as required to receive reports on the negotiations and to deal with issues arising in the course of negotiations.

At the same time, the special committee of adjustment would refine the impact analysis and adjustment issues in light of elements being pursued in the negotiating process.

Once negotiations were completed the committee of ministers would meet to examine the results and recommendations of the delegation with technical input from the subcommittee. The ministerial committee would then make their recommendations to a meeting of first ministers for their response to any negotiated agreement. Finally, the legal and constitutional issues involved in implementing the agreement would be further examined by the sub-group on ratification and implementation. Their views and recommendations would then be presented to a meeting of first ministers.

Current Federal-Provincial Mechanisms

At the beginning of January 1985, a continuing committee on trade negotiations was established under the chairmanship of Ambassador Reisman, with representatives from each province, the Yukon and the Northwest Territories. The committee is designed to serve two central purposes: one, to ensure communication between federal and provincial officials on the evaluation of the work program, including meetings with the United States and in the GATT; and two, to provide for exchange of information and views on the major economic, sectoral and policy issues whereby federal and provincial officials would have the opportunity to present information, review analytical work and discuss Canadian objectives in both Canada/U.S. and multilateral contexts.[23]

At the ministerial level, discussions were held as to how best to give expression to the principle of full provincial participation during the negotiating phase as agreed to at the first ministers' conference in Halifax in November 1985. On June 2, 1986, the first ministers agreed to a process for provincial involvement in the negotiations. The agreement called for the prime minister and the premiers to meet every three months and review the progress of Canada-U.S. negotiations.[24] It was also agreed that "designated ministers" would meet from time to time when required (the first meeting was held September 10, 1986).

Ottawa, however, has retained exclusive jurisdiction at the negotiating table. As a result, the premiers are cautiously optimistic about the agreement reached June 2. Ontario Premier David Peterson has commented "I'm satisfied that through these first ministers' meetings every three months ... we're going to monitor everything that's going on .... If the process isn't working well, we'll adjust it."[25]

Outstanding Issues

Norman Spector, who has recently been appointed secretary to the federal cabinet on federal-provincial relations, has commented, "Because of the provinces' role in implementing whatever bilateral agreement emerged, their full participation in forging a coalition (with the federal government) is critical. Not only must the provinces be 'sold' on any agreement resulting from negotiations with the Americans, the federal government will need the provinces to help 'sell' such an agreement to the Canadian people."[26]

The United States has a "fast-track" approval process, which ensures that Congress either approves or disapproves of agreements negotiated by the Administration.[27]

However, Canada lacks such a "fast-track" procedure. A number of proposals have been put forward, including amending the Constitution, to ensure political compliance with an international trade agreement.[28]

Premier Peterson has also indicated that a number of additional issues need to be addressed. Any trade agreement between Canada and the United States would likely require formal mechanisms to resolve disputes. The role of the provinces, and indeed the private sector, must be considered in formulating dispute settlement mechanisms. The implementation of binding dispute settlement mechanisms could have an impact on provincial autonomy.

Adjustment issues also need to be addressed. Ontario has emphasized that both levels of government need to start considering not only appropriate adjustment assistance programs, but also development of a negotiating strategy which fully integrates adjustment issues, taking into account the structural differences between the Canadian and U.S. economies.[29]

Positive adjustment will require both transitional arrangements, such as differential phasing of tariff reductions and duty remission schemes, as well as direct assistance. Provisions for adjustment must be an integral part of any agreement and receive the general support of the provinces. Responsibility for the cost of such measures must also be determined.

The prime minister, in his address to the nation regarding a comprehensive bilateral trade agreement with the United States, stated, "We will seek what, in the jargon of trade negotiators, is called 'national treatment'[30] whereby goods from Manitoba will be treated exactly the same as goods from Minnesota."[31] At its broadest theoretical level, national treatment on bilateral trade in goods, services and investment would mean that all commerce between the two countries would be conducted on the same basis as commerce within either country. To name but two of many issues, provincial autonomy over the licensing of trades and professions and control over American participation in such sectors as transportation and securities markets would be severely constrained.

Clearly, the concept of a broad national treatment standard in a comprehensive Canadian-American bilateral agreement raises a number of profound and difficult questions. While the concept would seem to present opportunities for certain Canadian sectors through increased access to American procurement markets and protection from American trade laws, it may also present considerable damage to others. Given the precedent-setting nature of these negotiations, careful sector-by-sector study and extensive federal-provincial discussions are clearly warranted.

Finally, producing goods and services for international trade has not obviously been the sole thrust of Canada's economic development. Trade **within** this country is significantly more important. Flows of goods and services are from the east to the west as well as from the west to the east, crossing provinces and regions. Provincial governments have frequently sought to diversify their economies by establishing restraints to the movement of goods, services, capital and labour from other provinces. Many of these constraints are a legitimate exercise of powers provided in the Constitution.[32] Examples of these restraints can be found in provincial residence requirements, content rules for government procurement, and in provincial production rules for selected industries. The intention of these programs and policies is to ensure a range of industry within each province. But the frequent consequence has been the development of small producers who are restricted to a limited market. Many economists worry that these producers, while they may be efficient within their market, lack the resources to compete internationally.

Significant restructuring must occur within Canada to create efficient international trading firms. At the same time the provinces should begin to eliminate their restrictions on goods and services from other provinces. The issue has such potentially serious consequences that the Ontario select committee on trade has commented "Canadian participation in discussions to reduce international trade barriers should be premised on initiatives to reduce provincial barriers."[33]

Conclusion

With the rise of non-tariff barriers, trade negotiations have become complex and involve commitments which increasingly enter into areas of provincial jurisdiction. The provinces, in response, have demanded an expanded role in formulating federal trade policy that affects their interests. This role will continue to increase as recent bilateral trade disputes between Canada and the United States have focused on a wide range of industrial and agricultural products which severely affect almost all provinces.[34] "The stage has been reached," states Michael Hart, "at which provincial involvement in issues affected by the international trading system must be dealt with as a matter of course."[35] In future, new mechanisms will have to be developed in order to ensure close federal-provincial cooperation, which will become an increasingly important dimension in the formulation and implementation of trade agreements negotiated by the federal government in both the bilateral and multilateral arenas.[36]

Notes

1. Unlike tariffs, NTBs rarely take the form of an explicit tax on imports. NTBs include quantitative restrictions such as quotas, administrative and bureaucratic procedures, such as burdensome customs regulations or national standards, contingency protection measures, such as countervailing and anti-dumping duties, and voluntary export restraints (VERs).

2. Seven sets of "rounds" of negotiations have been held since the birth of GATT, the most recent being the so-called Tokyo Round in the 1970s.

3. The major exception was a commitment made by the Canadian government at the end of the Tokyo Round to use its best endeavours to ensure the implementation of understandings reached with the province regarding the operations of provincial liquor boards.

4. A.J. Sarna, "The Evolving International Trading Environment," *Behind the Headlines*, Vol. 41, 6, 1984.

5. As negotiations proceeded on issues such as public procurement, it became clear that GATT members were prepared to enter into agreements of only limited scope and coverage, in part because other countries also had to deal with the issue of subnational jurisdiction.

6. C.D. Howe Institute, "Closing a Trade Deal: The Provinces' Role," *Commentary*, No. 11, August 1986, p. 3.

7. *Ibid.*, p. 3.

8. See comments made by Melvin Clark at the Research Symposium on Regional Considerations and Canadian Trade Policy in John Whalley and Roderick Hill,

ed., *Canada-United State Free Trade* (Toronto: University of Toronto Press, 1985), p. 307.

9. *Globe and Mail*, 12 July 1979, "Ottawa openness over GATT pays off," column by Ronald Anderson, p. B2.

10. For example, in the United States a system of sector advisory committees that met with considerable success during the negotiations was retained. See Denis Stairs and Gilbert R. Winham in *Selected Problems in Formulating Foreign Economic Policy* (Toronto: University of Toronto Press, 1985) p. 4.

11. Sylvia Ostry, "The World Economy in 1983: Marking Time," *Foreign Affairs* 62(3) (America and the World 1983) 1984, p. 548.

12. The five new agreements on non-tariff measures reached during the Tokyo Round are: an agreement on interpretation and application of Articles VI, XVI, XXIII of the General Agreement on Tariffs and Trade (the Subsidies Code); an agreement on technical barriers to trade; an agreement on government procurement; an agreement on import licensing procedures; an agreement on customs valuation procedures. In addition, the Anti-dumping Code negotiated during the Kennedy Round was revised in the Tokyo Round negotiations.

13. Effective delivery of a service to a foreign customer often requires an establishment in the foreign market. Therefore, some may argue that freer trade in services requires negotiation of such a right — in accounting, in legal, in health and engineering services among others.

14. See testimony of Robert Latimer to the Ontario Select Committee on Economic Affairs, *Ontario Trade Review*, August 5, 1986, p. E-13.

15. Declaration by the Prime Minister of Canada and the President of the United States Regarding Trade in Goods and Services, March 18, 1985, p. 1.

16. *Ibid.*, p. 13.

17. Mitchell Sharp, "A Different Kind of Negotiation" in *Policy Options* 7, 3, April/1986, pp. 6-7.

18. If the federal government negotiates a treaty dealing with a provincial matter, then only the provinces can give domestic legal effect to the treaty. See *Attorney General for Canada v. Attorney General for Ontario* (1937) A.C. 326 usually referred to as the Labour Conventions case.

19. First Ministers' Conference on the Economy, Halifax, November 28-29, 1985.

20. Proposal tabled by the Honourable David Peterson, premier of Ontario, "Ensuring Co-operation Between Ottawa and the Provinces for Trade: A Proposal," First Ministers' Conference on the Economy, Halifax, Nova Scotia, November 28-29, 1985, p. 2.

21. Speech delivered by Honourable Hugh P. O'Neil, Ontario Minister of Industry, Trade and Technology to Trade Ministers' Meeting, Toronto, February 3, 1986, p. 2.

22. Hereafter referred to as the "subcommittee."

23. During the period January 1985 to August 1985, a series of CCTN meetings were held to begin the preparatory work for the Canada/U.S. and multilateral negotiations under GATT.

24. The first of these meetings was held on September 6, 1986.

25. *Globe and Mail*, "P.M., Premiers plan regular reviews of free trade talks," June 3, 1986, p. A1, A10.

26. Norman Spector, speech delivered to the University of Ottawa/Public Affairs International Conference on Canada and International Trade: The Canada-United States Trade Negotiations, Ottawa, May 10, 1986, p. 16.

27. Under the *Trade Act* of 1974, Ch. 5, s.151, Congress has 60 days to react to any agreement signed by the president and amendments are not permitted.

28. A number of options are discussed in C.D. Howe Institute, "Closing a Trade Deal: The Provinces' Role," *Commentary*, No. 11, August 1986.

29. By 1980, Canadian output per hour was about 25 per cent lower than that of the United States. See D.J. Daly and D.C. MacCharles, *Canadian Manufactured Exports: Constraints and Opportunities* (Montreal: The Institute for Research on Public Policy, 1986), p. 15.

30. National treatment means that once goods have entered into the territory of a contracting state, the host country will treat imported goods no less favourably than goods of domestic origin in terms of taxes, law, regulations and other requirements.

31. Notes from an address to the Nation on the Trade Initiative, by Prime Minister Brian Mulroney, Ottawa, June 16, 1986.

32. Although the provinces are constitutionally prohibited by section 121 of the *Constitution Act of 1867* from levying tariffs on interprovincial trade in goods, they are not similarly constrained for imposing regulations on capital labour and services.

33. Select Committee on Economic Affairs, Ontario Trade Review, Interim Report, October, 1985, p. 11.

34. Products recently affected include wood products, steel, wheat, hogs and fish.

35. Michael M. Hart, *Canadian Economic Development and the International Trading System* (Toronto, University of Toronto Press, 1985), p. 76.

36. Any new mechanisms should also strengthen government-industry consultations, perhaps along the lines of the American industry sector advisory committees.

*Social Science, Social Scientists
and the Free Trade Debate*

Canada-U.S. Bilateral Free Trade:
A Perspective from Britain and Europe

Mel Watkins

My title — actually, my sub-title — may strike you as pretentious but it is meant only to recognize that, now being resident in London, England, I am somewhat out of touch with the day-to-day intricacies of the free trade debate in Canada and have no alternative in writing for an informed Canadian audience but to try to exploit my unaccustomed position as an outsider.[1]

Actually, news of the Canada-U.S. negotiations on free trade does occasionally make the British press, as when the United States put a countervailing duty on Canadian lumber and Canada replied with a punitive duty on American corn. The reason for this interest outside North America in a possible free trade agreement within North America is obviously not because it matters terribly to the world what Canada does. It is rather that everyone these days is at the mercy of the United States and what it does as it attempts to solve problems of its own making — a trade deficit that results from a budget deficit that results from an insane escalation in spending on arms — by alleging that other countries are engaged in unfair trade practices which they must either cease or suffer American protectionism.

Outside interest in the Canada-U.S. bilateral talks was greater before the new GATT round of multilateral talks was agreed to, though there is presumably still some potential for a bilateral deal with a compliant Canada to set precedents — for example, by covering services as well as goods, or by incorporating investment codes which extend "national treatment" to foreign firms and give them full "rights of establishment" — that the United States could try to generalize globally. Of course, with GATT negotiations

131

under way again, one of the reasons given initially by the Canadian government for proceeding bilaterally — that the multilateral road was blocked — is no longer valid.

What the United States is most concerned about are the protectionist implications of the Democratic victories in the mid-term American elections. What a world we live in, where a defeat for Reagan is a cause for concern among decent people! It does expose the inherent dilemma for Canada: a deal is presumably more than ever needed to protect against American protectionism, but is less likely to happen precisely because of that American protectionism.

The position of the American establishment on the bilateral talks with Canada — if the business section of the *International Herald Tribune* is properly reflective in its rare stories thereon — is that their failure would be bad for the world because it could doom efforts at multilateral liberalization of trade and investment. The tendency as often encountered in Britain, and in Europe generally, is to worry that the **success** of the talks could signal a North American protectionism against the rest of the world that would augur ill.

I recently spent a pleasant day in the library of the London School of Economics (LSE) reading up on the debate about British entry into the European Community (EC). Some economists, as befits their purism, were opposed precisely on the grounds that regional blocs were discriminatory and a violation of multilateralism and worldwide free trade. The opponents even included the late Harry Johnson, the eminent, wholly orthodox, Canadian-born economist who held a chair at LSE (as well as, fittingly, at the University of Chicago). This may surprise those of us who remember him best for his sermons to Canadians about the virtues of free trade. It should put us on our guard when proponents of a Canada-U.S. deal sell it as if it were free trade proper.[2] Certainly, the potential political consequences for Canada would appear to be vastly different.

In entering into these free trade talks, the chief object of the exercise for Canada was to get exemption from U.S. protectionism, to be inside rather than outside any U.S. tariff wall, to go back to the era of the 1950s and 1960s when Canada was regularly exempted from U.S. balance-of-payments provisions against the world. American protectionism, by incorporating Canada, becomes North American protectionism and would be so seen, and properly, by the world. Nor can we in fact rule out a scenario where the United States goes protectionist and does exempt Canada, because we are not seen as foreigners like the others.[3]

I have no idea whether the present bilateral talks will succeed or fail — and you don't either just because you're in Canada; only Washington knows for sure and it has other things on its mind. But ask me the main thing I have learned about a Canada-U.S. free trade agreement from being abroad and my answer is the clear realization that its consummation would tell the world that Canada, already perceived as at least "half-American," had gone whole hog.[4] It would risk ending whatever credibility we still have as an independent country with our own foreign policy. We cannot ask the Americans to exempt us from their policies and not treat Canada like a foreign country and expect foreigners to continue to see us as a separate and distinct people worthy of respect.[5]

On those many days when there is nary a whisper in the media about Canada-U.S. free trade, I have had to find ways to occupy myself. I have taken to reading widely and to reflecting grandly on the idea of free trade — the theory and the practice — since I am, after all, in the country where it all began.

Anyone who has taken introductory economics, and even many who have not, have heard of the law of comparative advantage. It was invented in the early nineteenth century by the great classical economist, David Ricardo. He offered, by way of proof of the mutual benefits said to inhere in free trade, England exporting cloth and Portugal wine. This example is still sometimes to be found in textbooks, but does it not ring false? For you and I know with the unerring benefit of hindsight that England prospered much and grew mighty while Portugal remained poor and was rendered marginal.[6]

The issue here is whether the benefits from trade are necessarily mutual. Put differently, must development within a free trade area be even, or can it be uneven? There is considerable evidence that there are inherent tendencies under capitalism or the market, towards uneven development or regional disparities, internationally and intranationally. Since free trade gives greater sway to the market, does it not risk worsening rather than lessening disparities? Canada has been a free trade area since 1867 but regional disparities, at least from the perspective of Atlantic Canada, have worsened over the century plus — which is surely a long enough time for them to have diminished if that was inherent in the process. One thing on which all commentators appear to agree is that, within Europe, regional disparities have widened since the creation of the EC. We should therefore take with a large grain of salt the sanguine views of the Macdonald commission that bilateral free trade will necessarily increase the standard of living of Canadians, reduce hinterland alienation, promote national unity and generally create the official federal version of heaven on earth.

Before Ricardo came the yet more famous Adam Smith, the founding father of liberal economics who gave us his powerful free trade bias in contradistinction to the protectionist and interventionist proclivities of the then prevalent mercantilism. He did so by linking free trade internationally and *laissez-faire* intranationally, or domestically. Now we know that that linkage has become the hallmark of neo-conservatism, which serves to remind us of the ideological baggage — today's advocacy of deregulation, privatization and limited government except for the military — that inhered in the idea of free trade from the outset.

We need look no further than the Macdonald report for candid confirmation of the connection. The commissioners tell us: "Our proposals to increase our openness to the international economy and, specifically, to enter into a free-trade arrangement with the United States reflect our general preference for market forces over state intervention as the appropriate means through which to generate incentives in the economy, from which growth will follow." The sentiment was spelled out to the press by the usually reticent Paul Reichmann (of the family with the massive interests in both Canada and the United States): "Not only should the government go ahead with plans to liberalize trade between the two countries, it should also follow Reagan's lead and cut regulations and taxes."[7]

The left, it turns out, has good and venerable cause to be — as the Canadian left is today — profoundly suspicious of free trade, particularly when it involves closer ties with the greatest citadel of neo-conservatism. We should not be surprised that the ideological dimension has come to constitute the most significant divide between the proponents and opponents of bilateral free trade, with the remarkable polarization between business and labour which has suddenly given Canadian politics an explicit class character.

Within economic analysis itself, Smith is famous for the dictum that the division of labour is limited by the extent of the market — by which he meant that productivity-enhancing behaviour by firms was induced by access to larger markets where economies of scale could be exploited. Two centuries later, this proposition is central to proponents of free trade arrangements, whether for Britain with respect to the EC or Canada with respect to the United States; we are endlessly told that only Canada and Australia of the industrialized countries do not have guaranteed access to a market of 100 million or more. Yet to live in Britain is to be painfully aware that access to the European market worked no magic for the British economy (on which, more in a moment). As for the free trade area called Canada, there are persistent differences in productivity within industries and among regions that are quite inconsistent with Smithian optimism. Though no great fan of markets, I confess I am myself surprised at how slight their magic is.

There is also the question of whether the market being referred to in the phrase "the extent of the market" cannot be domestic rather than foreign. Of course, it can be the external market giving us the export-led model of growth. But cannot it also be the domestic when that has come to be excessively served by imports to the detriment of home production? If we answer yes to that question, we stand the free trade presumption on its head. For the case can then be made for the import-substitution model of growth; in Canada, that means tariffs historically and domestic-content legislation (like the Auto Pact) today. It means using the **domestic market** to negotiate production and jobs under the aegis of foreign or domestic capital.[8] The Canadian model has been import-substitution for manufacturers combined with export-led growth from staples and it has served us reasonably well by global standards. Given the extraordinary extent to which the Canadian market for manufactures is serviced by imports, it might be thought to have continuing potential.

In spite of Smith and Ricardo, Britain did not adopt free trade until the mid-nineteenth century, when it abandoned the imperial preference system of the Navigation Acts and the Corn Laws. (Within Britain, the loss of agricultural protectionism devastated agriculture and drove people off the land; some fled to the colonies to farm there — including, I calculate, many of my great-grandparents, who then had the misfortune to settle on the unyielding land of the Parry Sound area). A century and a quarter later, the Macdonald commission tells us how Britain prospered **after** it saw the light, and cites that as demonstrating the virtues of free trade for contemporary Canada. Such nonsense! Britain moved to the practice of free trade only after it was politically and economically dominant. It did not do it to liven up its industrialists and thereby to render itself strong; rather, being already the workshop of the world, it did it the better to impose its manufactures on the weak. This is what historians mean when they write of the imperialism of free trade; though some haughtily approve of the process, others insist persuasively on its odious nature.

If there is a moral here for a weakly-industrialized and satellitic Canada, it is the exact opposite of what the Macdonald commission alleges. And, of course, in the latter part of the nineteenth century, Canada did not follow Great Britain down the free trade path but rather, emulating the United States and Germany, built high tariff walls and, like them, prospered in spite of, even because of, that. The world, evidently, never has been so tightly determined as the free traders would have us believe. Cases abound of free trade without economic success and economic success without free trade. Even when we do find the two together, there is the further point made throughout the debate about Britain and the EC by the distinguished economist Lord Kaldor, namely, that market behaviour—investing and innovating by the capitalists in the face of fresh opportunities—may be a symptom of growth already ongoing rather than its cause.

When I left Canada, free trade was nevertheless being presented as **the** way to create economic growth in Canada. I suspect this argument is still being used, though ironically Canada now has a rate of economic growth which is one of the highest, if not the highest, in the developed world of the OECD countries; we risk being sold an unreliable solution to a non-existent problem (which is not to say that the level of unemployment in Canada is anything other than intolerable—but the effect of free trade would be almost certainly to worsen it immediately and perhaps in the long run as well).

What I can report is a striking similarity in the rhetoric being used in Canada—about getting the economy moving again, giving it a competitive jolt, liberating the animal spirits of business, taking a cold shower and so on—and what was used in Britain over the years about entry into the EC. I am told that Harry Johnson himself made the point that cold showers have been known to cause pneumonia. A British government white paper of 1970 made claims about economic benefits that bear a remarkable resemblance to those now being made in official Government of Canada papers.

The fact of the matter is that these claims came to naught: Britain's industrial decline continued unabated after 1973; the best that can be said is that the **rate** of decline seems to have slowed. The income of the average Briton relative to the whole European Community fell from 85 per cent in 1972 to 78 per cent in 1979. There is a continuing productivity gap between Britain and much of the EC. British trade has been significantly reoriented to Europe but there has been a worsening of the trade balance with the rest of the EC in manufactured goods. Specialization there has been, but it has been towards industries which are declining on a European basis; nor has it been towards the service industries in which Britain has a significant comparative advantage.[9] This dreary record has resulted in spite of the fortuitous exploitation of North Sea oil at high OPEC prices (until recently) and in spite of the added fillip from the free marketeer's perspective of a neo-conservative Thatcher government promoting *laissez-faire* at home and diligently refusing to adopt a positive industrial policy.

The proposition—that free trade and access to larger markets is a necessary and sufficient condition for economic prosperity—has been well and truly tested in Britain in virtually laboratory-like conditions and it has been found to be woefully wanting. True, some of the proponents now say that it was not really a fair test because British entry just happened to coincide with the onset of a global economic crisis which complicated everybody's life. Of course, if they could foretell the future so well with respect to free trade, we are entitled to ask how they could have missed out on the big story. There is, in any event, slight solace in this for Canada, since the world is still mired in that economic crisis.

If orthodox economic theory be our guide, the impressive growth of the Canadian economy in the past century is inexplicable. The National Policy must have been a vast mistake from which must have flowed the most horrendous consequences. Canada must have paid a very high price for rejecting free trade with the U.S. in 1911 when it was offered, and again in 1947 when it was there for the taking but for the voices that caused Mackenzie King to pull back at the last moment. In the latter case, the senior officials who had negotiated a deal warned of impending doom if Canada failed to go along but, in fact, Canada kept right on growing and prospering. In the current debate, we find so eminent an economist as Richard Lipsey (writing with Murray Smith) stooping to scare tactics by conjuring up a scenario in which Canada, if it does not go the free trade route, could become another Argentina.[10]

The only sensible conclusion to draw from all this is that economists (among whom, for this purpose, I cheerfully include myself) know little or nothing with any certainty about what causes economic growth. On reflection that may not surprise; we could guess that growth is based on "inputs" like the quality of labour, of management, and (yes) of the state — plus the luck of the draw in natural resource endowments — all of which defy easy explanation. That probably means that the best that can be said about any one factor even when it seems to be quite important, like free trade or protection, is that it may sometimes help, sometimes hurt but will never by itself, in the nature of things, wholly or even substantially, determine the rate of economic growth. I will willingly rest my case on matters economic there, if my neo-classical colleagues, whose *obiter dicta* on economic growth figure so largely in the case for bilateral free trade, will likewise be appropriately agnostic and cautious.

If my memory serves me right, there is a further allegation made by the proponents of free trade in Canada, this time about its political effects. It is that increasing economic integration does not lead to equivalent political integration and loss of national sovereignty. The proof of that pudding, we are told, is the European experience. Against expectations — and, in this case, often hopes — political integration has been much more limited than economic integration; some has happened — tangible progress has been made toward a common foreign policy — but not massively so. Ergo, it will not happen all that much in North America either — particularly since all that is being talked about is a free trade area rather than a full customs union or common market — and the claims to the contrary of the Canadian critics can be ignored.

It so happens that this issue is examined in two studies done by political scientists for the Macdonald commission. I urge you to read them: Kim Richard Nossal and Charles Pentland in No. 29 of the commission's innumerable volumes; you did, after all, pay for them with your taxes and someone should read them, there being no evidence that the commission did in its headlong rush into advocating free trade.

What their findings boil down to is that the European Community analogy is inappropriate. First, there were 6, then 9, next 10, now 12; there were never 2. There is no superpower, nor even a dominant single power. Numbers matter — a point that economists should understand since it is central to economic theorizing about the behaviour of firms; this has, however, not stopped them (again, Lipsey is a leading culprit) from endlessly evoking the European example. The distribution of power matters. A two-country North America is what political scientists call a "disparate dyad," that being an asymmetrical monstrosity that is, from the perspective of the lesser part, as awful as it sounds. Common sense is confirmed; the best bet is that there would be politically constraining effects for Canada from a free trade arrangement with the United States, that is, that Canadian autonomy would, in fact, be significantly eroded.

There is a further insight available to anyone who has travelled both in North America and in Europe. Europe is a common market and North America is not yet even a free trade area, but Canada and the United States are already more integrated economically (meaning Canada into the United States) than is Europe. The relevant question then becomes: What if politically integrative effects among linked countries — like the so-called harmonization of policies that makes them similar notwithstanding borders — comes from economic integration *per se* and not from its specific forms? Then the fact that Canada is only contemplating a free trade area with the United States does not mean — as Canadian proponents take such great pains to insist — that there is nothing to worry about. Indeed, the Americans see free trade as a way to twist our tiny arms and make us bring our policies into line with theirs. That precisely means harmonization of policy — that very harmonization that has been at work, albeit slowly but nevertheless surely, eroding sovereignty and distinctiveness within the EC. And might it turn out that there was a moral for Canada in the evolution in the EC toward a common foreign policy? In that event, the fuller alignment of an already sycophantic Canadian foreign policy with America's would have devastating consequences for any pretence of Canadian independence.[11]

When I was in Canada, I was opposed to free trade with the U.S. Such views are sometimes thought to be merely parochial. So let it be duly recorded that, after a year of life as a cultured cosmopolitan, I've seen nothing to make me change my mind.

Free trade is hardly a new idea. The economic theory that justifies it between nations is two centuries old, yet it remains deeply flawed. Its virtues have long been preached and otherwise promoted by the powerful — which should be sufficient to make those of us at the periphery suspicious. It has always been difficult to distinguish economic analysis from pro-market ideology.

The United States and Canada, without the present benefit of a comprehensive free trade agreement, still manage to engage in an extraordinary exchange of goods that is unprecedented in volume by any other two countries in the world, and constitutes an impressive 6-7 per cent of world trade. Without proper access to the American market, we nevertheless manage to send about four fifths of our huge volume of exports to that market. The result has been to make Canada highly vulnerable and dependent on the United States. We are told that a bilateral free trade agreement is necessary to deal with that vulnerability; the problem is that it risks increasing the dependency.

It may be that a Canada-U.S. free trade agreement is an idea whose time has come; that certainly is what its proponents hope and its opponents fear. Should it come to pass, however, it will not prove that good ideas ultimately triumph. It may rather show that the 1980s, being a miserable decade, recycled every bad idea and stuck us indefinitely with one of the worst.

It may be that no agreement results — because the United States has a too-crowded imperial agenda, or because the United States becomes too protectionist to countenance even a deal with Canada, or because Mr. Mulroney remains unable to get his act together, or because opponents within Canada (the nationalist popular alliance led by the trade union movement) stop it. In that event, Canada must certainly continue, as it long has, to exercise eternal vigilance, on a day-by-day, sector-by-sector basis, to get the best access we can to the American market. But we should also take some steps toward a more self-reliant economy[12] — albeit cautiously, because that is the Canadian way and because it is anyhow the only way the Americans would let us.

Notes

1. This paper is based on notes used to address a colloquium at Carleton University in November 1986 and on a paper prepared for a lecture at Canada House in London in December; a shorter version has appeared in *This Magazine*.

2. Martin Wolf, of the Trade Policy Research Centre in London, in which Johnson played a leading role, has questioned a Canada-U.S. arrangement on these grounds. He is worried that the Americans are abandoning multilateralism and playing into the hands of European protectionists, though he does see great economic benefits for Canada from better access to the large American market. See his "Free Trade Agreement between the United States and Canada: A European Perspective" (Mimeo, April 1986).

3. I happened to see the December 12, 1986 issue of *Maclean's* which quotes Democrat Lloyd Bentsen, the new chairman of the U.S. Senate Finance Committee, to the effect that he did not intend "to witness the dismemberment of U.S. industry." It then continues: "At the same time, Bentsen voiced support for free trade negotiations with Canada and urged the administration of President Ronald Reagan to speed up the talks."

4. The term "half American" is used repeatedly by James (now Jan) Morris in the *Pax Britannica* trilogy.

5. The economist Albert Breton was a member of the Macdonald commission which endorsed Canada-U.S. free trade. He has, nevertheless, been quoted in the press as saying that, while he believed that such an arrangement would benefit Canada

economically, he feared that "to abandon a multilateral trade policy we've had since 1945, in favour of bilateral trade with a hegemonic power with global interests" would make it appear to Third World countries that Canada had become part of the United States "from at least a symbolic point of view." *Toronto Star,* February 27, 1986.

6. In the longest run, England, having risen, then falls; instead of Portugal coming to resemble England, England comes to resemble Portugal. The question of whether England's fate is in some part the ultimate unfolding of an excessive specialization consequent on free trade is too large a question to be dealt with in this paper.

7. See *Report of the Royal Commission on the Economic Union and Development Prospects for Canada* (Ottawa 1985), Volume I, p. 66; for the Reichmann quote, see *Toronto Star,* December 18, 1985. Likewise, Richard Lipsey and Murray Smith write with respect to Canada-U.S. bilateral free trade: "Most advocates of this option believe that investment and output decisions taken by the private sector, operating through relatively free markets, are a better guarantee of economic success than are similar decisions taken by the public sector, operating through Crown corporations or through directives to privately owned firms. They see Canadian-U.S. trade liberalization, therefore, as part of a larger package of economic policies designed to increase the importance of the free market in determining investment and output decisions"; they list as other parts of the package "a strong competition policy," "selective privatization," and an industrial policy limited to "climate" with actual decisions left "strictly to the market." See Richard Lipsey and Murray Smith, *Taking the Initiative: Canada's Trade Options in a Turbulent World* (Toronto, C.D. Howe Institute, 1985), pp. 69-70.

8. Details are spelled out in Abraham Rotstein, *Rebuilding from Within: Remedies for Canada's Ailing Economy* (Toronto, James Lorimer & Co. in association with the Canadian Institute for Economic Policy, 1984).

9. These data are drawn in particular from Robert Grant, "The Impact of EEC Membership upon UK Industrial Performance," in Roy Jenkins, ed., *Britain and the EEC* (London, Macmillan, 1983).

10. Lipsey and Smith, "Taking the Initiative," p. 25.

11. In this discussion of the politics of free trade, I have chosen to pass over the difficult question of whether the very existence of the EC is a good or bad thing for the world. On the one hand, the EC holds out the prospect of a third force that could mitigate the present insane and dangerous polarization of the world between the superpowers. On the other hand, the economic integration embodied in the EC militates against any one country pursuing the kind of interventionist policies, either Keynesian or structural, that the left favours.

12. See the publications of GATT-Fly for both a general discussion of the meaning of self-reliance and detailed proposals on how to achieve it for Canada.

Elegant But Not Helpful to Navigation: Social Sciences Research and the Free Trade Debate

Gilles Paquet *

"Beware of the man who works hard to learn something, learns it, and finds himself no wiser than before," Bokonon tells us. "He is full of murderous resentment of people who are ignorant without having come by their ignorance the hard way."

— Kurt Vonnegut

Introduction

From time to time, major issues of public interest provide an opportunity for social scientists to unpack their gear and show what new insights their "outillage mental" can generate and what new solutions their analyses suggest for tackling urgent and complex social issues. Such moments are always greeted with enthusiasm by practising social scientists as an occasion to prove their social usefulness; however, it is fair to say that most of those challenges have turned out in retrospect to be somewhat catastrophic for the reputation of the social sciences when such "insights" and "solutions" have been assessed with a bit of hindsight.

Such failures are not so much ascribable to the incompetence of the practitioners as to the fact that social sciences in Canada and elsewhere have promised more than they

* This paper is part of a program of research on the practice of social sciences in Canada. I am grateful to Allan Maslove and Stan Winer for offering me an opportunity to explore the implications of this work in the context of the free trade debate. The assistance of A. Burgess, G. Kippin and H. Nicoll is gratefully acknowledged.

could possibly deliver: they have been living beyond their means. This is nowhere seen more starkly than when social scientists leave the ivory tower to go to the forum.

Section 2 suggests that one of the major sources of this failure of the social sciences may be traced back to the positivist revolution which led social scientists to ape the postures of their colleagues in the physical sciences in the hope of achieving respectability by following the recipes physical scientists were using.

Section 3 reviews critically the social sciences input into the free trade debate and shows how limited its usefulness has been. Section 4 speculates on the likely contours of refurbished social sciences and on what such an "outillage mental" might be able to contribute to the free trade debate. In conclusion, some hopes for refurbished social sciences are shown to be less unrealistic than might first appear.

Social Sciences Research: A General Diagnosis[1]

There has been much dissatisfaction with the drift of the social sciences into positivism but also considerable praise for this development. Consequently, the social science community has been split into two factions: one group betting on the form of **explanation** propounded by positivism, the other defending **a mix of explanation and understanding** as the only warranted strategy for a sound social scientist.[2] A majority of practitioners has chosen positivism while a minority is on the other side.

Syntax versus Semantics

Much of the success of positivism in the social sciences is ascribable to the success of the physical sciences in explaining much of what is observed in nature through mechanical cause-effect connections. The machine model of reality was deemed to have worked well in the physical sciences, and it has slowly come to be regarded, since the nineteenth century, as more or less the only acceptable one in the social sciences also.

But to explain, in the sense of the physical sciences, one must presume the phenomenon to be explained to be both identical and repetitive: one can only explain identical phenomena and predict their repetition.[3] But social phenomena are rarely, if ever, truly repetitive or identical. Consequently, social phenomena must be reified, i.e., be made artificially identical and repetitive in order for explanations to take hold.

As a consequence of this process of reification (perpetrated on social phenomena to make them amenable to explanation) the social sciences have drifted further and further from the original questions that led to the emergence of inquiry into social phenomena.[4] They have come to focus more exclusively on method and methodological procedures instead of focusing on content and meaning: the social world has been reduced to a set of **facts** and knowledge made exclusively synonymous to the output of certain methodological procedures. Epistemology has been reduced to simple methodology and methodology itself to certain procedures that had been successful in the physical sciences.[5] A hypertrophy of syntax in the social sciences has ensured, much to the detriment of semantics: the social sphere has been reified, physicalism and analytical methods have become hegemonic, a polytechnician attitude prevails, and unrealistic ambitions have flourished within the social sciences community.[6]

Parsimony/Normalization/Regulation

The drift toward positivism has permeated the whole social science enterprise over the last 40 years. Originally, positivism had been nothing but one of many research strategies or approaches: but it has slowly become a set of norms imposed on the practice of social science and then the basis for a control apparatus to ensure the hegemony of those norms. There has been **progressive sociologization** of positivism.

Positivism is a parsimonious way to look at social reality. It constructs a collapsed, flattened and shrivelled version of the social world, a reduction to a single order, a single true version of the world — an order that positivism is supposedly best equipped to investigate.[7]

This parsimonious attitude would have been of little consequence, were it not that the social sciences of the nineteenth century had the tendency to respond to accusations of practical irrelevance or theoretical failures in a bizarre way. They were not so much led to take a less parsimonious view of reality but rather to neutralize such criticisms by efforts to normalize and regulate the practice of the social sciences. This is the purpose behind the production of **rules of method** codifying **the only way** to acquire meaningful knowledge.[8]

But every time a **rule** defining a norm — what is normal and what is not in the practice of any activity — is defined there must be reference to a regulatory power with the capacity to separate the normal from the abnormal. There is a need for a regulator. The dynamic of construction of regulatory instruments has been spelled out succinctly by Homa Katouzian.[9] He ascribes the emergence of the rigid paradigms in good currency in the practice of the social sciences to the growth of professionalism: the growth of a population of full-time mental workers operating in discipline-bound fields. There, narrow disciplinarian leaders rule through their control on the instruments of publication and dissemination of ideas but also on the mechanisms of research funding. In such a world, being normal translates into a higher probability of being hired and promoted, i.e., into a probability of survival in academe.

This enforced balkanization of the social sciences into fragmented disciplines has had important consequences for their usefulness. There has been a tendency toward a high degree of hyper-specialization, toward the concentration of the effort of full-time mental workers on the solution of real or imaginary problems defined by the leadership of the disciplinary professions, and toward a proliferation of publications for the sake of publications, i.e., much printed material with comparatively little addition to knowledge.[10]

In practice, this perversion has resulted in the social sciences' developing a predilection for small questions, a certain quantophrenic bent, an unmistakable theoretical twist, and a tendency to follow "in the footsteps of Monsieur Pangloss and Dr. Bowdler."[11] The smoke screen of jargon has grown exponentially, and the analytical/ tautological developments have mushroomed to the point where Nobel laureate Wassily Leontief has gone on record deploring the drift away from relevance and meaningfulness of much of the work in current journals in economics. The methods used to maintain intellectual discipline in the most important departments of economics, says Leontief, "occasionally remind one of those employed by the Marines to maintain discipline on Parris Island."[12]

The Need for Interpretation

Those trends in the current practice of the social sciences are well known even though they are not always appropriately acknowledged. Some continue to argue that positivism is **the only way** to make the social sciences truly scientific; however, a view that is becoming more widely held is that only through a more judicious mix of interpretation and explanation can we hope to extract the social sciences from their present crisis of confidence. Recently, Daniel Bell has argued, in a special issue of the *Partisan Review*,[13] that a "turn to interpretation, in the broadest cultural sense, signifies the turn of the social sciences — or of those practitioners of this art — from the models of the natural sciences and their modes of inquiry, to the humanities."

Interpretation is an ancient method of inquiry. It was the traditional method in vogue among scholars until the physical sciences developed and imposed their mode on the production of knowledge in all areas. What makes **interpretation** a necessary ingredient in the social sciences has to do with the nature of the human sciences. The difference between mechanical or animal societies and human societies mainly rests with the fact that human action is based on plans, i.e., on mental constructs elaborated before the action is effectively carried out. It is not really possible to reduce all human activities to such plans (which are often not carried through) or to the perceptions or significance such plans might have for the main actors, but it is not possible either to exorcise those dimensions from any meaningful effort to understand such actions.

This qualitative difference between the human sciences and the physical sciences commands a different methodological strategy. It focuses mainly on institutions as instruments of coordination of activities for human agents, as rules of the game, as social armistices likely to reveal the meaning of such actions. Institutions are the fabric of World 3 in Karl Popper's parlance: a sort of efficient reconciliation of the pressures emanating both from World 1 (the world of material realities) and from World 2 (the world of plans, values and "*faits de conscience*").[14] World 3 is a complex "text" that the human sciences must interpret in order to understand. This sort of interpretation would not be unlike a close interpretation of a collective agreement in order to reveal the texture of conflicts that it has refereed.

The Free Trade Debate

The free trade debate of the last year or two between Canada and the United States is a multilogue between different groups on both sides of the Canada-U.S. border about the optimal amount of impediments that should be tolerated to the trade flows between the two countries. As such, this multilogue should be analyzed like a multifaceted conversation. The instruments to be used to analyze such a multilogue must obviously draw on the body of theories and techniques in vogue in the study of rhetoric. For what is involved in this debate are attempts to persuade and, in assessing those attempts, rhetorical norms are in order. Indeed, much of science is rhetoric: "what distinguishes good from bad in learned discourse . . . is not the adoption of a particular methodology, but the earnest and intelligent attempt to contribute to a conversation."[15]

In such a context, the central question has to do with the standards of persuasiveness: whether or not the conversation about free trade is working well, whether the arguments put forward are persuasive. Our general point will be that the conversation about free trade is **not** working well, and that social scientists as persuaders have failed miserably in that debate.

Anatomy of the Free Trade Debate

One of the basic difficulties that might explain the poor performance of social scientists as persuaders in this debate may have to do with the confusion between three interrelated questions all subsumed generally under the same rubric: **free trade as an idea, free trade as a bout of negotiations,** and **free trade as construction of a new socio-economic space.** These are quite different issues, though they are obviously interconnected, but they have been debated interchangingly without the necessary care to specify which issue was addressed.

Free Trade as an idea does not refer to the design of a free trade arrangement. It pertains to the inception of the idea of a free trade arrangement as a source of opportunities for business enterprise. As such it is a potent economic force, even though it may never be realized. New opportunities are entertained and the prospective and plausible futures are significantly altered by the socio-psychological setting created by the beginning of a "conversation" about free trade.[16]

Since one may speculate on many different ways in which this idea might be implemented, everything is plausible, for the idea of free trade embodies what Leland Jenks would call "the dream of developing communities, regions, the continent." Corresponding to any number of different social partitionings of the community one may identify clusters of groups grappling with the idea, speculating on whether the costs and benefits are of comparable magnitude or not for them. This is the paradise of **simulators,** i.e., those who have a simulacrum of the socio-economy on which they are willing to play, for a fee, any imaginative scenario one might fantasize or build on this free trade idea. The simulacrum may be a simple supply-and-demand scheme, or an "issue-machine," or an elaborate econometric caricature of the socio-economy, but the process is largely of the same nature: a mechanical analog of the socio-economy is used to forecast different allocational, growth and distributional impacts.[17]

Whether these simulations are anchored in a "realistic" model or not is not the issue. Since any mechanical analog is a reification of the socio-economy — even if behavioural reactions and policy triggers are built in — such a construct is unlikely to generate very persuasive results. Indeed, the wide variability of "results" developed through those simulations has provided their consumers with very little in the form of robust persuasion. The basic reason is that too much of the reality of the socio-economy as instituted process is expurgated from even the most sophisticated simulations. An additional reason is that any built-in forecast of the reactions of the different groups to changes in the rules of the game in matters such as our trade relations with the United States is unlikely to be gauged reasonably well by a simple rule. Consequently, most of the results generated by such exercises are not very robust when they are not simply tautological.

One cannot expect much better results from social science analyses of the **free trade debate as bout of negotiations**. Modelling such an interactive process is so difficult that most analysts have been satisfied with simple general descriptions. It is because of the fact that, in order to perform a meaningful simulation of a game of negotiations, much is required: (1) an explicit set of actors together with their domains of possible actions, (2) a clear specification of mutual interdependencies, (3) a correct gauging of the extent of consciousness of each group of actors and (4) of the degree to which any group is aware that all groups are aware of each other's perceptions and of their interdependencies.[18]

Leif Johansen makes the point that standard social sciences do not admit of most of those points: in general, analyses considerably emasculate (2) and (3), do not deal with (1) very well and fail altogether to take into account (4). There have been some efforts to develop **the game paradigm**. But it is fair to say that the results to date are not very promising when one is confronted with complex non-zero-sum games with more than a few actors. The great merit of that paradigm has been to throw some light on the essential **social** character of the social sciences and on some of the requirements that status imposes on the practice of social sciences.[19]

The contribution of the social sciences **to the process of bargaining** in the free trade debate has been rather limited up to now. While a certain amount of intelligence is necessary in such a process, it was noted by the Macdonald commission report that there is a significant gap in the expertise of Canadian academics about the structure of the American political system and its behaviour. (Vol. II, ch. 18 of the final report). Therefore, whatever intelligent contribution might have been legitimately expected from the social sciences in ascertaining better what our trade partners are all about has not been provided. While this is ascribable partly to a lack of expert personnel, it is not entirely clear that their contribution (if it had materialized) would have been that significant, largely because of the limits of their tools.[20]

As for **free trade as construction of a new socio-economic space**, the process is so full of unforeseen and unintended consequences that social scientists have a rather limited ability to grasp its full scope. Attempts to gauge such broad transformations in the social architecture of socio-economies have been attempted through the use of **counterfactuals**, i.e., the use of alternative versions of the world to ascertain the net effect of a particular transformation or feature. Counterfactuals have to be reasonably precise to be of help. It has been a standard weakness of most general equilibrium analysis of counterfactuals that it left so much unspecified that nothing categorical can be stated with certainty from comparisons between the "world as it is" and the counterfactual version of it.

A good example, again taken from economic history, is the comparison made by Robert Fogel between a world with and without railroads in the United States. One is hardly persuaded by simple quantifications of the "social savings" generated by railroads, when they are based on a naive comparison of the costs of transportation by rail with the costs of transporting the same goods to the same places using the pre-existing mode of transportation. The assumption is that the same goods will be transported to the same places before and after the introduction of railroads. But if anything is clear, it is that railroads have triggered a complete transformation of the matrix of transported goods.[21] Therefore, the comparison is really meaningless and the notion of social saving thus defined somewhat spurious. The same general weakness plagues all attempts by social scientists to gauge the effects of the long-run adjustment to a "reality of free trade."

A sweeping transformation of the tariff arrangements between two countries is likely to promote economic growth through the expansion of trade, but it is not certain exactly how the benefits emanating from such a transformation will be shared by the different segments of the new socio-economic space. Depending on the assumptions one makes about reactions, adjustments, etc., one may obtain dramatically different though not necessarily inconsistent results. Moreover, many have expressed doubts about the wisdom of this policy initiative as a mechanism to solve Canada's economic problems: tariffs are not the issue any more, "the real issue is non-tariff barriers, such as regional tax incentives, government procurement policies, the treatment of foreign-owned firms, and the setting of currency exchange rates. These are the tools used in advanced industrial countries to pursue industrial strategies ... These tools are central to the economic power of the modern state, the key to sovereignty in the late twentieth century, just as tariffs were in the nineteenth."[22]

Since social sciences can throw no uncontroversial light on the impact of the "idea" of enhanced trade arrangements between Canada and the United States, nor on the best way to bargain for it, nor on the efficiency, economic growth and wealth redistribution the new socio-economic space is likely to trigger, nor even on the wisdom of such a policy initiative, it is hardly surprising that rhetoric has played such an important role in this debate. What has been accomplished in terms of public awareness and in terms of persuasion has been achieved often less by arguments soundly based on thoroughly persuasive social sciences research than through the use of rhetorical devices. Rhetoric may be inescapable, but even the conversation about free trade might be conducted more persuasively with the use of an enriched "outillage mental."

Some Paradoxes

Three paradoxes illustrate the degree to which social science research is bogged down when asked to illuminate the current debate.

1. Second-best results

One of the depressing results of economic analysis of the post-World War II period has been the development of second-best theorems in economics. This disquieting feature of general equilibrium analysis may be summarized as follows: there are many conditions to ensure welfare maximization in an economy; if for any reason, **one** of the many conditions for welfare maximization is unobtainable, it may be necessary to depart from **other** welfare-maximizing conditions. Because of the fact that perfect competition rarely exists (governments intervene via all sorts of taxes and subsidies, there do exist external economies and diseconomies in production and consumption etc . . .), it cannot be assumed that all marginal social costs and benefits are equal in every segment of the economy. Since this entails that some welfare-maximizing conditions are not met at some point in the economy, it becomes impossible to know with certainty any more whether a policy designed to remove a restriction to free trade (supposedly in order to bring the socio-economy closer to the point of welfare maximum for all) will leave members of the community economically better off than if the existing impediment to trade had been retained.[23]

This shattering result has not received the broad diffusion it required. Second-best is still regarded as an advanced subject and is not discussed in most intermediate textbooks. Yet, one may infer from it that there are very few *a priori* propositions that economists may offer to policy makers. Obviously, the more we know about the **facts** of the economy, the more we are in a position to compute *ad hoc* second-best optima. However, as the number of violations of efficiency conditions increase, and as the complexities of interdependency grow, computing such second-best solutions is both difficult and of necessity based on disputable assumptions.

In the great debate that surrounded the decision by Britain to join the European Economic Community, economists were very divided, and even free trade defenders like Harry Johnson campaigned against Britain joining the EEC on the ground that "the obvious economic benefits to Britain of joining are negligible and the obvious economic costs are large."[24] Other economists took a quite different stand, and their option prevailed; however, the force of their argument was much more rhetorical than substantive. The same conundrum faces experts when asked whether Canada should enter into a free trade agreement with the United States.

The broad consequence of this predicament is that there is no agreement among economists *a priori* about the desirability of free trade except even as an idea. When confronted with facts that can be read in a variety of different ways, one is faced with very different viewpoints: the full extent of the confusion can best be summarized by saying that it does not appear inconsistent any longer for an economist to say that even if economic integration is likely to generate more efficiency and growth in many cases, it cannot be presumed that economic disintegration is necessarily likely to generate inefficiency and slower growth.[25]

2. The framing of decisions

A second major paradox has emerged from the experimental work of Kahneman and Tversky: if one modifies the framework of presentation within which a decision is taken, one may dramatically transform the nature of the decision taken.[26] For instance, their studies have shown that medical personnel may be led to choose diametrically opposed strategies of cure if the same "objective" information is cast in terms of probability of death instead of probability of survival.

This work raises fundamental questions about the predictability of decisions by groups, and therefore about the reliability of simulacra, since it would appear that "objective" conditions are **not** the determining factor in decision making. This increases still more the importance of the rhetorical elements in debates such as the one about free trade. For the activities of the "*définisseurs de situation*" will trigger continuous "reframing" of the decisions context, and consequently a modification in the decisions taken. In the case of complex issues, it makes it futile to model decisions and strategies as anchored in "objective" conditions. This casts a shadow on much work based on rational man and his predictable behaviour.

In the free trade debate, much is based on presumptions and assumptions and the complexity of the choices proposed are of such a magnitude that the framing dimensions are even more determining than they might be in laboratory circumstances. Consequently, there is little hope of developing an objective data base on which to construct a sound simulation of decisions to be expected from different groups. Not only is the knowledge and data base necessary for good social science work non-existent, but even if it could be arrived at, nothing would lead us to believe that the objective facts would have a determining impact on real decisions. In this world, as in the world of Heisenberg, interventions by opinion moulders using the instruments of rhetoric have more chance of being determinant than the so-called basic facts of the case.

3. Balkanization and multistability

The efficiency/growth/redistribution effects of a freer trade arrangement are unclear, but the relative weights of these performance indicators in a dynamic socio-economy living through extremely rapid change and transformation are not clear either. Departure from the world of perfect competition does not only deprive economists of simple rules for policy advice, it also imposes a different set of weights for those different performance dimensions. In a world of perfect competition, it is argued that "there is an optimal amount of instability and inequity; this is the one that makes the human economy as efficient as possible in the broadest sense."[27]

This may be questionable even in a world of perfect competition, but it is clearly neither warranted nor reasonable in a world which departs from the competitive ideal. In such a context, the whole notion of performance indicators has to be "reframed", and the problem must be addressed by a decision to "select **a set of targets or objectives for**

the economy and then analyze the performance of particular sectors of the economy in terms of whether or not this performance aids or impedes the achievement of these overall goals."28 *De facto*, the pursuit of equity and stability (or of growth/employment objectives or the construction of a particular socio-economic structure or the achievement of some cultural goals) overrides the concern for efficiency.29

This shift in emphasis in evaluating performance has not always been given sufficient recognition in the practice of social scientists. This is so despite important work recasting the image of the economic system as a non-zero-sum game in which the parts devise rival strategies taking into account conjectures about what other parts might do and the interactions between strategies. Such work has shown our capitalistic socio-economies to be dynamically inefficient and therefore calling for other performance indicators to be used.30

What makes this shift to other gauges of performance fundamentally important in the free trade debate is the fact that as soon as efficiency considerations cease to be dominant, there is little or no agreement on what might be alternative gauges. Moreover, optimizing in other directions seems condemned to violate blatantly the efficiency norms. For instance, a fragmented/fractured economic system may be shown to be **multistable**, i.e., to have a relatively greater ability to adapt than a fully integrated one. Through the fragmentation of an economic system into "sub-systems subject to slightly different rules and interacting incompletely or only through the mediation of specific channels," one may ensure that an adjustment in some key or essential variables is "delegated, so to speak, to a partial system enabling the overall process to adjust to important shocks in the environment in a manner which would have been either impossible or very time consuming had the overall process been forced to adjust *in toto*."31

This might lead one to argue that while an expanded zone of freer trade might generate efficiency benefits, it might also reduce the capacity to transform a socio-economic system. It is possible to argue along the same line on the basis of some fundamental social objective like the **primacy of culture** or the **preservation of sovereignty**: this leads to a situation in which no technical advice based on simple efficiency norms can ever be persuasive, for the ground has been shifted to moral choices and one cannot displace a fundamentally **moral** basis for decision by a **technical** argument.32

It is far from evident, therefore, that social science research can produce unambiguous answers to the questions of the day. The combination of second-best and framing-of-decisions constraints, together with the possibility that static and dynamic contexts or narrow and broader contexts might call for different policy initiatives, have led social scientists to make many statements in general (and therefore on the basis of the most extremely reductive assumptions) but to contribute little except some interesting rhetoric — nothing that might be regarded as providing solutions to the practical problems facing the community.

Anamorphosis of the Free Trade Debate

An extensive literature has been triggered by the free trade debate in Canada over the last two years. Our ambition is not to review that literature. We have only sampled it in order to identify some of the major strands of argument, to illustrate the interesting rhetorical ploys used, and to show the general unpersuasiveness of the social science contributions to that debate. Since the free trade issue has a dominant economic flavour, the place of economists in this anamorphosis may be larger than life. We have also made some efforts to sample some magazines and we have had a look at the financial press in order to gauge what had filtered down to the citizens from the social sciences community through the press.[33]

Since it is our claim that rhetoric has played a dominant role in the free trade debate, an anamorphosis through the prism of the four tropes that have so generously spiced the economic discourse in the past has appeared useful.[34] Those figures of speech (metaphor, metonymy, synecdoche and irony) have played a crucial role in the free trade debate. The pro-free trade participants have tried to persuade by making use of those tropes. Their opponents, in turn, have often used figures of speech in lieu of proofs. The rationale for such posturing is simple: neither side is really able to prove much.

Trade as Synecdoche

A socio-economy as instituted process cannot be reduced to the process of trade: this is a synecdoche, i.e., taking a part for the whole. The manner in which the economic process gets instituted at different places and times vests that process unity and stability, and defines the nature of specific human economies.[35] A socio-economy is fundamentally an organizational/institutional reality, of which trade is only a portion.

Any analysis of an economy partitions it into sub-processes. This reveals the extent to which trade is but a small part of the picture. One such partitioning which has proved particularly useful in analyzing the Canadian socio-economy is based on six sub-processes (the demographic sub-process, the financial sub-process, the production and exchange sub-process, the distribution sub-process, the state sub-process, and the ecology of groups and their motives).[36]

By making trade relations **the fabric** of the economy, some social scientists have reduced the complex process of private, social and public production, consumption, cooperation and exchange to simple trading relations. This is a bold synecdoche.[37] In fact, one is led to postulate a frictionless world in which monads trade relentlessly in all dimensions, and where any trade impediment generates waste in preventing the realization of first-best optima in all dimensions.

This elevation of trade relations to absolute eminence has meant that all other dimensions have been either occluded (except for their trade-related traits) or at least emasculated to a great extent. For instance, the whole production process and its technological dimensions are naively simplified to a problem of scale economies.[38]

The Mythical 100-million Market

The trade bias leads naturally to an interesting metonymy—a procedure through which a thing associated with the matter under discussion becomes a symbol for it. The whole productive dimension of national economies has simply been subsumed under the rubric of **scale**. All the complexities of modern economies are reduced to one feature: the size of the market. Consequently, all problems of productivity and competitiveness are ascribed to lack of opportunity to gain access to a market of 100 million.

This is the foundation on which the Macdonald commission builds its argument in favour of freer trade: without such a market, it is presumed that a socio-economy cannot really achieve efficiency and therefore competitiveness. Yet there is more to the making of our daily bread (as McCloskey would say) than scale economies, and there is plenty of evidence that small open economies have succeeded in doing extremely well even without full access to a market of 100 million.[39]

This reduction of the whole productive side of the human economy to scale economies, and therefore to the extent of the market, has been challenged by most opponents to free trade as bogus. They argue that there is plenty of evidence of economies with small domestic markets but skilled productive capacity and good marketing that have forged a strong international presence for themselves in the world economy.[40] But the figure of speech has a great resiliency and it has had an extraordinary impact on the citizenry, as can be seen in the popular and in the financial press which have reproduced this argument hundreds of times. This is so despite the fact that the same financial press ("Small is Beautiful Now in Manufacturing," *Business Week*, October 22, 1984) has also shown unambiguously that economies of scale alone would no longer guarantee an advantage in manufacturing. Shorter product cycles and computer-assisted design and manufacturing (CAD-CAM) have "made it economical to turn out products in small customized batches."

The Metaphorical Flavour of the Basic Argument

By focusing exclusively on trade and on the extent of the market, the pro-free trade participants are led to infer that from competition in a large market flows efficiency, and from efficiency flows welfare. This pivotal reliance on efficiency enables the pro-free trade argument to stand; however potent the forces of competition may be, they cannot by themselves eliminate "natural protection" bestowed by transportation costs or "unnatural protection" bestowed by collusion, cartels, price manipulation, and other such techniques. Moreover, the surge of employment and growth and per capita income purported to ensue from free trade (on the grounds that efficiency is the key to prosperity) is dependent on a large number of factors about which we know little. What about investment?; what about the independence of Canadian policy making?; what about the differential institutions that characterize Canada in comparison to the United States? On those matters, we can speculate, but we know little. The trick of the free trade promoters has been to force the argument on the ground of competitiveness and efficiency and to presume that employment, growth and welfare are **necessary** consequences flowing from efficiency. In fact, efficiency **may** promote growth but it is hardly sufficient to ensure growth. Indeed, "inefficiencies" like tariffs would appear to have been associated historically with periods of rapid growth in Canada.[41] The basic argument stating the following connotation chain – large market/competitiveness/ efficiency/growth, employment, welfare – may hold as **a perfectly competitive world metaphor** but it does not capture the essence of real socio-economies.

The thrust behind the basic argument is that the optimal amount of protection is zero. The counter-argument is that it is not so, that there is a "scientific tariff" that may well be different from zero if one is intent on achieving certain social objectives like economic growth, the creation of jobs or the pursuit of certain objectives of political sovereignty or cultural development. The counter-argument adds that there is an "imperialism of free trade" as present today as it was in the middle of the nineteenth century. Free trade as panacea or free trade as economic and cultural genocide – those are rhetorical stands one cannot buttress with persuasive arguments.[42]

The Use of Irony in the Free Trade Debate

Irony is the most sophisticated of the rhetorical techniques. It uses humorous or slightly sarcastic expressions in which the "intended meaning of the words used is the direct opposite of their usual sense." The trade literature in Canada has always had a strong ironic strand: some may remember the famous Bladen Plan, a proposal to reduce tariffs on the import of auto parts but retaining them on whole cars which, even though designed to increase protection for local assembly plants, was billed as a step toward free trade.[43]

For instance, in order to defend his belief in a more aggressive and forceful effort toward a complete liberalization of trade, Ron Shearer has no hesitation in characterizing the more careful urging by the Macdonald commission to liberalize trade in industrial products only as "a new face of Canadian mercantilism."[44]

Simon Reisman, in the face of attacks on the free trade initiative as a threat to Canadian independence, refers to studies that supposedly show that "there is not much to worry on the independence issue in a free trade context that we don't already worry about." This is an argument that Anthony Westell also uses, although Westell reserves his most biting words for those "romantics" who keep referring to the "national character" and the "national identity."[45] There is also something suave about the U.S.-Israel free trade area agreement being proposed as a model for Canada. Or about the suggestion by the prime minister (in his television address of June 1986) that the growing protectionism in the United States (*Fortress U.S.A.*) was putting our markets in peril and the only way out was to negotiate a trade deal. The rest of the year has shown how little the ongoing negotiations would affect the dynamic of countervails and how vulnerable the Canadian sovereignty over its own policy instruments turned out to be!

The other group has not been without its own capacity to use irony. James Laxer handles this trope exceedingly well: he accuses "economists of harbouring dark feelings about Canada" and he understands "that Canada is the scene of heinous outrages against economic theory." Mel Hurtig is also a master of irony in his many speeches and articles where he uses variations on the theme of the famous blindfolded leap of faith through the window of opportunity into the cold shower of international competition and ending up on a cement floor.

The final irony about the free trade debate is that the very notion of free trade connotes and has been made to connote explicitly in the mind of the public some sort of reduction of the importance of the state in trading relations. We are told that free trade, deregulation and privatization constitute a trinity of policies designed to reduce the role of government in the socio-economy. In fact, as Bruce Doern has shown, free trade is bound to mean expanded activities by the state.[46] In this context, it is enlightening to read the briefing document outlining the communications strategy of the Canadian government to sell free trade to the Canadian public. It shows clearly that the intent was less to educate the general public than to bamboozle the citizenry by emphasizing the **free** of free trade.[47]

It is hardly surprising that the free trade debate has generated more heat than light. The notion of free trade has maintained throughout a certain strategic vagueness nurtured carefully by all participants in the debate. Attempts to promote other versions of the notion (freer trade, enhanced trade) have been perceived as decoys for the real thing and never could take hold. This strategic vagueness compounded with a certain tactial imprecision when dealing with the coverage of any possible free trade arrangement (industrial production *à la* Macdonald or a wider coverage including services, agriculture, culture, etc.) and with the shifts between free trade as an idea, as a game of negotiations and as a redesigning of the socio-economic space of North America have maintained the debate out of reach of most Canadians.

The lack of focus of this conversation about free trade is obviously partly strategically planned, but it is also in great part ascribable to the lack of rigour of the language of problem-solution provided by the social sciences. Otherwise, much of this mumbling would have been exposed forcefully much earlier. But since very little of substance can be generated from general social-scientific rules, debaters have been forced to construct *ad hoc* policy recommendations derived from analyses of second-best or third-best possibilities; the framing of decisions has become such a key variable that the same "objective" information is now seen as capable of triggering quite diverse reactions depending on the way it is presented: rhetoric is queen. This is nowhere more transparent than in the communications strategy document revealed on September 20, 1985. Government would appear intent on shaping the framework for decisions rather than attempting to deal with so-called "objective" dimensions of the issue.

The multilogue is fundamentally flawed: on a bold **synecdoche** of a socio-economy fully defined by trading relations, academics and bureaucrats have attached the **metonymy** that the only operative force in the productive process is scale economies; this has served as a foundation for a metaphorical connotation chain rooted in the extent of the market and leading to an efficiency-seeking policy recommendation that had to be free trade; an occlusion of key substantive features of the socio-economy as instituted process ensued. All this appropriately spiced with irony could only be tonic but not enlightening.

What Refurbished Social Sciences Might Contribute

An alternative practice of the social sciences might be able to go further and deeper in making sense of the free trade debate. In this section, a general sketch of what refurbished social sciences might look like is presented, together with the sort of new model for policy research that should ensue. We try to show that it might carry the debate on free trade into more promising directions.

This is quite a voyage deep into *terra incognita*. It cannot be certain therefore that we can deliver as much as we would like to promise. The intent at least should be clear: we wish to map out this new terrain in a preliminary way.

Nature of the Repairs[48]

Refurbished human sciences must take a turn toward interpretation and the fundamental **sociality** of the social sciences must become the central dimension of interest. To explore sociality, a new methodological strategy focused on institutions is necessary. This strategy calls for a reconstruction of the institutional schemata (as social armistices and parameters of possible actions) and for a re-creation of their genesis: the central concern is not to explicate the reified social context from **without**, but to try to understand from **within** the unity, complementarities, consistency, permanence and development of the institutional texture of World 3.[49]

But this cannot be done without some effort to go beneath historically contexted traditions to the real forces determining their shape. This is where hermeneutics comes in. It considers human social life as text-analogue calling for interpretation in the same manner as old incomplete and fragmented texts from past ages used to be interpreted. The **contexted** traditions are almost of necessity interpreted overtly by different actors or groups of actors in a biased, ideological way. This is why **depth interpretation** is in order.[50]

What is called for is not unlike a Freudian-type interpretation seeking beneath the observed speech pattern of ordinary life unsuspected patterns of distorted communication of an individual as a result of the repression of needs and wants. What appear to be forms of neurotic symptoms in the individual may transpire as forms of "false consciousness" and ideology in societies. Habermas suggests that in the same manner that Freud, by methodical interpretation of dreams, behaviour, speech, etc., can penetrate beneath the surface to the underlying forces, one may interpret societies' pathologies and unearth what might account for the false consciousness of groups in society.[51]

In the same manner that bringing out the latent repressed significance of the patient's life history leads the patient to give to those repressed areas new significance, Habermas would hope to apply the same therapy in social life. Through revealing the preconditions of power and domination that gave rise to distorted communication, one might improve the degree of communicative competence within a socio-economy and come closer to realizing a less imperfect community.

To do so, one needs a better decoder than the language of problem solution in good currency — the language of progress. This language of progress is based on **freedom as an absolute** and on a blind faith in continuing progress through the use of instrumental reason and technology. This has been the decoder used to analyze our societies. The language of progress is not capable of throwing any light on the essential **sociality** of human communities, on their inter-subjective fabric or on the various ways in which communication can be and is systematically distorted within human communities. It decomposes the institutional fabric of our societies into reified rights and thereby dissolves it into a contractual texture that gives no voice or reality to those that have no contracting power: marginals, non-conformists, the unborn, etc. It cannot take into account fundamental categories like goodness or justice.

What is required is **a language rooted in what makes us human rather than in what makes us free**. Michael Ignatief has proposed one such language — a language of the good, a language of needs — more capable of appreciating fully our essential sociality and consequently also the relevant deformations of the social space, i.e., deviations *vis-à-vis* situations promoting the good and the just.[52] Such a language rooted in the civil society recognizes the centrality of the good society, the good polity, the good economy, and strives to eliminate impediments standing in the way of their realization, i.e., a socio-economy that meets not only efficiency standards, but also standards of reciprocity and stability.[53]

Toward a New Model of Policy Research

Most policy research on big questions is such that goals are ambiguous or in conflict, **and** that means-ends relationships are highly uncertain. It is hardly surprising that policy research should be of little use. Researchers have a great latitude to specify unreasonably narrow or naive goals, or to presume some deterministic link between means and ends when there is at best a remotely possible one. However cleverly one may wish to package the results of such policy research, it is bound to be irrelevant.

This often leads to deception, but most of the time to some conniving between the producer of the metaphorical research and the policy maker that has paid for it. The rationale for this connivance comes from the fact that such policy research is of no consequence: it leaves the policy maker entirely free to follow the strategy that proves electorally expedient, for the research results are demonstrably impertinent. David Slater was not challenged when he wrote that little in the successes or failures of economic policy in the post war period in Canada could be ascribed to economic research.[54]

The only way to generate policy research of import is to renounce scientism and to develop policy research in the full context of social practice. This in turn calls for a simultaneous taking into account of four sub-processes in interaction: "the formulation of a theory of reality, the articulation of relevant social values, the selection of an appropriate political strategy, and the implementation of practical measures or social action."[55] John Friedmann has proposed one such model in which "cognition is linked to the world of events via social action (SA) and the results of that action. The adequacy of the theory of reality (TR) and/or the political strategy (PS) is therefore dependent on the results of action (SA) and the extent to which these results satisfy the given social values (SV). Such knowledge is useful in solving social problems, but it is not formally cumulative knowledge. Indeed much of the knowledge obtained may leave no visible traces of itself; it is experiential or tacit knowledge."[56]

Such a policy research model incorporates normative assertions explicitly instead of "smuggling" them in, and is based on a transactive style of planning that accepts boldly the underlying conflictive process implied in the political system. It is also based firmly on the belief that **social learning** must be promoted at all possible locations within a social system and that social experimentation should be promoted wherever possible. Indeed, it would appear to lead exactly to the converse of the present manipulative strategies hinted at in note 47. In a world freed from the totalitarianism of the knowledgeable elite, there is a "commitment on the part of the policymaker to the idea of social experimentation, practice, and learning as the principal methods for public intervention."[57]

Dimensions of Interdependence

The remaining question is whether refurbished social sciences might throw some new light on the free trade debate. We feel that it would. An attempt to examine the Canadian socio-economy as a text-analogue and to **socioanalyze** it to unearth the foundations of the different ideological discourses we hear might indeed reveal a great amount of false consciousness in the Canadian political economy. Moreover, a model of policy research taking explicitly into account the socio-cultural and the socio-political dimensions of the free trade arrangement might significantly redirect the thrust of the debate.

Many "deformations of the social space" might serve as *révélateurs*: Canada is a small, open, dependent and balkanized socio-economy living in the shadow of the United States but intent on preserving a separate and different cultural identity and social fabric. Whatever the rectitude of this view, the coherence and permanence of the existing Canadian social order is perceived as jeopardized by an economic *rapprochement* with the United States. Richard Lipsey has labelled this sort of opposition to free trade "visceral rather than intellectual."[58]

There are widespread concerns about free trade because it would seemingly lead irreversibly to a complete submission of the operations of the Canadian socio-economy to the imperatives of the market. The strictly commercial dimension of the arrangement has already become hegemonic in all discussions: culture which used to connote for Canadians a profoundly different "program" (in the sense computer scientists use the word), i.e., a different way of life, a significantly different way of tackling issues and solving problems, is in the process of becoming synonymous with cultural industries;

social programs, that used to connote the style of society Canadians had chosen, are now referred to as forms of export subsidies.

If the **free** in free trade has been used to market the idea that Canadians could have their cake and eat it too, for other Canadians, the abandonment of their life styles to the whims of the **free** market makes no sense. In many ancient societies, the market mechanism was used for the allocation of widgets, but banned in regard to food and essential goods, because it was believed that the free market might not allocate or shape ideally (i.e., fairly and appropriately) such essential commodities. The same might be said about such important intangibles like culture and social mores. Free trade has therefore been a major source of fear.

The only way to incorporate fully those social and cultural dimensions (but also the regional, distributional, technological, financial, human, political and demographic objectives) into the discussion about trade is to recast the debate in terms of **fair trade**. This would ensure that in the process of bargaining over trading arrangements, the collection of goals Canadians have chosen would be kept in perspective and explicitly brought forward in an attempt to negotiate a fair deal with the United States.[59]

Fair trade is an expression which is likely to generate some negative reactions from those who feel that **fairness** is not a sound enough basis to serve as a benchmark. Yet courts have for years refereed cases on the basis of such criteria without too much difficulty. This is most certainly better than the "leap of faith" that might simply end up in a process of "Ukrainization" of Canada.[60]

The fair trade scenario poses many important challenges to Canada. Such negotiations would have to be developed on the basis of the Charter of the Economic Rights and Duties of Nations approved by the General Assembly of the United Nations in 1974. The 34 articles of the charter (including the right to control foreign investment, the right to share in the advantages that result from technological and scientific innovations, the duty to cooperate to ensure fair terms of trade, etc . . .) were approved by a majority of 120 votes to 6 but it should be known that the United States voted against the charter. Consequently, it is not sure that efforts to negotiate a fair commercial, technological, financial and social deal with the United States would either be welcome or feasible. But is anything less than such an arrangement but another form of "imperialism of free trade" and, if so, do Canadians really want it?

A social science research program intent on examining the new trading relations with the United States within the context of a model of social learning might reveal that, as it has been mentioned by some observers, free trade as an idea is not such a good one, that Canada may have been imprudent in jumping into such negotiations without the necessary preparatory work at the provincial and at the grassroots level, and that the economic benefits from such a new trading space are doubtful while triggering irreversible social, cultural and political consequences. It might also dispel those fears and help prepare the documentation necessary for the negotiation of a fair deal.

Such a research program does not exist for the time being. Many intelligent appraisals of the situation have been put forward but they are mostly speculations and opinions couched in different figures of speech. Little has been done to analyze the "deformations" of our social space, to dispel the high degree of false consciousness that inhabits the debate, or to hasten the social learning about the price Canadians might be willing to pay to maintain "their good society." And when such analyses have been put forward they have been ignored or disparaged as "nationalist" or "socialist." This has not helped the conversation about what a fair deal with the United States might be. Canadians have been bombarded by messages from many Cassandras and many Candides when they have not simply been dis-informed. What they need is an orderly framework for their thought. Only refurbished social sciences can help in this construction.

Conclusion

It may appear unduly optimistic to believe that after a century of positivistic indoctrination one might feel that a turn to interpretation is likely to breathe some fresh air into the social sciences. Yet there are many signs that we are entering a crucial transition period. The disciplinary guilds have been led to excesses in their regulation and there has been "a crisis of abstraction" in the 1970s. As a result, it can be argued that the social sciences have become more disconnected from the original questions that had led to the creation of the social sciences than ever in the past.

According to Homa Katouzian, no amount of moral suasion, sporadic dissent and no quantity of sermons will provoke the needed change, "only a combination of public consciousness and the growing proximity of the abyss" will do the job. Those two forces may be at work. A crisis of confidence has developed over the last 15 years within the social science community. It has been echoed within the broader social context as practical irrelevance and theoretical failures showed up more and more frequently. Consequently governments and patrons have become less willing to fund the activities of the social scientists. The matching grants policy of the Mulroney government should bring that crisis to a head.[61]

While not determinant in this process, the free trade debate may have exposed social scientists more than they would have liked. There seems to be a convergence of developments (both in current philosophical thinking and in the demands by society) that would appear to promote the development of "an epistemology of practice which laces technical problem solving within a broader context of reflective inquiry, shows how reflection-in-action may be rigorous in its own right, and links the art of practice in uncertainty and uniqueness to the scientist's art of research."[62] An alternative to positivism now exists and there is a demand for it.

At a time when those who gave us positivism — the physicists — apply terms like **colour** and **charm** to the quark, this elusive and invisible ultimate element, it may be time for social scientists to recognize at last that they should cease to be slaves to some defunct physicist.[63]

Notes

1.   The diagnosis put forward in this section has been developed more fully in G. Paquet, "Le goût de l'improbable: A propos d'une stratégie de sortie de crise pour les sciences humaines" in G. Paquet & M. von Zur-Muehlen (eds), *Higher Education: Crisis or Opportunity?*, (Ottawa: Canadian Higher Education Research Network, 1987), (in press).

2.   G.H. von Wright, *Explanation and Understanding*, (Ithaca, N.Y.:   Cornell University Press, 1971), Chapter 1.

3.   S. Latouche, *Le procès de la science sociale*, (Paris: Anthropos, 1984), Chapter 2.

4.   J. Monnerot, *Les faits sociaux ne sont pas de choses*, (Paris: Gallimard, 1946); C.O. Schrag, *Radical Reflection and the Origin of the Human Sciences*, (West Lafayette, Ind.: Purdue University Press, 1980).

5.   Jürgen Habermas, *Knowledge and Human Interests*, tr. by Jeremy J. Shapiro (Boston: Beacon Press, 1971), Part II; also G. Paquet, "Two Tramps in Mud Time: Social Sciences and Humanities in Modern Society." In B. Bu-Laban & B.G. Rule (eds), *The Human Sciences: Contributions to Society and Future Research Needs*, (Edmonton: The University of Alberta press, 1987) (in press).

6.   F. von Hayek, *Scientism and the Study of Society*, (Glencoe, I11: The Free Press, 1952). This is probably the most vehement denunciation of this perversion of the social sciences. Hayek shows how, from Francis Bacon to Auguste Comte, there have been efforts to reduce the human sciences to the status of natural sciences of man. While there is much merit in this approach in many sub-areas of the study of man, it is unacceptable, says Hayek, to reduce all of social sciences to this sub-segment.

7.   A.O. Hirschman, "Against Parsimony", *Economics and Philosophy*, I, 1985, pp. 7-21.

8.   J.S. Mill, J.N. Keynes, E. Durkheim, etc., produced different sets of rules defining the different appropriate methodologies that characterized the diverse disciplines in the nineteenth century.

9.   Homa Katouzian, *Ideology and Method in Economics*, (New York: New York University Press, 1980), pp. 119-122.

10.   R.D. Beam, "Fragmentation of Knowledge: An Obstacle to its Full Utilization" in Kenneth E. Boulding & L. Senesh (eds), *The Optimum Utilization of Knowledge: Making Knowledge Serve Human Betterment* (Boulder, Col: Westview Press, 1983), Chapter 13. See also G. Paquet, "Un appel à l'indiscipline théorique" in M. Lebel & C. Marchand (eds), *Présentations à la Société Royale*, (Québec, 1978), pp. 109-118; also G. Paquet, "The Optimal Amount of Coercion is not Zero" in Science Council of Canada, *Social Science Research in Canada: Stagnation or Regeneration?*, (Ottawa: Supply and Services, 1985), pp. 98-115.

11. Stanislau Andreski, *Social Sciences as Sorcery*, (Harmondsworth: Penguin Books, 1974); Scott Gordon, *Social Science and Modern Man*, (Toronto: University of Toronto Press, 1970); see also Scott Gordon, "The Political Economy of Big Questions and Small Ones," *Canadian Public Policy*, I.1, Winter 1975, pp. 97-106.

12. Wassily Leontief, "Academic Economics", *Science*, Vol. 217, July 9, 1982, p. 107. One might make similar statements about other disciplines and observe the same drift away from empirical, policy-oriented or problem-solving work in other disciplines also.

13. D. Bell (ed), "New Directions in Modern Thought", *Partisan Review*, 51, 2, 1984, pp. 215-320.

14. For an introduction to the method of interpretation (verstehen), L.M. Lachmann, *The Legacy of Max Weber*; three essays, (Berkeley: The Glendessary Press, 1971); also G. Shapiro & A. Sico (eds), *Hermeneutics: Questions and Prospects*, (Amherst, The University of Massachussetts Press, 1984). On the three worlds of Karl Popper, see his *Objective Knowledge*, Oxford, 1972, Chapter 3.

15. D.N. McCloskey, *The Rhetoric of Economics*, (Madison: The University of Wisconsin Press, 1985), p. 27.

16. In economic history, it is often argued that tariffs are not unlike "negative railroads" since the impediments to trade that they generate are the exact obverse of the facilitation of trade generated by the introduction of railroad transportation. L.H. Jenks ("Railroads as an Economic Force in American Development," *Journal of Economic History*, IV, 1944, pp. 1-20) has analyzed the impact of railroads on American development under three rubrics: railroad as an idea, railroad as a construction enterprise, railroad as a producer of transportation services. We have adopted a somewhat similar approach albeit in a modified way in our own analysis.

17. These mechanical analogs might be almost entirely unspecified as in the case of John M. Culbertson ("The Folly of Free Trade," *Harvard Business Review*, Sept-Oct. 1986, pp. 122-8) although one may easily gather from the analysis what sort of model Dr. Culbertson carries in the back of his head; or it might be a very elaborate econometric construct as in the case of the work of Richard G. Harris & David Cox, *Trade, Industrial Policy, and Canadian Manufacturing*, (Toronto: Ontario Economic Council, 1983) or in the very many simulations performed by management consultants like *Informetrica* for a variety of clients. Such elaborate constructs need not be economic in nature. For instance, David Braybrooke, *Traffic Congestion Goes Through the Issue-Machine; A Case Study in Issue Proceedings, Illustrating a New Approach* (London: Routledge & Kegan Paul, 1974).

18. For a general discussion of the difficulties posed by bargaining for social scientists, see Leif Johansen, "The Bargaining Society and the Inefficiency of Bargaining" *Kyklos*, 32, 3, 1979, pp. 497-522.

19. For a good review of the limited accomplishments of the game theorists despite valiant efforts, see Martin Shubik, *Game Theory in the Social Sciences; Concepts and Solutions*, (Cambridge, Mass.: The MIT Press, 1982). On the treacherous nature of the analytics of the bargaining process, see Alan Coddington, *Theories of the Bargaining Process*, (Chicago: Aldine, 1968); also see J.G. Cross, *The Economics of Bargaining*, (New York: Basic Books, 1969). For a recent review essay on the state of the art, James A. Schellenberg & Daniel Druckman, "Bargaining and Gaming," *Society*, 23, 6, September - October 1986, pp. 65-71.

20. It is interesting to note that in many instances the "social scientists" that have been making the most interesting contributions to this debate have been those least constrained by the trappings of the traditional disciplines: journalists, situationologists or leading academics. The first two groups have provided "débrouissaillages" guided somewhat by social-scientific frameworks but not trapped in it. As for the prominent senior academics, freed from the need to abide by the rules of the discipline to an extent, they would appear to adopt a style and a form of analysis that is not without reminding those adopted by journalists and situationologists. An example of the journalistic pieces might be J. Blouin, *Libre-échange vraiment libre?*, (Québec: Institut Québécois de recherche sur la culture, 1986), or R.I.G. McLean, "Three Men in a Boat—A Discussion of Free Trade", *The Idler*, 9, pp. 17-27. For a very lucid piece by a prominent academic economist, see Richard G. Lipsey, "Will there be a Canadian-American Free Trade Association?", *The World Economy*, 9, 3, September 1986, pp. 217-38; for a good piece by a situationologist, G. Bruce Doern, "The Tories, Free Trade and Industrial Adjustment Policy: Expanding the State Now to Reduce the State Later" in Michael J. Prince (ed), *How Ottawa Spends 1986-87; Tracking the Tories*, (Toronto: Methuen, 1986), pp. 61-94. On the notion of situationologist, G. Paquet, "Econocrats versus Situationologists: A Question of Rationalities" (mimeo 1982, 17p.).

21. Robert W. Fogel, *Railroads and American Economic Growth: Essays in Econometric History*, (Baltimore: Johns Hopkins University, 1964), see also Robert W. Fogel, "Notes on the Social Saving Controversy." *Journal of Economic History*, 39, March 1979, pp. 1-54. For an evaluation of the Fogelian approach as a form of rhetoric, see D.N. McCloskey, *Rhetoric of Economics*, p. 27.

22. J. Laxer (*Leap of Faith—Free Trade and the Future of Canada*, Edmonton: Hurtig, 1986) argues that a market-driven approach is not appropriate; he suggests that a business-government partnership is required to rebuild Canada's socio-economy. (The specific quote is taken from page 11). See also, Abraham Rotstein, *Rebuilding from Within; Remedies for Canada's Ailing Economy*, (Toronto: James Lorimer & Co. in association with Canadian Institute for Economic Policy, 1984).

23. This phenomenon has been noted for quite some time but it was analyzed carefully only in the postwar period. James Meade, the Nobel Laureate, coined the phrase J.E. Meade, *Trade and Welfare*. The Theory of International Economic Policy, v. 2. (London: Oxford University Press, 1955). The fact that a first-best solution is ruled out by the existence of imperfections in one sector means that a second-

best solution has to be found. Such a second-best solution has to be derived from an examination of the particulars of the case. It cannot be inferred from the use of a general rule like the equalization of marginal costs and benefits. Obviously such a line of reasoning may be used to justify the existence of trade restrictions.

24. H.G. Johnson (*Spectator* 13, February 1971) - quoted in T.W. Hutchinson, *Knowledge and Ignorance in Economics*, (Oxford: Blackwell, 1977), p. 181.

25. In Canada, the debates at the time of the Quebec referendum of 1980 and in the years preceding it, together with those that have been going on about free trade in the 1980s, have provided numerous examples of such apparently contradictory statements. In fact, there is, most of the time, no inherent contradiction: as soon as they stray away from tautologies or truisms, practitioners can hardly answer any question pertaining to the world of facts (as perceived by the citizenry) except by saying "it depends," and many of the conclusions that follow are simply an echo effect of the assumptions on which they have built their argument.

26. Amos Tversky & Daniel Kahneman, "The Framing of Decisions and the Psychology of Choice", *Science*, 211, 30, January 1981, pp. 453-458.

27. This is the view upheld by neo-classical economists and their policy advice is anchored in the assumption that the standard rules in force in the ideal competitive world should be used whatever their inappropriateness. For a critique of this view and some suggested alternative approaches to the gauging of performance, see Gilles Paquet, "The Regulatory Process and Economic Performance" in G. Bruce Doern (ed), *The Regulatory Process in Canada*, (Toronto: Macmillan of Canada, 1978), pp. 34-67.

28. James B. Herendeen, *The Economics of the Corporate Economy*, (New York: Dunellen, 1975), p. 230.

29. Gilles Paquet, "The Regulatory Process..." p. 46.

30. Kelvin Lancaster, "The Dynamic Inefficiency of Capitalism", *Journal of Political Economy* 81, Sept. - Oct. 1973, pp. 1092-1109. Lancaster presents capitalism as a differential game and demonstrates the sub-optimality of this regime because of its built-in coordination failures. Social waste ensues. In the face of such inefficiency, it is futile to argue for a return to competition (and therefore freer trade) as a way out of this inefficiency. Such a focus on efficiency criteria is not only unwarranted but assumes away too many of the complexities, uncertainties and strategic dimensions of the real game that underpin the human economy.

31. The argument is developed at some length in Gilles Paquet, "The Regulatory Process..." pp. 52; see also G. Paquet, "Federalism as Social Technology" in *Options: Proceedings of the Conference on the Future of the Canadian Federation.* (Toronto: University of Toronto, 1977), pp. 281-302 where an argument is developed showing that to the extent that federalism fragments a socio-economy, it may improve its capacity to adapt. To the extent that regulation and other non-

market mechanisms balkanize the socio-economy, the same argument may be made that regulations promote multistability.

32. Such attempts to persuade the population that **the technical has replaced the moral** has been dubbed by N. Wiley as "a methodological or epistemological coup" perpetrated by social scientists on the population. (Quoted in G. Paquet, "Federalism . . ." p. 296.) It has proved effective but only in the short run. Questions of **sovereignty** or **culture**, for instance, would appear to be almost *ultra vires* for traditional social sciences: it is easier for some, like A. Westell, to simply occlude such dimensions from their analysis or to transmogrify them: "To be a Canadian citizen does not signify a way of life, or a set of values beyond attachment to the community and loyalty to the national state. So the fear that closer association with the United States will erode a Canadian identity in the making or abort a Canadian culture about to be born is unfounded." (p. 22); in the same spirit, he argues that free trade would entail "no sovereignty loss"; it is simply that "both governments would have to look very carefully before implementing domestic policies" (p. 18), A. Westell, "Economic Integration with the USA", *International Perspectives*, November - December 1984.

33. Given the publication lag and the insensitivity of much of the academic community to current issues, it has been important to sample journals and magazines with a stronger interest in current policy issues. We have scanned a number of publications without any intention of being exhaustive. In alphabetical order they are: *Alberta Report, The Business Quarterly, Canadian Business, The Canadian Business Review, Canadian Dimension, Canadian Forum, Canadian Labour, Canadian Public Policy, International Perspectives, Queen's Quarterly, Policy Options,* and *The Idler.*

34. D.N. McCloskey, *Rhetoric of Economics*, p. 83ff has analyzed the prose of Robert Solow and others and he has shown that figures of speech have played a great role in "scientific" arguments.

35. Karl Polanyi, "The Economy as Instituted Process" in K. Polanyi, *Primitive, Archaic and Modern Economies; Essays of Karl Polanyi,* (New York: Anchor Books, 1968), Chapter 7.

36. Gilles Paquet, "Putting it All Together: A Political Economy Perspective of the Early 1980s" in Charles A. Barrett (ed), *Key Economic and Social Issues of the Early 1980s,* (Ottawa: The Conference Board in Canada, 1980), ch. V. One may suggest alternative partitioning of substantive socio-economies but, in all cases, trade would not represent more than a portion of that reality.

37. For a more realistic look at the fabric of real economies, see Oliver E. Williamson, *The Economic Institutions of Capitalism,* (New York: The Free Press, 1985).

38. Harris has underlined the fact that comparative advantages are not inherited from nature but made largely through institutional build-ups and structures. (Richard G. Harris, *Trade, Industrial Policy and International Competition,* (Toronto: University of Toronto Press (Macdonald Commission Study No. 13,

1985). Even though Harris underlines the limitations of the classical approach to international trade, his entry barriers approach still focuses unduly on the trade side of the economy and ignores the institutional fabric except as it generates barriers to trade.

39. The 100-million market as a necessary basis for achieving economies of scale is an argument one finds everywhere in the free traders' prose. It was there already in the 1982 Senate Report (Standing Committee on Foreign Affairs, Vol. III). It is repeated by A.J. Sarna, "The Impact of a Canada-U.S. Free Trade Area," *Journal of Common Market Studies*, 23, 4, June 1985, p. 302, but also by Richard G. Lipsey, "Will There Be . . .", p. 225, and by a large number of participants in that free trade debate.

40. For instance James de Wilde, "Global Competitor or Farmteam Economy: Canada's Real Trade Debate," *Business Quarterly*, Winter 1985, p. 37-40. Even those who have been leaning toward free trade as the favored option have expressed concerns about the weakness of the argument when it relies exclusively on scale economies (Ian M. Drummond, "On Disbelieving the Commissioners' Free Trade Case," *Canadian Public Policy*, 12, Supplement, Feb. 1986, pp. 59-67.)

41. This argument has been made by Ian M. Drummond, "On Disbelieving . . .". There have been many challenges to this representation of free trade as a necessary/sufficient condition to ensure efficiency and of the suggestion that efficiency is a necessary/sufficient condition for increased welfare. Some have argued that free trade is not sufficient (Richard G. Harris, *Trade, Industrial Policy* . . ., but also Pierre Paul Proulx, "Free Trade is not Enough," *Policy Options*, January 1986, pp. 11-15). Others have challenged the link between efficiency and welfare for the very reasons mentioned in section 3.B.(3). They claim that other goals are more clearly correlated with the welfare of the population. The priorities may differ among those opponents to free trade (need to preserve our independent use of policy instruments – J. Laxer; need to design an industrial strategy – S. Smith; need to combat unemployment and poverty – E. Kierans; cultural objectives – B. Anthony) but the agreement is that efficiency considerations cannot be regarded as sufficient to lead to increased welfare.

42. On the notion of scientific tariff, see Harry G. Johnson, "The Cost of Protection and the Scientific Tariff" *Journal of Political Economy*, 68, 4, August 1960, pp. 327-345. Economic history provides ample evidence of both imperialism through protection **and** through free trade. Albert O. Hirschman, *National Power and the Structure of Foreign Trade*, (Berkeley, California: University of California Press, 1945) has shown how Nazi Germany used trade relations and protection for the purpose of domination and penetration in Southeast Europe and elsewhere. John Gallagher & Ronald Robinson "The Imperialism of Free Trade," *Economic History Review*, 6, 1, 1953, pp. 1-15 have shown how one of the most common political techniques of British expansion in the nineteenth century was "the treaty of free trade and friendship made with or imposed upon a weaker state." Therefore one cannot necessarily associate free trade with benefits, and protection with costs, mechanically. Each country must design the mix of free

trade and protection that suits its priorities. In the free trade debate of the last few years, this simple groundtruth has seemingly been forgotten.

43.   For a critical examination of this sort of economic sophistry conveniently putting aside the well-known principle that reducing the tariff on an input increases effective protection, see Harry G. Johnson, *The Canadian Quandary*, (Toronto: McGraw Hill, 1963), Chapter 11.

44.   Ronald A. Shearer, "The New Face of Canadian Mercantilism: The Macdonald Commission and the Case for Free Trade," *Canadian Public Policy*, 12, Supplement, February 1986, pp. 50-58.

45.   S. Reisman, "Canada-United States Trade at the Crossroads: Options for Growth," *The Canadian Business Review*, 12, 3, Autumn 1985, p. 19. A. Westell, "Economic Integration . . .", p. 22.

46.   For samples of the irony of the anti-free trade argument, J. Laxer, *Leap of Faith* . . ., Chapter 1; M. Hurtig, "Giving Away the Store," *Canadian Business*, 58, 6, 1985, pp. 265-271. Even the labour movement would appear to have been persuaded that free trade would mean state action being reduced (Bob Baldwin, "Free Trade, Deregulation and Privatization" *Canadian Labour*, 31, 4, 1986, pp. 6-7). For a review of the different ways in which the state will expand as a result of free trade (negotiations necessary, state agencies and rules to operate what has been arrived at, adjudication mechanisms, adjustment policies, etc.) see G.B. Doern, *The Regulatory Process* . . . .

47.   This document was published in the *Toronto Star* on September 20, 1985. Excerpts are telling: "The popular interpretation of free trade appears to be keyed to the word 'free.' It is something for nothing – a short cut – to economic prosperity. It is bigger markets for Canadian products, more jobs, more of everything. It is, as Terrence Wills of *The Gazette* puts it, having your cake and eating it too. The strategy should rely less on educating the general public than on getting across the message that the trade initiative is a good idea. In other words, a selling job." Late in 1986, this document has been reprinted in a book of readings attempting to collect a representative sample of the documents generated by the free trade debate. D. Cameron (ed), *The Free Trade Papers*, (Toronto: Lorimer, 1986). A.N.T. Varzeliotis (*Requiem for Canada*, Vancouver: Alcyone Books, 1985, Ch. 21) has analyzed the strategy document as an invitation to "keep the people ignorant, impact upon them false impressions, prevent the opposition from exposing myths, encourage apathy and rule the society." (p. 296).

48.   Some of the material in this section has been developed more fully in G. Paquet, "Le goût de l'improbable", sections 4-5.

49.   A sketch of this methodology is available in John B. Thompson, *Critical Hermeneutics: A Study in the Thought of Paul Ricoeur and Jürgen Habermas*, (Cambridge: Cambridge University Press, 1981), pp. 173ff. Some interesting examples of the manner in which such a methodology might be implemented are provided by Pierre Bourdieu, *Esquisse d'une théorie de la pratique*, (Genève: Droz,

1972), Deuxième partie. Another example of the use of this methodology at the macroscopic level might be Interfuturs, *Face au futur: pour une maîtrise du vraisemblable et une gestion de l'imprévisible*, (Paris: OECD 1979).

50. For a simple introduction to hermeneutics and a sketch of the manner in which Jürgen Habermas has used it in a manner parallel to Freudian analysis, see R.J. Anderson, J.A. Hughes, W.W. Sharrock, *Philosophy and the Human Sciences*, (London: Croon Helm, 1986), Ch. 3. We have drawn from their presentation (pp. 76-81) in the next few paragraphs.

51. For a lucid analysis of the parallel between neurosis and schizophrenia in the individual and ideology and false consciousness at the social level, see Joseph Gabel, *La fausse conscience; essai sur la réification*. (Paris: Minuit, 1962).

52. For a critical evaluation of the flaws of the language of progress, see Alberto G. Ramos, *The New Science of Organizations; A Reconceptualization of the Wealth of Nations*, (Toronto: University of Toronto Press, 1981). On the language of needs, see Michael Ignatief, *The Needs of Strangers*, (New York: Viking, 1985). See also F. Schick, *Having Reasons — An Essay on Rationality and Sociality*, (Princeton: Princeton University Press, 1984).

53. For a sense of what these concepts refer to see John Friedmann, *The Good Society*, (Cambridge: MIT Press, 1979); S.C. Kolm, *La bonne économie*, (Paris: Presses Universitaires de France, 1984). Any major departure from those norms would constitute a "deformation of social space" (L.M. Lachmann, *The Legacy of Max Weber*, Berkeley: The Glendessary Press 1971, p. 83.) One may regard, in this context, policy-making as the elimination of misfits or the search for a good fit (C. Alexander, *De la synthèse de la forme, essai*, Paris: Dunod, 1971).

54. David W. Slater, "Economic Policy and Economic Research in Canada since 1950," *Queen's Quarterly*, 74, 1, 1967, pp. 1-20. One might make the same argument about social policy or social change in general. A case in point of a fundamental change in which social scientists played little or no role is the civil rights movement in the United States (M.L. King, "The Role of the Behavioral Scientist in the Civil Rights Movement," *Journal of Social Issues*, 24, 1, 1968, pp. 1-12.

55. Such a model is sketched in J. Friedmann & G. Abonyi, "Social Learning: A Model for Policy Research," *Environment & Planning* A, 1976, 8, p. 933. The "paradigm of social practice" is stylized as a process of intercreation between the following four sub-processes: theory of reality, political strategy, social values, social action.

> "These processes come to life only in the context of a concrete situation, and they are so connected that a change in any one of them will necessarily affect all others, either producing a substantive change or confirming the existing practice."

56. John Friedmann, "The Epistemology of Social Practice: A Critique of Objective Knowledge," *Theory and Society*, 6, 1, July 1978, p. 86. For those schooled in positivism, such a statement may appear rather vague and all encompassing. It should be clear however that the exploration of those dimensions is more apt to

generate useful knowledge than the attitude in good currency that leads one to declare not answerable and therefore irrelevant questions intractable with their disciplinary tools.

57.   John Friedmann & G. Abonyi, "Social Learning..." p. 939. On the manner in which one might implement such transactive planning, see J. Friedmann, *Retracking America: Theory of Transactive Planning*, (New York: Doubleday, 1973).

58.   Richard G. Lipsey, "Will There Be...," p. 235.

59.   A general statement about a policy of fair trade has been sketched in Christian Mégrelis, *Keys for the Future: From Free Trade to Fair Trade* (Lexington, Mass., Lexington Books, 1980).

60.   The expression is used in A.N.T. Varzeliotis, *Requiem for Canada*, (Preface).

61.   This is a policy that imposes a sort of market test on the funding of research by the federal government. The granting councils will get additional money only to match funding by the private sector. This should put the demand for social science research through a market test from which social scientists should emerge somewhat humbled. For the details of that policy, see *Strengthening the Private Sector/University Research Partnership — The Matching Policy Rules*, Ottawa, 1986.

62.   Donald A. Schön, *The Reflective Practitioner; How Professionals Think in Action*, (New York: Basic Books, 1983), p. 69.

63.   On the recent evolution of physics and its departure from naive physicalism, see R.S. Jones, *Physics as Metaphor*, (New York: Meridian, 1983).

And Common Sense is No Port in a Storm:
A Comment on Gilles Paquet's Paper

Sharon Sutherland

I have listened to Professor Paquet's discussion of the contribution made by the discipline of economics to the debate over freer trade, rapt with enjoyment. As a political scientist now working in the area of public administration, whose main field of training was social psychology — that is, as someone who is almost dangerously eclectic — I in particular enjoyed his characterization of economics as a set of rules run by a guild. That guild and those rules have done remarkably little to really illuminate the various aspects of the debate over the feasibility and consequences of a bilateral agreement for much freer trade between Canada and the United States, Professor Paquet says, because the treatable sub-topics, the rules and routines of mainstream economics are terribly marginal to the really important facets of the debate.

Professor Paquet would have us — if I may telescope the gist of his talk — return to ordinary forms of discourse for this particular debate. We should substitute a more basic intellectual calculus for the trained lunacies of the econometrician, a calculus that would allow us to use non-quantifiable decision rules such as simple fairness.

All that really remains for me, being ardently in sympathy with the main lines of Professor Paquet's arguments, is to question whether or not faith in ordinary argument and educated good sense as a "method" better fitted to illuminate large political questions is indeed well-placed or misplaced.[1] Do we citizens who sincerely want to cope well with this complex political question really have any basis for thinking that we can do better with ordinary knowledge, and ordinary intellectual processes?

I am going to say that the most honest answer is no. The new-ish branch of social psychology that investigates cognitive routines — not just of ordinary people but of all people, including experts—has generated a number of telling insights into the human capacity to really think deeply and well. The basic finding is that our cognitive routines are exceedingly simple and fragile. In a computing analogy, people as "thinking machines" have immense amounts of core, but unreliable operating systems that can neither reliably address the information stored nor manage the power.[2] We run extremely small programs in these ambiguous big machines—programs using perhaps four or five variables. These programs, like the Stupid Peanut Program in the Usborne children's book on computing,[3] are ridden with flaws that lead to quixotic outcomes. Further, the human computer is subject to continual shorts of electricity and "brown-outs" which affect whether or not programs, once started, are executed. In addition, the whole wonderful set-up is assisted by a robot arm that habitually unplugs the whole apparatus at the first sign of a serious application.

Contrary to the rules of ordinary logic, but in keeping with the way we actually operate, people **can** have it both ways. We manage to plan to have everything, not by holding opposing principles in our minds at the same time and working out a transcending principle or even a new method of scheduling, but by thinking in fits and starts, one thing at a time, maximizing isolated values in succession—by being, as an economist might say, utterly inconsistent. As thinking machines, expert and inexpert alike, perhaps our major feat is what I would think of as inattention.

Ordinary knowledge, I am going to argue, naked of its emperor's clothes of quantitative economics, is not an Olympic athlete stripped for speed. It is, rather, a strange little Pinnochio with clumsy joints and one leg on backwards. Let me give an example of the kind of thinking of which ordinary people are normally capable. In the days before this conference I found myself in front of a large poster on the face of a voluntary social services agency on a street near my home. "Have you always wanted to read and write?" it asked me. Down the right side were listed for the reader all the life factors that literacy would affect: better job, a sense of control in one's relations with government, the ability to protect oneself in dealings with one's employer . . . On the left were provided for the writing passer-by the name and telephone numbers of the literacy coordinator of the society. Someone had actually forgotten that a written sign was not an appropriate way of reaching the unlettered for long enough to print the text and find a photo of the classroom.

Rather than portraying human cognitive limitations as poor programming, perhaps because the computing analogy is new, it has been customary in mainstream social psychology to pin most of the blame for the extremely limited role pure reason has been able to play in social affairs on the emotional motility of "mass man." The notion of "attitude" toward social objects as determining an individual's ultimate overt behaviour choices or action in that sphere dominated social psychology from the 1930s through to the 1970s[4]. Affect, although it has some cognitive determinants, is likely more accurately described as a psychic grunt than a clear thought. Thus, in classical attitude theory terms, whether or not a person will ultimately vote or even argue in favour of freer trade with the United States will be determined by an unexamined amalgam of largely accidental "found" impressions and emotions, owing little if anything to rigorous intellectual debate on the subject. Elites and specialists are thought to be subject to many of the same frailties, but more capable of improving their own rationality through retrospection. Even psychology of individual differences (except for academic psychology and its behavioural developments) has tended to regard ordinary man as tentatively or potentially ruled by reason, but more or less often subjected to overrides of passion, bursts of id through the civilized veneer of logic and reason. That is, "good logic" has generally been thought to be a state that is potentially attainable by well trained and well motivated people, even if it is not necessarily the normal state in which we go about most of our daily business.

What is really telling about the newer cognitive psychology is that it addresses **intrinsic** limitations to our capacity — ordinary people and experts alike — to do what we like to think of as "thinking clearly" and without bias. It addresses our limitations as thinking machines, leaving aside all the traditional assumptions as to the kinds of "human" (and sub-human) variables that were traditionally accepted as spoilers of normal/ideal functioning. Of course this kind of cognitive psychology is not really all that new, having many of its roots in the seminal piece by Miller, "The magical number seven, plus or minus two: Some limits on our capacity for processing information," which was published in 1956.[5] People, Miller showed, can, as a feat of memory rather than in preparation for any detailed analysis or comparison, hold in mind only four to nine simple elements at a time. And, as all list-writers know, in ordinary life many of us do not remember so many as two or three things we may set out to do.[6]

Working from Miller's propositions, other cognitive psychologists have shown that even aspiring experts are not all expert when it comes to integration of disparate bits of knowledge. That is, even the people who deliberately set out to consume specialized information will have grave difficulties in "fairly" assimilating it. Once affect, that psychic grunt, is embedded, its general character as simple approval or disapproval holds. Not only the Bourbons were like the Bourbons — forgetting nothing and learning nothing. People are Bourbons.

Sadler, in a piece titled "Intuitive data processing as a potential source of bias in naturalistic evaluations," talks about typical errors the mind is likely to make even once it has self-consciously begun a process of judgment and inference.[7] One can paraphrase his main conclusions. The unassisted mind — that is, the thinker bereft of equations and the straitjacket rules of the guild — suffers very quickly from data overload. The restructuring of information into different (fewer and cruder) categories is about the only way to increase the amount of information held simultaneously.[8] In a way, the choice of beginning categories importantly pre-figures the finding or outcome of the cognitive process. Second, the power of first impressions, i.e. "anchoring" of affect, is profound. Next, the colour of evidence is important — we seize on any evidence with novelty value or bizarre interest and over-weight it. We are blind to disconfirming instances, rather ruthlessly selecting information to confirm our favoured (first) hypotheses. As thinkers, we also over-weight extreme data, forgetting about middle values or instances that ring in at an average for that phenomenon. Perhaps most important, we suffer from premature closure: once we have begun to see any kind of a pattern in our evidence and in our categories, we tend to quickly sketch it in and become basically unable to continue processing. Thus even the simple conditional "do loop" in programming is an advance on ordinary logic: computers do not routinely become bored. Finally, we suffer from extreme over-confidence in our own capacities as assessors and predictors. In short, ordinary thinking is rich and racy stuff in comparison to formal treatments of the same subjects because it is supremely unpredictable and supremely indifferent to its own totemic decision rules.

Even when we try to calm ourselves with decision rules and groups of respected colleagues, we do not do very well. L.R. Goldberg in the late 1960s and early 1970s, Robin Dawes writing in 1971 and 1976, and David Faust, writing in 1982, have provided interesting work that suggests that even very simple formulae are at least as good as impressionistic human judgments arrived at after great labour and deliberation, and are still better if executed by a computer than by a person. In his piece "Shallow Psychology," Dawes reports briefly on his earlier work on graduate admissions. A three-variable formula could have screened out 55 per cent of all students who would eventually be refused entry on the expensive and time-consuming basis of personal interviews and committee assessments of qualifications. It eliminated none who would eventually be admitted.[9] Faust's work was with radiologists who were asked to use seven major signs of malignant gastric ulcer in diagnosis. Eighteen professionals viewed nearly 200 X-rays, each X-ray for each case being presented twice. Test re-test by the same person was reported at .6, and the average correlation between all pairs of radiologists was .38.[10] Goldberg has shown that computers can improve the consistency of decisions by revisiting them with algorithms drawn from the decider's very own criteria.[11] The process is called bootstrapping – the computer picks us up by our bootstraps.

Slovic, in 1966, and later working with MacPhillamy in 1974, has dedicated himself to showing that most individuals are unable to perform what is called "configural analysis," where elements are held in a more complex relation to one another than a simple linear, time dependent story-telling. Indeed, people are very often unable to integrate even two or three simple clues to solve a problem.[12] In fact, most non-linear strategies are quite radically simplifying strategies that people resort to in order to lessen cognitive strain. One can recall the hero's decision in *Raiders of the Lost Ark* to shoot a challenger rather than respond to a dazzlingly complex display of swordsmanship.

Finally, Faust argues that, in principle, simultaneous group attacks on a problem do little to advance our knowledge. That is, "wars" on drugs, poverty, tariffs and so forth do not suddenly help advance hard problems: ". . . the combined working of minds does not make possible the comprehension of patterns at a level of complexity beyond that which the single most complicated mind can grasp."[13] The process of science[14] works to the extent that it does because it consists of sequential critiques in which people teach themselves each stage before they move on to the next.

The overall conclusions, then, seem quite clear. First, Donald Macdonald's prescription for a "leap of faith" into freer trade with the United States does not seem so absurd. It may have been his best guess after working with many factors over a long time and realizing that he was going in circles, perhaps each of them slightly different but nevertheless too sickeningly similar to keep processing. Second, maybe we shouldn't "decide" suddenly in 1988, after a big push of research and discussion, to sign an agreement. A decision is an artificially rushed process which means that it will often be wrong. That is, massing evidence and argument is not a substitute for developing a critique over time. So let's not sign. Let's not even decide. But if we have to, if only because politicians become hyperactive at election time, let's work out the criteria as closely as possible, weight them with great care – and let a computer make the ultimate decision.

Notes

1. Most of the other social "sciences," apart from some streams of psychology, are generally characterizable as guilds frantically in search of a set of rules.

2. We, of course, build computers in something like our own idealized image. Compaq's new desk-top computer has four or five jigabites of memory in a world where the most memory that any disk operating system can handle is something like 640 K. The hardware outstrips the software. Like people, it needs a DOS.

3. Brian Reffin Smith, *Usborne Guide to Computers: A simple and colourful introduction for beginners*, London: Usborne, 1981.

4. See S.L. Sutherland, *Patterns of Belief and Action*, University of Toronto Press, 1981. It would be more true to say that the attitude concept has been abandoned, rather than effectively discredited, which means that it will likely become the rage again in 15 to 20 years.

5. G.A. Miller, in *Psychological Review 63* (1956) pp. 81-97.

6. There is help available all the way up to five or nine. See Alan Baddelely, *Your Memory: A user's guide*, New York: Macmillan, 1982.

7. D.R. Sadler, in *Educational Evaluation and Policy-Making 3*, (1981) pp. 25-31. See also Lee Ross and Mark R. Lepper, "The Perseverance of Beliefs: Empirical and Normative Considerations," *New Directions for Methodology of Social and Behavioral Science*, 4 (1980) pp. 17-36. The references for their article are particularly varied and interesting.

8. One can speculate that the reason that people always divide a topic up into three or four aspects is that that is as many as they can remember – or that they think we can handle.

9. Robyn Dawes, "A case study of graduate admissions: Application of three principles of human decision-making," *American Psychologist* 26 (1971) pp. 180-188, and "Shallow Psychology," in John S. Carroll and John W. Payne (eds.) *Cognition and Social Behavior*, New York: John Wiley, 1976, pp. 3-11. In the latter piece Dawes provides a useful round-up of studies to that date.

10. So don't let your doctor discourage you. See D. Faust, "A needed component in prescriptions for science: Empirical knowledge of human cognitive limitations," *Knowledge 3*, pp. 555-570.

11.   L.R. Goldberg, "Man versus model of man: A rationale, plus some evidence, for a method of improving clinical inferences," *Psychological Bulletin*, 73 (1970), pp. 422-432.

12.   See Paul Slovic and Douglas MacPhillamy, "Dimensional commensurability and cue utilization in comparative judgment," *Organizational Behavior and Human Performance 11* (1974) pp. 172-194.

13.   *Op. cit.*, p. 564.

14.   Unaided by either computer or other researchers, I have also been puzzling about why the natural sciences progress while the social sciences engage in largely repetitive cycles of reasoning moved along by fads and collegial fits of inattention. Part of the answer, I think, is in the social scientist's "ordinary knowledge" idea of what would constitute a solution to any given dilemma, like the question of whether and how Canada should join with the United States. First it must be new, illuminating, and of the same power and scope as the most traditional definition of the problem, it must be simple and clear enough to explain to each other over coffee, it must be rational along contemporary lines of definition and it must subsume any trade-offs that would smack of politics — that is, it must make political discourse unnecessary.

An Economist in Wonderland: Comments on Papers by Watkins and Paquet

Richard G. Lipsey

Probably the most interesting message that I derive from the contributions to this volume is the difference between the political scientists' and the mainline economists' perceptions of the issues involved in the great Canadian free trade debate. This volume gives a sampling of views of political scientists and political economists; the reader must go elsewhere to read in detail the contrasting views of mainline economists.

It is high time that someone convened a conference in which political scientists and mainline economists discussed in detail the bases for their radically different typical perceptions of the issues. Disagreement would, of course, remain at the end of such an interchange, as it always does on any complex social issue, but the open-minded in both groups would gain from subjecting their views to such critical assessment — particularly where each group deals with issues that are part of the particular expertise of the other group.

I could not carry out such a task single-handedly under any circumstances, and certainly not in the space allotted for one reactive comment. (I was not a contributor to the original series that gave rise to this publication). Neither can I present the economic arguments for bilateral trade liberalization in the space available; for that I must refer readers to other publications (my bibliography gives some of the relevant material). Here I can do no more than make a few marginal comments on two of the papers in this volume.

The Watkins Paper

Mel Watkins provides some interesting perspectives on the arguments of those who oppose bilateral trade liberalization with the United States. His comments are, as always, thought provoking. Readers should be warned, however, that he often appears to be speaking facetiously — which is good fun for those who know the facts, but potentially misleading for those who come to this volume to learn. Here are a few examples.

In his second paragraph Watkins writes, "the United States put a countervailing duty on Canadian lumber and Canada replied with punitive duty on American corn." Of course, Watkins knows that in both countries countervail proceedings are initiated by complaints from the private sector and that they take a year or more to grind to a final result. The proceedings in the corn case were initiated by a complaint by the Ontario corn producers and were under way long before the preliminary decision by the U.S. Department of Commerce on softwood lumber. Although the Canadian government's subsidy decision on corn came after the U.S. subsidy calculation on softwood lumber, Canada applied narrower and stricter criteria for calculation on subsidies. The unwary reader could be forgiven, however, for concluding that the Canadian duty was levied in response to the American one.

On page 154 we read that "... with GATT negotiations under way again, one of the reasons given initially by the Canadian government for proceeding bilaterally — that the multilateral road was blocked — is no longer valid." As we all know, few, if anyone, inside or outside the government thought that the negotiations would not take place. What many thought, and still think, is that the prospects are poor that the negotiation will produce a significant liberalization of trade in goods and services.

On page 154, we hear that with a free trade area (FTA) "American protectionism, by incorporating Canada, becomes North American protectionism." This, of course, confuses a free trade area, under which Canada and the United States have their own individual trade barriers against third countries, with a customs union, which requires a common set of trade barriers against third countries. The reason why the Canadian government is pursuing an FTA rather than a customs union is that it wishes to preserve its autonomy with respect to the trade policy that it directs at third countries — as do the members of all other free trade associations in existence today.

In the next paragraph, we read that "only Washington knows for sure" whether the free trade talks will succeed. Given the early confusion in the American camp on what its demands would be, a confusion that was due to a deficiency of in-depth preparation which was in sharp contrast to the enormous preparation on the Canadian side, the suggestion that the Americans knew exactly what they wanted at the time that Watkins was writing, let alone whether or not they would get it, is not even exaggeration, it is distortion. In any case, who is "Washington"? As Watkins well knows, one of the problems of dealing with the Americans generally is that the administration often speaks with one voice while the Congress speaks with several other voices. In this specific case, it is almost certainly true that what a representative member of the administration wants from the Canadian negotiations is very different from what a representative congressional committee member wants.

Having alerted readers, I will forbear from boring them with further examples of amusing statements that are, presumably, not meant to be taken seriously.

An issue that runs through much of Watkins' comments is that "(t)he proposition – that free trade is a necessary and sufficient condition for economic prosperity – has been well and truly tested . . . and has been found woefully wanting." Of course, someone can always be found who has advocated any unreasonable or silly view that one cares to mention. So I am sure Watkins could fill in the missing references of those who hold the view of necessity and sufficiency. However, I know none whom I regard as serious researchers who do. I try to be careful in pointing out that liberalizing trade with the United States is not a **sufficient** reason for anything (see Lipsey 1987, p. 51) – although I am more careful now than I used to be since it did not occur to me earlier in the debate that such an unreasonable view would be ascribed to supporters of a Canadian American Free Trade Association (CAFTA).

I do not believe that Watkins is correct in saying that orthodox economic theory predicts that trade restrictions are negatively associated with the domestic growth rate – although some orthodox economists do believe that proposition. Comparative advantage is a static theorem about the efficiency of resource allocation. There is no economic theory of which I am aware that forges a **necessary** causal link between efficiency of resource allocation and growth – although circumstances can be posited under which such an association will exist and under which that association will either be negative or positive.

Under the headings of human capital and dynamic comparative advantage, modern theory gives good reasons why protecting the home market in order to build up an industrial base and acquire the necessary human capital – defined in the broadest sense to include attitudes as well as skills – may be the fastest route to growth. (For a recent detailed discussion see Lipsey and Dobson 1986). Particularly for a small country, however, there is a presumption that once this early stage is past, the best route to further growth is to lower trade restrictions and integrate the domestic economy into world trade, letting those industries that have succeeded prosper while those that have not shrink. This is the route followed by most of the so called newly industrializing countries (the NICs). Thus, there is nothing inconsistent in approving of both Canada's policy of maintaining high tariffs until 1935 and of slowly lowering tariffs after that date (a policy that a CAFTA would bring very near to completion).

The above discussion illustrates that at least one orthodox economist believes that **no** single economic policy will be a necessary and sufficient condition for achieving **any** broad social goal. Those who argue otherwise are rarely the serious researchers and those who argue against those who argue otherwise are usually attacking straw men.

As Watkins points out, Britain's economic history since its entry to the European Community (EC) certainly refutes those who hold the naive "necessary and sufficient" view. As far as Britain's decline, which was a concern to observers as far back as the first decade of the twentieth century, I personally think that Ralf Dahrendorf (1982) got as close as anyone to an explanation when he analyzed the British rejection of the values of the new industrial class that was spawned by the industrial revolution, a rejection that was in sharp contrast to the acceptance of those values that occurred in the United States and, to a lesser extent, in continental Europe.

Having played some small part in the debate about Britain's entry into the EC (which, along with my good friend Harry Johnson, I opposed), I disagree with Watkins that the rhetoric being used in the current debate is similar to that used in the earlier British debate. In the United Kingdom, there was concern over the long-term failure of the British economy to compete and over what was thought of as a failure of both business and labour to adopt modes of behaviour that encouraged growth. The chill winds of foreign competition were advocated as a shock to force a change in basic economic and social behaviour. At the time I pointed out the deficiencies in this view and argued (see Lipsey 1967) that the failure of British policy in the 1960s led

> to a search for a panacea — to the search for a mystical formula that would solve all the problems at one swoop. This panacea became the common market. ... most of the arguments in favour of our (i.e., the United Kingdom) joining the common market was suitable to a mystical solution to an intractible problem.

Aside from believing that a little more competition was not going to change such deep-rooted social attitudes as were studied by Dahrendorf, many of us who opposed Britain's entry believed that the British economy was too rigid in its capacity to adjust, partly because of economic and social policies that resisted change and partly because of social attitudes.) We feared, therefore, that a severe shock might do more harm than good. The chill winds of competition may be salutory if the recipient is healthy enough to be braced by them and harmful if the recipient is not in such good shape. All of which illustrates that, contrary to the allegations of many of our opponents, supporters of a CAFTA do not all blindly advocate the same cure for all illnesses. Just as the punishment should fit the crime, so should the economic prescription fit the economic condition.

The Canadian case is different from the British case. Supporters of a CAFTA do not see the need for the chill winds of foreign competition to revitalize a moribund business community and to discipline a recalcitrant labor force. Instead, proponents of a CAFTA tend to believe that Canadian business is already able to compete with American business. What is needed, they argue, is security of access to the American market to prevent the all-too-successful Canadian exporters from securing that access by emigrating to the United States — as they are currently doing in disturbingly large numbers.

At the time of its entry into the EC, Britain already had secure access to the European market by virtue of its membership in the European Free Trade Association (EFTA); Canada has no such secure access to the United States. At the time of its entry many believed, and rightly in my opinion, that the British economy was too rigid to withstand a major shock without very serious repercussions; this is not, I believe, true of Canada as a whole, although I worry about the Atlantic provinces. So, under different circumstances, I advocate different behaviour: I think Britain should have stayed out of the EC in 1974, and that Canada should form an FTA with the United States in 1987.

Another important issue touched on by Watkins, and one on which the Macdonald commission is particularly weak, is the effects of a CAFTA on regional inequalities. In a static neo-classical world, markets work to equalize the net advantages among regions. (Note that they do not equalize monetary advantages; if people prefer to live in the Atlantic provinces, then equilibrium average income will be lower in the Atlantic provinces than in the central ones). The late Nobel Laureate, Gunnar Myrdal, has championed the dynamic theory of cumulative causation. According to this theory, drastic reductions in trade barriers between several regions allow the already dominant areas to pull in capital and talent from the peripheral areas, making the strong regions more prosperous and the weak regions poorer. Thus, although liberalizing trade might raise average living standards, it is likely, according to this theory, to exaggerate regional differences in living standards.

Of course such a complex (and interesting) issue is not easily handled, but there is some evidence relating to it. It will surprise only the committed dogmatists on both sides to learn that there are cases in which freer trade seems to have frozen or exacerbated existing inequalities, and cases in which it seems to have reduced them.

The evidence, however, is not easy to interpret. First, other things besides changes in trade rules are going on. For example, Britain's industrial decline predated its entry into the EC by decades and few can doubt that the fate of Manchester and Liverpool would have been much different if Britain had stayed out of the EC and the EFTA (although the fate of the now-booming southeast, an area which includes London, would probably have been different). Second, public policy affects the outcome. A plausible case can be made that much of the persistent regional inequality in Canada is the result of public policy which, although directed at ameliorating inequalities, actually exaggerates them. In this respect, the United States provides an interesting comparison. Here the index of regional inequality has not varied greatly over this century, but individual states have alternated between being towards the bottom and towards the top of the pecking order. Inequality has not been frozen as it has in Canada; instead individual states have typically gone through alternating periods of relative prosperity and relative decline. Of course, the issue is not settled but the existence of such different behaviour and of such different explanations, each with plausible factual support, shows that we can no more accept the proposition that freer trade will always increase regional inequalities than the proposition that it will always diminish them.

Watkins' treatment of the argument that a CAFTA will not cause a major loss of national sovereignty is a little wanting in depth. The argument will never advance and thus help those who wish to learn from it, if protagonists insist on attacking straw persons. The context in which the EC is quoted by advocates of a CAFTA is to point out that a vastly tighter association than is contemplated in a CAFTA has not led, and shows no sign of leading, to a political union or loss of national identity. For harmonizing pressures, which seem to me to be a more serious worry than political integration, the EFTA provides better evidence, since it is the model for a CAFTA (although, of course, no two historical cases are identical). The EFTA seems to have avoided serious unwanted harmonization pressures on domestic economic and social policies. (On the lessons for Canada from the EFTA, see Curzon Price 1987).

One of the important considerations is that Canada's sovereign ability to follow many of its current domestic policies is under severe attack now. This was illustrated in the softwood lumber case when a long-standing Canadian resource policy was suddenly and unilaterally declared an unfair trade practice by the United States, and Canada was forced to change that policy in self-defence. Supporters of a CAFTA argue that treaty-secured access to the United States would constrain **American** sovereignty by making it impossible for the United States to pressure Canada to change Canadian domestic policies by unilaterally declaring them to be unfair trade practices, as it did with softwood lumber.

Reasoned argument about this, and other important sovereignty issues, is to be welcomed. In a recent volume, Murray Smith and I (Lipsey & Smith 1986) have tried to address some of these issues in a way that they can be critically assessed. No doubt in the sovereignty issue, as in most other issues, it will be a case of winning some and losing some, so that a careful balance sheet of gains and losses will be needed in order to assess the net sovereignty effect of a CAFTA. But this calls for serious research rather than platform rhetoric.

Watkins buttresses his arguments on loss of sovereignty by referring to two essays in Volume 29 of the Macdonald commission's research reports (Stairs and Winham 1985) by Nossal and Pentland. I particularly enjoyed the Pentland essay—although I must record that the author makes two strong assertions about the economic effects of a CAFTA which run counter to much available evidence, while making no attempt to explain why the evidence can be dismissed. I leave the reader to judge between Watkins' view that Pentland's analysis (as distinct from his questionable assertions on economic matters) lends support to Watkins' argument and my view that it does no such thing.

The Paquet Paper

This paper is so rich in ideas that there is little I can do with it in a short space. Where it discusses methodology, a long critique would be necessary to go further and where it discusses free trade, each paragraph would need to be reconsidered and further references discussed.

The general thrust of the paper is a call for a new methodology in the social sciences. I am acutely aware of many of the shortcomings of methods currently used by economists. I wish the reformers good luck. In the meantime, I will go on using the current methods because, in spite of their all too evident shortcomings, they work better than any of the available alternatives. Indeed, new methods will replace the old ones when practitioners perceive that new methods give better results (broadly interpreted) than do the methods currently in use.

I would like to make just one point about Paquet's methodological criticism. In the usual zest for overstatement to be found in proselytes, Paquet tells us in his first paragraph that most attempts of social scientists to tackle "urgent and complex social issues." Let me mention four of the many cases to the contrary in which I have been involved personally.

First, recall the great debate between the structuralists and the Keynesians on how to alleviate American unemployment in the early 1960s. The Keynesians were finally victorious, their policies were adopted, and they worked. The debate also left a lasting set of still-useful concepts such as the full-employment deficit and the unemployment-creating bias of fiscally neutral growth.

Second, consider the debate about stagflation in the 1970s. Critics called for the abandonment of all conventional economic analysis – indeed with hindsight, it is hard to believe the extent to which the critics underestimated the resiliency of conventional economic theory. In the event, the working out of the full explanation, its integration into Keynesian macro-economic theory, and its incorporation into text books right down to the first-year level took less than a decade.

Finally, in the current debate over the causes of the U.S. trade deficit, mainline economists take the view that the deficit is largely the result of such macro-economic forces as the U.S. domestic budget deficit and the low U.S. savings ratio, and not the machinations of unfair foreign trading practices (which no doubt exist). I have little doubt that economists are right on this one and that the evidence in favour of their view is quite strong. (The various alternative explanations are laid out in Lipsey and Smith 1987).

One could go on at length. The moral is that denunciations of economics as being totally useless are as wide off the mark as are defences of it as being nearly perfect. If one wishes to have a rational assessment of its current social value, one needs to understand not only its failures, which Paquet points out, but also its successes, of which Paquet's readers are left ignorant.

Let us now pass to Paquet's specific theme: "social scientists as persuaders have failed miserably in the free trade debate." He uses this theme to assert – I hesitate to say argue an anti-free trade position. Indeed, when Paquet comes to consider matters of economics, he seems to me to provide an example of the kinds of treatment that he castigates in others. Again I have space for only a few isolated issues.

Consider first his treatment of the "mythical 100-million market." First, he gives no example of the "small open economies that have succeeded in doing extremely well even without full access to a market of 100 million." So we cannot assess his assertions because we do not know their subject. Second, he does not even consider the reasons advanced for worrying about the lack of secure Canadian access to such a market – the shift in Canadian exports from primary products to manufacturing products and the disturbing exodus of Canadian manufacturing firms who are successful in the North American market and who go to the U.S. to avoid American trade barriers. (I have briefly considered these reasons in Lipsey 1987). Third, the technological changes to which he refers permit small markets to be economic for individual **product lines** but still seem to require large markets and multiple product lines for individual **firms**.

Paquet also tells us that "the trick of the free trade promoters has been to force the argument on the grounds of competitiveness and efficiency and to presume that employment growth and welfare are **necessary** consequences flowing from efficiency." I find it hard to reconcile this assertion with the list of advantages given on page 78-81 of Lipsey and Smith 1985. (See also my earlier discussion of this issue in relation to the Watkins' paper).

Paquet tells us that "the notion of free trade has maintained throughout a certain strategic vagueness **cultured carefully** by all participants. Attempts to promote other versions . . . have been perceived as decoys for the real thing and never could take hold" (boldface added). This travesty ignores the reason why the issue has been referred to as one of free trade. As pointed out by Lipsey and Smith (1985), free trade is an unachievable ideal, while the real debate is about reducing trade barriers in a number of dimensions. However, some term has to be used to describe it, and "free trade" is used because that is the name the CAFTA will be known by when, and if, the two governments apply for exemption under GATT Article XXIV so that their bilateral tariff cuts will not be subject to the GATT's normal most-favoured-nation requirement.

Of the countless other statements which could be debated, let me choose just one more. Paquet tells his readers that I labelled opposition to the free trade association based on concern about the "coherence and permanence of the existing Canadian social order (being) jeopardized by an economic *rapprochement* with the United States" as "visceral rather than intellectual." If I believed that, Lipsey and Smith (1985) would not have contained an entire chapter entitled "Political and Cultural Concerns." In that chapter, we tried to treat these issues as subjects for rational debate, hoping not to say the last word on the subject, but to say enough to get the debate on a plane where it could be rationally discussed. The "visceral" quotation comes from Lipsey (1986) where I said that "when all of the rational arguments (on economic, political, social and cultural issues) have been heard and discussed, a deeper Canadian opposition is found at a visceral, rather than an intellectual, level." I now add the same comment about a deeper Canadian support. Can anyone doubt that this comment can be made about our opposition to, or support for, any complex social issue? The moral of this discussion to me is that those who would be highly critical of the nature of the debate should be very careful of their own quality control.

What surprises and depresses me most about this essay is how the author of such a sweeping denunciation of the debate could ignore so many of the economic writings that try to get the debate focused onto specific questions which are amenable to rational debate and on which evidence might be brought to bear. There is substantial work by the Economic Council of Canada on the adjustment issue (see 1983 for one example). There is much work by Ed Saffarian on the foreign investment issue (see 1985 example). There was a serious three-day conference by the Ontario Economic Council (1985) that ranged over many issues. Murray Smith and I (1985) wrote an entire book on the subject in which we tried to treat the issues seriously and invite reasoned criticism and which, it is worth noting since Paquet is interested in the process of the debate, was widely read and apparently influential in Ottawa. The C.D. Howe Institute hosted a symposium on the important issue of harmonization in which Smith and I (1986) tried to come to grips with the mechanisms by which harmonization pressures might be felt, and several other experts examined various specific harmonization issues. The list could be extended to some considerable length, yet all of the items on it are ignored by Paquet who chooses from my extensive writings on the subject to notice but one descriptive piece that I wrote to explain in general terms to a European audience what I thought was at issue in the great Canadian debate.

I am an advocate of a free trade deal with the United States. But this is a complex social issue and I may be wrong in believing that it would, on balance, be a benefit to our country. Views such as mine can only be challenged effectively by considered attempts to rational criticism. It is more than a little depressing to find someone dismissing the debate as a failure while failing to notice any of the serious attempts made by economists to treat it as a subject for rational discourse, let alone to meet the arguments and evidence that they have advanced.

References

Curzon Price, V. 1987. *Free Trade Areas, The European Experience: What Lessons for Canadian-U.S. Free Trade?* (Toronto: C.D. Howe Institute).

Dahrendorf, R. 1982. *On Britain* (London: British Broadcasting Corporation).

Economic Council of Canada. 1983. *The Bottom Line: Technology, Trade and Income Growth*, (Ottawa, Supply and Services, Canada).

Lipsey, R.G. and Dobson, W. (eds.). 1986. *Shaping Comparative Advantage* (Toronto: C.D. Howe Institute).

Lipsey, R.G. 1967. "The Balance of Payments and the Common Market," *Economics*, Vol. 7., No. 3, pp. 5-17.

_____ 1986. "Will There be a Canadian-American Free Trade Association," *The World Economy*, Vol. 9, No. 3, pp. 217-238.

_____ 1987. "The Economics of a Canadian-American Free Trade Association," in *The Future on the Table: Canada and the Free Trade Issue*, M.O. Henderson (ed.) (Toronto: Masterpress).

Lipsey, R.G., and Smith, M.G. 1985. *Taking the Initiative: Canada's Trade Options in a Turbulent World*, (Toronto: C.D. Howe Institute).

_____ 1986. "Preface: An Introductory Overview" and "Chapter 1: An Overview of Harmonization Issues", *Policy Harmonization: The Effects of a Canadian-American Free Trade Area* (Toronto: C.D. Howe Institute).

_____ 1987. *Global Imbalances and U.S. Policy Responses: Implications for Canadian U.S. Relations*, (Washington: Canadian-American Committee).

Ontario Economic Council. 1985. *Canadian Trade at Crossroads: Options for New International Agreements*, D.W. Conklin and T.J. Courchene (eds.).

Saffarian, A.E. "The Relation Between Trade Agreements and International Direct Investment," Ontario Economic Council (1985) as cited above.

Stairs, D., and Winham, G.R. 1985. *The Politics of Canada's Economic Relations with the United States*, (Toronto: University of Toronto Press).

Contributors

John Baldwin, Queen's University, Kingston

David Barrows, Government of Ontario, Toronto

Mark Boudreau, Government of Ontario, Toronto

Peter Cornell, Economic Council of Canada

Donald J. Daly, York University, North York

Richard G. Lipsey, Queen's University, Kingston and the C.D. Howe Institute, Toronto

Allan M. Maslove, Carleton University, Ottawa

Gilles Paquet, University of Ottawa

Denis Stairs, Dalhousie University, Halifax

Sharon Sutherland, Carleton University, Ottawa

Michael J. Trebilcock, University of Toronto

Mel Watkins, University of Toronto

Bruce W. Wilkinson, University of Alberta, Edmonton

Glen Williams, Carleton University, Ottawa

Stanley L. Winer, Carleton University, Ottawa

Gilbert R. Winham, Dalhousie University, Halifax

Related Publications Available
–June 1988

Order Address

The Institute for Research on Public Policy
P.O. Box 3670 South
Halifax, Nova Scotia
B3J 3K6

Keith A.J. Hay (ed.)	*Canadian Perspectives on Economic Relations With Japan.* 1980 $18.95 ISBN 0 920380 72 7
Donald J. Daly	*Canada in an Uncertain World Economic Environment.* 1982 $3.00 ISBN 0 920380 07 7
Rodney de C. Grey	*United States Trade Policy Legislation: A Canadian View.* 1982 $7.95 ISBN 0 920380 86 7
John Quinn & Philip Slayton (eds.)	*Non-Tariff Barriers After the Tokyo Round.* 1982 $17.95 ISBN 0 920380 61 1
Douglas D. Purvis (ed.), assisted by Frances Chambers	*The Canadian Balance of Payments: Perspectives and Policy Issues.* 1983 $24.95 ISBN 0 920380 83 2

Roy A. Matthews	*Canada and the "Little Dragons": An Analysis of Economic Developments in Hong Kong, Taiwan, and South Korea and the Challenge/Opportunity They Present for Canadian Interests in the 1980s.* 1983 $11.95 ISBN 0 920380 87 5
Charles Pearson & Gerry Salembier	*Trade, Employment, and Adjustment.* 1983 $5.00 ISBN 0 920380 89 1
F.R. Flatters & R.G. Lipsey	*Common Ground for the Canadian Common Market.* 1983 $5.00 ISBN 0 920380 92 1
Yoshi Tsurumi with Rebecca R. Tsurumi	*Sogoshosha: Engines of Export-Based Growth.* (Revised Edition). 1984 $10.95 ISBN 0 88645 008 X
Frank Stone	*Canada, The GATT and the International Trade System.* 1984 $15.00 ISBN 0 88645 004 7
Pierre Sauvé	*Private Bank Lending and Developing-Country Debt.* 1984 $10.00 ISBN 0 88645 009 8
Samuel Wex	*Instead of FIRA: Autonomy for Canadian Subsidiaries?* 1984 $8.00 ISBN 0 88645 012 8
R.J. Wonnacott	*Selected New Developments in International Trade Theory.* 1984 $7.00 ISBN 0 88645 010 1
R.J. Wonnacott	*Aggressive US Reciprocity Evaluated with a New Analytical Approach to Trade Conflicts.* 1984 $8.00 ISBN 0 88645 011 X
Richard W. Wright	*Japanese Business in Canada: The Elusive Alliance.* 1984 $12.00 ISBN 0 88645 005 5
Michael Hart	*Some Thoughts on Canada-United States Sectoral Free Trade.* 1985 $7.00 ISBN 0 88645 014 4
Conference Papers	*Canada and International Trade. Volume One: Major Issues of Canadian Trade Policy.* 1985 $15.00 ISBN 0 88645 016 0
Conference Papers	*Canada and International Trade. Volume Two: Canada and the Pacific Rim.* 1985 $15.00 ISBN 0 88645 017 9

A.E. Safarian

Foreign Direct Investment: A Survey of Canadian Research. 1985 $8.00
ISBN 0 88645 018 7

Joseph R. D'Cruz &
James D. Fleck

Canada Can Compete! Strategic Management of the Canadian Industrial Portfolio. 1985 $18.00
ISBN 0 88645 020 9

W.R. Hines

Trade Policy Making in Canada: Are We Doing it Right? 1985 $10.00
ISBN 0 88645 019 5

Bertrand Nadeau

Britain's Entry into the European Economic Community and its Effect on Canada's Agricultural Exports. 1985 $10.00
ISBN 0 88645 024 1

Petr Hanel

La technologie et les exportations canadiennes du matériel pour la filière bois-papier. 1985 $20.00
ISBN 0 88645 028 4

Russell M. Wills,
Steven Globerman &
Peter J. Booth

Software Policies for Growth and Export. 1986 $15.00
ISBN 0 88645 029 2

William D. Shipman (ed.)

Trade and Investment Across the Northeast Boundary: Quebec, the Atlantic Provinces, and New England. 1986 $20.00
ISBN 0 88645 031 4

D.M. Daly &
D.C. MacCharles

Canadian Manufactured Exports: Constraints and Opportunities. 1986 $20.00
ISBN 0 88645 025 X

N.G. Papadopoulos

Canada and the European Community: An Uncomfortable Partnership? 1986 $15.00
ISBN 0 88645 042 X

James Gillies

Facing Reality: Consultation, Consensus and Making Economic Policy for the 21st Century. 1986 $15.95
ISBN 0 88645 044 6

G.E. Salembier,
Andrew R. Moroz &
Frank Stone

The Canadian Import File: Trade, Protection and Adjustment. 1987 $20.00
ISBN 0 88645 046 2

Richard W. Wright
with Susan Huggett

A Yen for Profit: Canadian Financial Institutions in Japan. 1987 $15.00
ISBN 0 88645 050 0

Edward R. Fried,
Frank Stone &
Philip H. Trezise (eds.)

Building a Canadian-American Free Trade Area. 1987 $15.00
ISBN 0 8157 2973 1

A.R. Riggs &
Tom Velk (eds.)

Canadian-American Free Trade: Historical, Political and Economic Dimensions. 1987 $15.00
ISBN 0 88645 055 1

Robert M. Stern,
Philip H. Trezise &
John Whalley (eds.)

Perspectives on a U.S.-Canadian Free Trade Agreement. 1987 $17.00
ISBN 0 8157 8131 8

Michael B. Percy &
Christian Yoder

The Softwood Lumber Dispute and Canada-U.S. Trade in Natural Resources. 1987 $20.00
ISBN 0 88645 057 8

Allan M. Maslove &
Stanley L. Winer (eds.)

Knocking on the Back Door: Canadian Perspectives on the Political Economy of Freer Trade with the United States. 1987 $20.00
ISBN 0 88645 058 6

Murray G. Smith &
Frank Stone (eds.)

Assessing the Canada-U.S. Free Trade Agreement. 1987 $15.00
ISBN 0 88645 061 6

James J. McRae &
Martine M. Desbois (eds.)

Traded and Non-traded Services: Theory, Measurement and Policy. 1988 $22.00
ISBN 0 88645 066 7

William M. Miner &
Dale E. Hathaway (eds.)

World Agricultural Trade: Building a Consensus. 1988 $19.95
ISBN 0 88645 071 3

Zhang Peiji &
Ralph W. Huenemann (eds.)

China's Foreign Trade. 1988 $12.95
ISBN 0 88645 065 9 (IRPP)   ISBN 0 88982 079 1 (Oolichan)

Jeffrey J. Schott &
Murray G. Smith (eds.)

The Canada-United States Free Trade Agreement: The Global Impact. 1988 $15.95
ISBN 0 99132 073 0